STUMBLING INTO SOBRIETY

And the Things I Learned on the Way Back Up

TRACY COLLINS

JACKSONVILLE

This memoir reflects the author's life faithfully rendered to the best of her ability. Some events have been shifted on the timeline for flow purposes only. Some names and identifying details have been changed to protect the privacy of others. All Greenfield Center patients who participated in this book sharing their stories did so willingly in the hopes their experiences will help another.

Edited by Lynn Skapyak Harlin
Cover Graphic/Layout/Design by Michael Hadden
Photo by Renee Parenteau Photography
Published by KENMAR Media

1st Edition
October 2018

The information contained in this book is the author's personal experience and should not be considered a substitute for the advice of a qualified medical professional specializing in addiction disorders.

Scripture citation is from NET Bible® copyright ©1996-2006 by Biblical Studies Press, L.L.C.

P.O. Box 17713
Jacksonville, FL 32245

Printed in the United States of America
2468097531

DEDICATION

If you suspect you might be an alcoholic, but you're not sure.
If you keep setting controlled drinking boundaries
and then breaking them.
If you know you need help, but you're too afraid to ask.
If you're afraid of what sobriety will do to your social calendar.
If you worry what other people will think.

THIS BOOK IS DEDICATED TO YOU.

Or, if you just like taking a glimpse at someone else's train wreck,
then this book is not *dedicated* to you, but it's definitely *for* you.

ACKNOWLEDGEMENTS

Tragedy + Time = Humor and I am grateful to anyone who stuck around long enough to laugh. Because for a while, it was not funny.

Thank you to my dad, for pushing outside your comfort zone to confront me and tell me you love me just in the nick of time. To my mom, for loving me no matter what crazy adventure I'm stirring up next. To my sister, for being the reason I needed to live when I couldn't find one.

Kerry "The Specktator" Speckman, your constant outpouring of love, phone calls and texts during the darkest times were some days the only human contact I had. Hank Watson, your begging and pleading finally paid off. Liz Morgan, there would be no Dot Com without you. Kimberly Clarke Jackson, your positive energy and spiritual wisdom is an inspiration. That goes double for you, Heidi Glynn. Julie Haskell, your home is an author's paradise. Pastor Joby Martin, I'm pretty sure I was still drunk from the night before, the first time I walked into your church. I don't remember what you said that morning, but I left knowing two things. You love Jesus. And you had my cray kind of humor. And that was enough to get me started on the right track. For at least one more week.

Lynn Skapyak Harlin. If it weren't for your tough love during the entire process—teaching me how to 'show' the story, blowing up my phone to keep the deadline on track, molding the proper tone of the message without smothering my voice—you and everyone close to this project knows it wouldn't have gotten done. Period. I know God placed you in my life as more than a good book editor. Your kind heart and knowledge of the disease was mandatory. Without it, this manuscript is just words on a page. With it, understanding and compassion for those still hurting.

My Greenfield Center peeps. What can I say? This would have been a book of only internal dialogue and one-sided conversations if not for your participation. Thank you for your willingness to share your stories. And thanks to Dr. Brian Jackson, for all your wise counsel and for answering a thousand follow-up questions.

Thank you to Marlene Zent, Rodney & Laurie Oberlander, Phyllis Staines and Chris Shriver for your tremendously generous financial support of this project. It was because of you I was able to keep the project rolling. And to everyone who contributed at every level, including money, silent auction items, fundraiser planning and professional courtesies. Especially Mike Hadden, who designed this entire book.

TABLE OF CONTENTS

FOREWORD

I've had the pleasure of knowing Tracy Collins since 2003. I was her boss and occasional mentor at the Florida Times-Union/Jacksonville.com for several years. I recruited her as an intern, hired her, trained her, eventually slid her into my job, and encouraged her to move on to a TV career.

The Tracy Collins I've known has been honest, positive, generous, enthusiastic, intelligent, overly chatty at times, respectful, kind and caring.

From time to time, I did notice a dark cloud cast a shadow across Tracy's usual smiling, sunshiny veneer, but it always seemed to quickly drift away. As her boss, I warned her against blurring the professional line between doing good works and having a good time; to put down that microphone or camera before picking up that drink. I thought she heeded my advice and made the necessary corrections.

Tracy went on to work with countless nonprofits and local businesses to benefit diverse arrays of people on the First Coast. To this day as her media persona, 'Tracy Dot Com', she regularly adds high-energy doses of entertainment fare and community-minded content on local TV and radio programs, as well as in print, on the Web and via social media.

Here's a twist: I was completely snookered. Played for a fool. I didn't really know Tracy's story at all. It's likely that nobody did. So, read on and dig deeper. Forget her 'classic story of success' and dismiss everything you know of her good works, at least for now. Because all of that pales in comparison to Tracy's real story.

This memoir can be a tough read. It's gritty and grimy in parts. Downright disgusting in others. Words like ugly, pathetic, heartbreaking and shameful come to mind. My jaw dropped when I read parts of this memoir. Yours probably will too. And like me, you'll probably wonder how on earth Tracy could even function, never mind succeed to any significant degree, as she battled her insidious disease.

You'll read how she gives mascara and makeup much of the credit for her cover-up, but I think the devil played a bigger role in it. Encouraging her cravings. Concocting lies that his demons told, until she believed them, and they ran the show.

So, here's another twist: Tracy's story is about how light overcomes darkness. Good wins over evil. It is a memoir about a victorious spiritual journey. Tracy's real story is so much bigger, so much brighter, so much more joyful, and so much more meaningful than I ever could have imagined.

It's a raw, unvarnished and honest account about overcoming many of the trappings of this physical world, including addiction, to focus on what really matters: following God and helping others. Tracy's prayers as a little girl to become something in this life were never answered (like she thought they were) when she achieved modicums of fame and success. I think God's answer to her prayers from long ago are being answered now—through this memoir and everything that follows, as Tracy humbly serves as a vessel for God to shine his love and light upon others.

My hope is that others will learn from Tracy's story. Maybe some will become more aware of the devil's oh-so-subtle snares. Possibly others will be motivated to reach out for help and face their own addictions. Maybe some will bow down, acknowledge their limitations and rely on God's strength to defeat the demons they're battling. Perhaps a few, in turn, will help others to avoid the temptations of this world and cast their eyes on God.

Tracy's story is of faith and redemption. Rejoice in it! Revel in it! Thank God for it!

Rich Ray
Partner, Rally Media Group, Ponte Vedra Beach, FL

CHAPTER 1
BLACKOUT, PASS OUT, COMA & DEATH

February 20, 2017

I can feel it in my soul. I am dying. I mean, we are all actively dying. But my demon of choice has already stolen my spirit. Now, it is coming for the case it was born in.

February 21, 2017

Tears gush down the side of my face to smelly, sweaty sheets below. My stomach convulses, warning me that I better take another drink or pay the price at the porcelain altar. My legs thrash back and forth and anxiety pin-needles pierce my skin in waves I cannot control.

I fan the covers back and forth to quell the hot flashes. It's either too hot or too cold. Never just right. Another convulsion sends me into a crunch position. I can't take it anymore.

I reach to the sky and scream out loud through my sobs.

"God, please. Take this disease away. I'm begging you, please."

More sobs. Gasps for air. Dry heaves.

Nobody hears me. Nobody has heard me for a long time.

But they see me. The *me* I opt to broadcast. The *me* who knows how to apply makeup just right to hide the truth. And right now, I have to pull that me together. I'm on television tomorrow. Guest hosting a popular local television show.

Eden hand-picked me to fill-in for her. I take the honor very seriously. She's a mentor. The person who gave me the shot that catapulted my career. I can't fill her shoes, but I'll darn sure hold down the fort.

Media is the only glimmer of passion left that hasn't been drowned in alcohol. When the on-air sign lights up, there won't be even a trace of my secret.

February 22, 2017

Liver sonogram results came in. The fact I had to get one is an indication that all is definitely not good in the hood. I've spent the last decade inching closer to this day. Typically, an annual 30-day cleanse put out of control liver enzymes in check. Then it was back to business as usual. Not this year.

"Do I need to come in?" I ask. Fingers cross in hopes the receptionist is just stating a fact. As in, *Hey. Just letting you know they're here. Alright. Carry on with your fabulous day.* It isn't that type of call.

"Yes. You need to come in," she says. No nonsense. No negotiation. She set up the appointment for today.

"The graph shows spots indicating fatty deposits," the doctor says. "You will need to slow down on the drinking." He's matter of fact. This could be his first or his fifth fatty liver conversation of the day. Hard to tell.

It's certainly not a death sentence, but dang it. The limits are busting at the seams. How do I ask what that specifically means in terms of use without letting on to my secret abuse?

There is no way. I avoid the topic. We've done this dance before. Usually after bloodwork. I make myself a deal. I get to drink. Not up until I'm knocking on death's doorstep, but just before. I'll quit just before irreversible damage.

That logic comes with personal negotiations. Like, only drinking on the weekends, or no liquor this week, just wine or beer.

My belly burns. My conscious is screaming, "Nobody knows your body better than you do. Listen to it." I study the doctor's face. Searching for non-verbal communication.

Certainly, he would say something if it were dire. Fat doesn't equal cirrhosis. I'm smart enough to know it is the beginning though. I promised myself I would quit before the death sentence. How far is it from fatty liver to cirrhosis? I search his face again. Looking for a trace of concern. *I'm sure I'm fine. Yeah. I'm fine. He would say something. Wouldn't he?*

The doctor pulls a script from my chart for an MRI. "This is just to be sure there isn't something worse going on."

That sounds serious, but his passive attitude gives me hope. Hope that it's okay to go home and drink. Just one more day. I need to quit. Just not today.

It's not like I didn't expect this conversation. The foreshadowing burning gut pain clued me in. Ignorance is bliss. I don't ask any more questions.

I know I need to quit. I'll do what he said and slow down. I leave without scheduling the MRI and head to the liquor store.

February 23, 2017

My eyes open and see nothing but carpet. Drool joins my left cheek to the floor below. Where am I? I lift my face and can feel the impression of hard fibers embedded in my skin. I recognize my bedroom door. I must have been heading up the stairs to sleep and passed out on the landing.

Painfully dehydrated. Arms at either side did nothing to break the fall. I can feel my feet dangling dangerously over the top step. I roll over and look down the staircase. Whoa.

I wince at the burning sensation on my right knee. A nasty rug burn means I'll be wearing slacks to work again today. I'm running out of excuses for bruises and bandages dresses expose.

March 1, 2017

It's precisely 7:30 p.m. Eastern Standard Time when I glance at my ringing phone. The word in white block letters lights up the iPhone screen: DAD. I let out a small gasp. *Something must be wrong.*

My boyfriend of 24 days drives us through the backroads of the Arlington community in Jacksonville, Florida. The sun has started its descent here, but I don't know what time it is in Phoenix. They don't participate in Daylight Savings Time, so I lose track.

Having moved to the East Coast 28 years earlier, it is always my habit to look at the current time. I calculate what time it is back home and try to decipher in nanoseconds the intention of the caller based on their daily habits. *Oh dear. Is Mom Facebook stalking a stranger again and wants to discuss what changes they need to make to better their life, or is she just calling to tell me what she's making for dinner.*

It's nothing more than a fun game I play with myself. But this call from the Grand Canyon state? This one can't be good.

"It's my dad?" I say to the driver. He drives a beefed-up Ford F-150 and is chauffeuring my drunk ass to the gym.

I brace for bad news. "Hello?"

"Tracy?" It's him. He always says my name like he's questioning if he got it correct, or if it was, in fact, me on the other end of the line. "I just wanted to call. It was great having all you kids out here at the same time."

It was the first time in 30 years we were all together at the same time. Dad almost didn't make it, spending 10 days in the hospital with double pneumonia the week before.

"Thanks. It was fun."

"Your mom's been showing me pictures of your kitchen. It's looking good."

"I'm doing it in steps so I can pay cash for it. The way you always taught me," I say.

"No, Dad. I don't have any credit card debt. Yes, Dad. I did recently finance a car, but my house payment is really small, smaller than my car payment.

"Yes, I am dating someone. No, it's not serious." *In fact, he's driving me to the gym drunk right now. But you probably can't tell because I am really good at over enunciating my words to cover it up.*

"Well," he says in a deep exhale. "I, uh, told your mother I should probably give you a call about your drinking."

There it is. Busted. Just like that, POOF, I'm 49 years old going on 12. But why now? Why are we finally discussing this now?

I feel the shame tightening my chest. I bite the right side of my lower

4

lip and push my words passed my teeth without letting up.

"Yeah, I know."

A fleeting look at Jake. There's nowhere to go. I'm stuck in this truck with a guy I barely know. I can't say I'll call you back. Talking with my dad on the phone is like approaching a bunny. Give him a reason to flee and I risk never getting this deep with him again.

I rub my left temple with three fingers, shielding my face with an open palm of wishful privacy.

"Your mom and I went out drinking quite a bit when you kids were young."

"Uh, huh," I say.

"But then I started going to the bar more often. I'd go after work, just to have one drink. That's what I told myself. One drink. But then the guy down the bar would buy me a drink, and I'd have to stay to return the favor. And it ... well, it got out of control and I finally had to stop going.

I don't know if that's what you're doing. But, jeez. I don't think you stopped drinking the entire time you were here. You've got your mom really worried."

"I know," I say. "She caught me sneaking wine out of the fridge at noon. She didn't even know the half of it."

"You've got to stop, Tracy. It's not going to get any better."

"I know. I will, Dad."

"You promise?"

"I promise. I know I need help."

The lengthy pause that follows signals our goodbyes are coming. I sit quietly waiting for it. The usual, apathetic farewell.

"I love you." His words hang in a cloud of my shocked silence.

I cannot believe what I am hearing. He has never said those words to me. Reluctantly mumbling, "I love you, too," yes. But I. Love. You.?

I already knew the phone call was difficult for him. He hates conflict. My mother was the disciplinarian. But this? This was a game changer.

"I love you, too, Dad. Bye."

"So ... what'd he say?" Jake asks. He turns the truck into a parking spot away from the rest of the gym rats and kills the engine.

He props his right elbow on his seat, resting his hand on the back of mine. I reach for the soda bottle in the center console and take two generous swigs of the clear liquid inside. No chaser necessary. I haven't needed one for more than 5 years.

"Hey," he says. He grabs the bottle and twists the cap back on. "What did your dad say?"

I open my door. *Maybe by the time we get to the treadmills, he'll forget.*

No such luck. As soon as I hit 3.2 mph, he pushes me to answer again.

I look over at him with a clenched jaw. Moving with the motion of his machine, he reads my face and looks back at me with puppy dog eyes pleading for information. Those crazy, almond eyes. They could make me give up my credit cards, Social Security number and the name of my 5th grade teacher. Fortunately, tonight he only wants to know about my conversation.

Jake is classically handsome. His dark beard is perfectly groomed, and his hair is trimmed short in the back with long bangs in the front. If a New York model and a Jax Beach surfer had a baby, he would look like Jake. I roll my eyes in surrender and tell him.

"He said, 'I love you.'"

"Well, that's good, right?"

"Yeah, but you don't understand. My dad never says 'I love you.' Hell, my dad never calls." I look at him intensely for five strides. "Like ... never." I swipe my right hand in front of me. "Never ... ever." This time I do it with two hands like an umpire calling the runner safe.

"What do you think that's about?"

I look away, pretending to adjust my speed. "He was calling to talk to me about my drinking."

"Well?" He shrugs his shoulders and holds the position in case I can't see it with my peripheral vision. I look over at him. Puppy dog eyes again and another shrug. "I told you. You really need to go to treatment."

"I don't want to talk about it." I slowly rub away imaginary sweat on my right eyebrow. Hoping the motion will wipe away the very real new wave of shame I'm feeling.

We walk quietly on the treadmills. He usually stays 10 minutes with me to warm up for the weight lifting reps that keep his shoulders broad. Tonight, he stays a lot longer. I know we're on the same team. Even if I don't like what he's telling me.

I know the choice is mine. He's not going anywhere.

Dad said, 'I love you.' He must REALLY want me to quit drinking. He doesn't even know how far gone I am. He only sees me once a year. It's too much to process. I'll quit. Just not tonight. Maybe tomorrow.

Am I an alcoholic?

It was a question I asked myself from a very young age.

As a 13-year-old. The only drunk teenage passenger to walk away from a rusty Oldsmobile crumpled into a pile of twisted steel and broken glass. Setting at the base of the old oak tree it slammed into at 120 mph. Silence broken by sirens.

As a 15-year-old. Chasing a handful of aspirin with my sixth beer. Calling 911 in a fake attempt at suicide because I'm sure the boy down the street will take me back out of pity.

As a 17-year-old. Screaming obscenities at my midnight reflection. Staring into bloodshot, dilated pupils. "I *hate* you. I hate you. Nobody likes you. You are so ugly."

As a 21-year-old sailor. Waking up in a half-naked daze on the floor of an abandoned trailer after a night of skinny dipping and making out with strangers. Screaming at my shipmate, "Get up! We're about to miss ship's movement."

As a 35-year-old. Divorcing the kindest person on the planet—and the only man ever allowed to love me—because things got a little tough. Foolishly believing there must be greener pastures somewhere in this town.

As a 48-year-old. Binging to blackout while bemoaning yet another failed relationship. Leaving behind a path of destruction littered with empty vodka bottles and venomous, unwarranted insults slurred at the latest man I claimed to love.

I wonder why I can't find a nice Christian guy who is age appropriate and makes a good living?

There was never a need for a Magic 8 Ball when I had a bathroom mirror for the answer. And like every day before it, I shut off the bathroom light, crawl under the covers and tell myself I would figure it out. Tomorrow.

So, was I an alcoholic?

For the majority of the years, I would say, no. I would classify myself as a problem drinker for sure. After all, I checked all the appropriate boxes on the National Council of Alcohol and Drug Dependence questionnaire.

- Do you drink heavily when you are disappointed?
- Do you feel uncomfortable if alcohol isn't served?
- Has a family member complained about your drinking?
- Have you ever missed work as a result of drinking?
- Do you drink to get drunk?

I consider drinking to get drunk completely normal. Do you eat to get full? Do you poop to purge? Do you have sex to climax? I can't comprehend another reason. And the day after the Super Bowl is the most missed work day of the year. So, I'm not alone here.

Black and white actions. My color chart no longer contains grey.

I'm not sure when it happened. I've tried to think back to when there was a clear shift from problem drinker to full-blown, tragic binge drinking, blackout-to-pass-out alcoholic.

But I've learned this is a progressive disease. I started moving my lines in the sand so slowly, so methodically that I liken it to the sun crossing the sky. Sometimes I'm aware it is in the east or the west. But most days I'm only conscious it is either light out or dark out.

I don't remember the moment moving from an open container in the car to minis in the glove box was perfectly justified.

I only know at some point the checked box list started to grow.

• Do you try to have a few extra drinks when others won't notice?

• Have you ever been unable to remember part of the previous evening?

• Are you in a hurry to get to your first drink of the day?

• Do you want to continue drinking when friends say they've had enough?

Check. Check. Check and check.

But I am leaving unchecked boxes. No DUI. No loss of income. No serious consequences. So, I'm okay, right?

March 4, 2017

My dad's words have not stopped cycling through my cloudy membranes for three days. Since then, I've been camping out on the road of good intentions. Each night, failing again to make a change. I wake to Jake standing next to the bed.

"Get up," Jake says. "Tracy, please."

"No. I'm tired. I don't feel well." I roll over away from his gaze.

"Come on. It's a beautiful day. Let's go do something."

"I can't. I told you. I don't feel good. I'm shaky and I feel like throwing up." His pleading is getting on my nerves.

"Tracy, please. I need to get you out of this house. You've been in bed since you got off work yesterday. Come on."

I don't respond. It's not an argument if only one person is talking.

"Okay. I'll make a deal with you. Just run an errand with me, and then I'll get us something to eat and we'll pick up some more vodka. Please, Tracy. I don't want to go alone."

I immediately start to feel empathy for him. I hate running errands.

They're so annoying. Even a grocery run 1.3 miles away grates my nerves. I roll towards him and pull back the covers.

"You'll come? Awesome."

I stand up and take off my nightshirt. Before I can reach for my bra, weakness rushes over my entire body. I wrap my arms around my waist and start weeping.

"I can't." I take a deep breath and sit back down, bending at the waist, tears rolling down my face.

Why? Why do I keep doing this to myself?

Jake reaches down for me, afraid I'll drop all the way to the ground. "I just can't."

He stands up, drops his head back and lets out a long, frustrated groan. I can feel him staring at me and he finally sighs.

"All right. I'll go. It shouldn't take me longer than a couple of hours."

I put on my robe and walk him downstairs. He kisses me goodbye and tells me to get some rest.

"What do you want me to pick up to eat?"

"I don't care." I don't have an appetite. I haven't for four months.

He leaves. I walk into the kitchen and pound back two double shots as his truck door slams.

***

God. What's that noise? Maybe I didn't hear any... No, there it is again.

I pull the curtain back and see Jake's truck in the drive. I can't see him at the front door from this angle but I hear him pounding on my door again followed by five hard, frantic pushes on the doorbell. I run downstairs and pull the door open. He's standing three feet away with his back to me, phone to his ear. He whips around. His eyes are like daggers. He fills his chest with oxygen from his enflamed nostrils and blows it out his mouth.

"Never mind. She's here. Yeah, I'll tell her to call you." He jams his cell into his back pocket and pushes past me.

"What's going on?" I'm completely confused, and frankly, still a little buzzed. *He just left, right?*

"I've been standing out there pounding on the door for 15 minutes." It's the first time I've heard him raise his voice. "I thought you were dead."

Seems a little overly dramatic.

"I fell asleep. You know I can't hear my door when I'm upstairs with the fan on."

"Listen to me." He brings his fist down like a gavel with every word. "I. Have. Been. Banging. For. Fifteen. Minutes. I called Hank to find out if there was a key hidden somewhere. I didn't know what to do next. My next call was going to be to the police."

A call to Hank was worse than the police. Her name is Henrietta, but her masculine nickname is true to her enforcer nature. Until now, she has been protecting my secret. Begging me in private to get help and keeping me close to her on most weekends to save me from myself. Or anyone else I might accidentally kill in a blackout. If she believes I have made it to death's doorstep …

"Okay. Jeez. I was sleeping." I start to turn around and he grabs me by my shoulders, staring intensely inches from my face.

"Do you even know how close you are to death? Do you even get it?" *I really don't. But I don't tell him.*

"When you pass out at night and I'm awake watching TV, you stop breathing. I don't know half the time if you have sleep apnea or if you're just checking out for good."

His voice and his hold on me softens. "You must get help."

"I know. I will."

"And not just outpatient either. You need inpatient treatment where you can't get to alcohol. I have never seen anyone love vodka as much as you do."

"Okay, fine. But not today. Today I just need to sip on some more to calm my stomach. I can't go to your family reunion feeling like this."

The clear liquid burns my gut. Poison. I am willingly putting poison into my body. I should hate it, but it's so comforting and instantly raises my mood.

I put on my face and straighten my hair. The green hue of my roadie Perrier bottle conceals its true contents. Time to meet the fam.

I don't know why he stays with me.

March 5, 2017

My stomach grumbles in anger over the previous day's festivities as we pull into the church parking lot. I reach behind Jake's seat. A stashed water bottle contains a not-so-mysterious liquid. Before I can get a grip, he does. A large hand snaps fingers around my forearm.

"What are you doing?" He's angry. "Not before church."

Dangit! Only a few weeks ago he found my mischievous behavior adorable. What happened?

"But after?" I ask. Raised eyebrows. Sly smile.

He's not amused.

March 10, 2017

Finally Friday. Free at last. Free to forget the stressors of the work week. Free to numb the gerbils in my head. Free to take a break from making excuses for the physical signs chasing me.

My plan is to stick with wine this weekend to subside the burning gut. Also, occasional dulled stabbing has me concerned. I did promise my dad I would quit, so I should probably figure out when I'm going to do that. Not this weekend, but I do need to come up with a game plan. Maybe I'll just drink on the weekends.

I don't know. I keep going back and forth.

It's the forgetfulness that really has me worried. Is it age? Older girlfriends keep saying they have the same problem. I don't think they do. Not this bad. I've started bringing a pen and paper to all my work meetings. I get back to my office and can't remember conversations minutes prior.

I'm genuinely scared that early dementia is in my future.

Then there's the eyesight. When I got Lasik more than a decade ago, the doctor said natural aging would require glasses later in life. I did get a prescription a couple of years ago for driving. I haven't been back since. I'm afraid to. I've started using readers, which my older girlfriends also say is normal. I don't think it is. Not the way I'm seeing typed print.

What is this fluttering eyeball movement? Am I going blind?

I keep hearing the voice in my head. "Listen to your body. Nobody knows it better than you."

I'm scared of the answers, but inexplicably more afraid of asking for help. That would require being honest. Honest with myself. Honest with the people who love me. I'm not ready for that.

March 11, 2017

The alarm jolts me awake. *Ugh! 7:15 a.m. What day is it? Oh, wait. It's Gate River Run day. Yay!*

"C'mon. Get up." I nudge Jake. He hates waking up as much as I do. Except on the morning of the official USA 15K Championship. It's a glorious excuse to start day drinking.

"Why do we have to do this again?" he asks.

"Because it's my annual tradition. Ray and Betty will be here by 8. Usually it's a bunch of people, but they're the only ones coming this year. We'll drink mimosas and watch the gun go off on TV, then wait about 30 minutes for the runners to get a good start. We'll pack up some travelers to drink while we cheer on the runners about to take on the green monster."

The green monster is what runners call the Hart Bridge because it's green and it is the final, brutal uphill battle before the end of the race at the bottom of the other side.

"Oh, and what's super fun is they have their names printed on their bibs, so we yell out, 'Go, Mary, you go this. Good job, John.' And they look around like, 'Do I know you?' Then we'll head back here and I'll make us all breakfast."

Jake puts a pillow over his head to block the bathroom light I flip on. I can barely hear his muffled voice.

"Can I get up when they get here?"

"Yup." I flip the bathroom light off and skip downstairs to pop a bottle of champagne. No sense opening the orange juice yet. OJ in a mimosa is nothing more than a useless additive that says, "See, I'm not really drinking this hoping to get a buzz. It's merely a festive breakfast drink."

So, if no one is looking, what's the point. I push the champagne flute to the side, fill up the biggest wine glass I own, flip on the TV for the pre-race coverage, and shoot Ray a text.

Me: I can't wait to see you guys!
Ray: Well, I guess we'll get up.
Me: Heck yeah, you're the only reason I'm getting up.
Ray: I'm hoping to be with you guys by 8:30. That will be fast for Betty.
Me: Dude we are moving slower than you. I'm on the couch waiting for you to show up. He's in bed, hoping you never show up. We're gonna have an awesome day.

I polish off the bottle of champagne just as the call comes in. Ray and Betty are not going to make it. Jake's wish came true.

Crap. What to do now? I'm buzzed and bored.

I go upstairs. Grab an Ambien from the bedside pill bottle. In minutes, the morning melts away.

***

Ringing slowly pulls me from the fog. It's 3:07 p.m.

"Who is it?" Jake asks.

"It's my sister." I hit the button on the side to hush the annoying noise. "I'll call her later."

Seventy-eight minutes later, she wakes me again.

"Are you okay?"

Weird question. "Yeah, I'm okay. Why?"

"Because Dad died."

I shoot straight up from the waist. "What?"

"Dad died."

"When? How?" I'm yelling. Sobbing. Yanking at the bedsheets with no purpose.

Jake sits up. "What happened?"

I pinch the bridge of my nose and drop my head. My whole body is shaking and I can hear myself moaning. It sounds like someone else coming out of me. I don't recognize my own voice. Jake jumps up and puts his hands on his hips. His eyes are wide and he shifts his weight, pivoting only his right foot with each change of movement.

"This morning," Nancy says. "We've been trying to call you. Didn't you get our messages?"

"No. I've been sleeping." *You mean, you've been passed out in a self-inflicted coma, you dumbass.*

I look at the freaked-out man standing next to my bed and mouth the words: *My dad died.* I pull a pillow on my lap and face-dive into it. My tears quickly make a mascara-soaked stain on the beige fabric.

I hang up and check my missed calls. Looking at Jake. Tears streaming down my face.

"Four hours. My mom called me four hours ago." An anxious shiver rolls through me. I can't believe what I've done.

My poor mother. All alone in Phoenix, and I couldn't even regain consciousness at 12:32 p.m. to console her. I know I was the first one she called. Her only biological child. The daughter she wouldn't give up when she was an abandoned single mom. And here I am, abandoning her in her darkest time of need. She lost the man who took us in and made us a family for 43 years, and I am nowhere to be found to tell her I love her. To tell her everything is going to be okay. I am the worst daughter in the world.

I dial her number. No answer. I dial my dad's number. No answer.

I listen to her voicemail and I want to die. I want a hole to open up and swallow me whole. I want to pull my heart out of my chest so I can't feel this excruciating pain anymore. Instead, I lay flat on the bed, bury my face in the covers, slam my fists into the mattress and scream.

The message is six seconds. Her voice is pure despair. A woman barely pushing her vocal cords past her tears. "Tracy, this is Mom ... You have to call me back as soon as you can."

I am immediately haunted by visions of her alone with my dad.

"She must have been so scared." I sit on the edge of my bed with my face in my hands, elbows resting on my knees, sobbing for six minutes straight. Jake stands as a silent guard over me until the phone rings. I lunge for it.

"Mom, what happened?" I let the tears freefall off my chin to the bedroom floor.

"We were getting ready to go to the doctor. I told him I was going to the garage to smoke a cigarette. He sat down on the couch to put on his shoes. When I came in, he was gone."

When tragedy strikes, I fight back with a self-induced coma.

Breakups. Death. National tragedies. I drink to forget. I drink to stop the pain.

A friend once asked, "Do you think you spiral out of control because of sadness? Or do you use your sadness as a good excuse to spiral out of control?"

It's a good question. Who can blame me for going crazy? My dad just died. I deserve a bender. Right? Unfortunately, I can now guzzle with no chaser.

Meaning I can consume faster than my body can go through the phases.

0.200 - 0.299	0.300 - 0.399	0.400 +
BLACKOUT	PASS OUT	COMA/DEATH

At what point is my blood alcohol level going to accidentally cross from 0.399 into 0.400 territory? The real coma. The no-joke coma. Untreated, the death coma.

CHAPTER 2

DEFECATION, URINATION & OTHER MORTIFYING MEMORIES

March 12, 2017

Dishonest, sexually irresponsible dream stealer. I wish I were describing someone other than myself. I don't recognize the person I've become.

March 17, 2017

In the light of day, this Miss Hyde character seems implausible. At least Monday through Thursday. That's when I keep my blackout to pass out episodes to the evenings. But slowly, cunningly, Hyde starts to impede on the entire week. I don't know when it happened. It's all a blur. But I found myself stopping at the liquor store on the way home every Friday for a handle of vodka. Then to the grocery store for enough food to sustain me through the weekend.

I know I need to heed what I now recognized as my father's dying wish. With Jake's help, I spent the last five days sober. It felt good. Coming home every night. Eating healthy food. Watching TV. Falling asleep with my head in his lap.

But like every good alcoholic, I uttered the ridiculous mantra: I got this.

On Friday night, Jake pops a beer. And I follow. That's all it takes. Not only to return to the land of excess, but also to cross yet another boundary. Socially unacceptable public intoxication.

March 18, 2017

"I don't want to get to the restaurant until a quarter after."

"Why?" Jake stops brushing his teeth and steps into the bedroom to look at me. "I thought you said the brunch starts at 11?"

I avoid his gaze, take another sip of wine, and slip my feet into jeweled flip flops.

"Because I've already been drinking this morning and I don't want anyone to smell it."

Jake looks confused. He turns to spit the toothpaste into the sink and rinse. He wipes his mouth with a towel and takes another stab at sorting out my madness.

"Well, aren't they going to smell it on you no matter what time you get there?"

"No," I say. "It's a champagne brunch. If I wait until everyone has had at least one, it won't seem odd that I have, too."

The party is for Melissa Ross, a highly respected talk show personality in Jacksonville. She's been voted Best Local Radio Host and Best Local Radio Show by Folio Weekly readers every year since I can remember.

During her daily morning show, the seasoned journalist flows seamlessly from hard-hitting political issues, social injustices and environmental debates to in-the-know entertainment news. Controlled delivery with serious conversation. A hearty laugh while interviewing local and international celebrities.

Her broad knowledge caught the attention of NPR and she was tapped as a possible replacement for Diane Rehm. When the offer was made to someone else, Jacksonville breathed a collective sigh of relief. It is a well-verbalized fact whispered at all the prominent parties. The beautiful, fierce blonde would leave a gaping hole if she left.

So, I feel fairly confident her milestone birthday luncheon will be a River City Who's Who soiree. Turns out, I'm right.

As we pull up, I spot social photog and friend Tonya Austin. It's a well-known fact, if Tonya is at your event, you're kind of a big deal.

"How do I look?" I ask. "Can you tell I've been drinking?"

"No." Jake shakes his head. "You look really pretty."

It is one of the nice things about being a girl. With enough hairspray and makeup, I can mask just about anything. I pulled out a dress I had not worn yet, so I'm feeling extra fancy in my new duds.

Jake opens the passenger door, and I give one final heavy exhale and a hug.

"Okay, here I go. Pick me up at one, please."

Turns out I pegged the temperature of the crowd correctly. The variety of the all-female gathering is as diverse as her radio topics. And much like the animal kingdom, we all congregate to the corner of the jungle we feel most comfortable.

My camouflage jungle tribe includes a pink-haired media personality, a PR superstar, and a celebrity photographer. I'm in my comfort zone, completely shielded from the possibility of the higher food chain in the room noticing these mimosas are going down a little too easy.

Unfortunately, my comfort zone is also being the center of attention.

***

"How did it go?" Jake's standing at the bottom of the steps to the restaurant holding the passenger truck door open.

"Fine," I say through a forced smile. Somebody might still be watching.

I reach behind his seat for a flask I've hidden as he slides behind the wheel. He stops short of turning the engine.

"You okay?"

"I'm good. Just drive."

I try to relay the story the best I can on the way home, taking swigs in between sentences.

"We were all supposed to write out and bring a personal message to Melissa. Like a letter, kind of."

He looks over at me intently.

"Somebody asked if anyone wanted to get up and share theirs."

19

"Let me guess." He chuckles. "You were the first one."

His laugh makes me laugh, prompting sarcasm.

"Ee-yus," I say. "Only I didn't just volunteer, I jump up, go all the way to the front from the back, and read it to her at an awkwardly close proximity."

I lean my head back in frustration and stare at the truck's beige rooftop while Jake laughs some more.

"It doesn't sound that bad. You're overthinking it," he says. "You read it to me this morning. It was really thoughtful. I'm sure she appreciated it."

"I got really emotional while I was reading it." I stare blankly in front of me. "And as if that wasn't bad enough, nobody else came up. Some others read what they wrote, but they did it from their table. Some of them didn't even stand."

"Well, not everybody's as outgoing as you."

"I feel like I tried to make it all about me," I say. "It's Melissa's big day and there I am going, Look at me! Look at me!"

"Was that what you were thinking at the time? Was that your intention?"

"No."

"Then you're being a little ridiculous. I'm sure that's not what anybody was thinking. And if they were, it's only because they don't know you. They don't know your personality or your heart."

He continues to try to console me, but it's not working. The only thing working are the gerbils on the wheel inside my brain. Spinning and spinning and spinning.

March 19, 2017

The light of the next morning does not feel like a new day. In fact, it only exacerbates the existing walk of shame.

I lay my head in both my hands and let out an exasperated growl of embarrassment.

"What's wrong?" Jake hollers from his home office.

He runs into his bedroom to find me sitting up from under the covers. The combination of two days without hair washing after two evenings of night sweats is not attractive. He stops short in the door.

"Wow," he says.

"Still perfecting my look for that modeling career." I take a failed attempt at running fingers through ratted locks. "Did we go somewhere after Melissa's party?"

"Yeah. The arts market."

My mouth drops. I'm shocked but shouldn't be. I've just located the evidence in my phone.

Sunshine-lit selfies using Jake's long right arm as the photographer. Two lovers on a walkway with the St. Johns River racing from south to north in the background. Ray-Ban sunglasses protect from UV rays and hide dilated eyes.

A valiant attempt, but there is no way my intoxication could possibly be covered up by a fancy pair of shades and an even fancier pair of pumps. Not if I can't remember it. Not if I am looking at a stranger in my body, out on the town, taking selfies with my camera less than 24 hours before.

Slamming back against the pillow, I drape my arm across my eyes to block out the brightness in the room. Visions of my spaghetti legs stumbling past families picking out farm-raised tomatoes and crocheted bracelets brings on a cringe.

"Will you go get some more vodka?" I sit up and give him puppy dog eyes.

He tries to argue but quickly gives up. This six-week ridiculousness is running its course and he knows it. Arguing is a waste of time and oxygen.

"Give me some money." He's disgusted but sticks his hand out.

Between the shift in financial obligation and whose house we spend our time, I realize the power is now his. I don't like it. But I need him to go get the liquor and hand over a twenty.

The front door closes. Chug. Chug. Chug. The warm beer on the nightstand, left over from the night before, goes down almost as fast as I do.

"Nothing good ever happens in a blackout," Comedian Amy Schumer says in one of her standup acts. "I've never woken up and been like, 'What is this Pilates mat doing out?'"

***

"Did you pee?" Jake's shrill voice startles me awake. "Hey! Did you piss yourself? You did. Unbelievable." He slams a new paper bag next to the empty Michelob.

"What? What's going on?" My eyes adjust in time to see him shaking his head storming out of the room.

"You wet the bed," he screams back. "Get your crap. I'm taking you home."

I should be embarrassed. Humiliated, really. But for some reason, I'm not. I'm also not upset about the breakup. Logically, I know this isn't how I normally react. But for some reason, my give-a-damn is busted.

Inexplicably, I decide to capture this moment with video.

"Sooooo ... he says he's done with me."

My reflection stares back at me from my phone. Puffy face. Smudged eyeliner. Unbrushed teeth. Tangled hair. I scrunch up my face.

"Can anyone deny him?" My eyes go to the ceiling in heavy thought.

This conversation with no one drags out in three slurring sessions totaling a minute and 13 seconds. I end with some sense of rationale.

"I need to get some sleep." I tell the camera. "I do have to work tomorrow." My head falls back onto the pillow. It's only 2 p.m.

At Jake's urging that "this bull crap is really over" and a final cry of "let's go," I change my clothes and put the soiled ones in a bag. Along with the new bottle of vodka. I can't forget that. I paid for it. I'll be damned if I'm leaving it here.

"I'm guessing this means we're not going to church today?"

March 20, 2017

I wake on my right side, facing the wall in the early morning darkness, and immediately sense I am not alone. The wicked energy makes my skin crawl and frozen muscles ache. A panicked mind scrambles to inventory the situation.

Where am I? Home. What time is it? Has to be about 3 a.m. What is that sound? Is that someone breathing behind me? Or is that my own exhale?

I hold my breath. And wait. And wait.

Definitely still hear it. Low, rumbling lungs. Behind my back. Close to my left ear. Just outside of my peripheral night vision. Like a lion leaning over his prey. Daring it to move. An excuse to pounce.

Did Jake stay the night? No. We broke up. Wait, did he?

My mind wants to reach across the sheets behind me and search for familiar flesh, but my body won't respond.

Move. On the count of three. Move. Turn around.

If I can look behind me, I can prove to my mind it's not real. All terror will disappear like every time before.

One. Two. Three.

Nothing. Muscles will not respond to the screaming mind.

The edge of the mattress gives under pressure. A knee—or is it a hand—bends the cushion. I hold my breath again.

It's not real. It's muscle memory. It's not real. It's not real.

The sound of box springs in motion tells a different story. Skin on the back of my left arm prickles. Shoulder blade recoils on my otherwise frozen frame.

What is that other noise?

A foreign melody plays from behind the closet door. It sounds like a radio broadcasting the final, foreshadowing evening on the Titanic. A string quartet. The clinking of glasses. Muffled voices.

What is that?

I fight for conviction. To be released from this mental prison.

Say it. Say it out loud.

I part my lips. With a locked jaw, I force the inaudible words out of my mouth.

"In the nah uh Jesus Christ. I cuh and you tah go."

Slowly, the night terror melts into a shout.

"In the name of Jesus Christ. I command you to go."

With gnashing teeth, I force my back to the mattress. The physical shift breaks the spell. The malignant spirit vanishes. The music silences. The only sound is my labored breathing.

Sleep will only come with the light on.

Hours later, stuck in a windowless work office, my mind is consumed. Spinning. And spinning. And spinning.

I probably shouldn't drink today. I'll just take a break until Friday. Maybe one mini. Or ... three. Three will be enough to get happy. No. No. I shouldn't drink. At least just for today. Maybe I'll grab some wine. That won't be too bad. Ugh! STOP THINKING ABOUT IT!

My brain ignores the command, and once again, an entire part of my day is wasted, negotiating in my head.

It might be time to get help. Might. I'll decide tomorrow.

That night I skip in to European Street, excited to spend a rare evening with Kerry and her brother, Billy.

"Hi, kids." My high-pitched delivery is a result of reaching my happy place at home before ordering an Uber to the restaurant. It would be a red flag for a normal person, but I always exude that style of excitement when I see people I love.

"I'll take a white wine, please." Beer and wine is all they serve, so I took three long pulls on the vodka bottle to set the tone before walking out of my house 20 minutes earlier. And in the car on the way, I pulled a mini from my purse at the halfway mark, leaned forward in the backseat to block the Uber driver's view, and downed it without a wince.

That extra swallow is the reason ordering the wine is all I can remember before time jumps to the Uber ride home.

That's how blackouts work. At least for me. I can carry on conversations for a long time in a composed manner until I no longer can. The difference is I usually do this on the phone and then pass out in private. Just me and my dirty little secret, snuggled in for the night.

But not on this night. On this night, I am lulled out of dreamland by a masculine voice.

"Tracy. Tracy! TRACY!" Billy's stern but controlled public voice rallies me from my slumber. "Tracy, I need your credit card. And give me your phone."

What follows next is called a brown out. A new term in my vocabulary arsenal. It's when you remember spotty parts of an event, similar to watching an anesthesia patient's point-of-view video. You have a general overview of what happened, but large chunks are edited out.

I remember Billy helping me and my sea legs to the car and asking the driver if my address came up on his app. He put my seat belt on and everything goes brown.

The next thing I know, I'm aware we're in my driveway, but I can't find my keys. I keep fumbling and making slurred small talk, but Uberman is growing annoyed.

"You have to get out," he says. I oblige and stumble up to my screen door, plop down on the ground and dump out the purse contents. It's still light out, so I'm sure somebody on my street of rowed townhouses is probably observing this, but the I-give-a-damn ship has sailed.

Next memory, I'm on my neighbor's doorstep, crying, begging for help.

Joan is a sweet, retired woman I have lived next to for 15 years. I trust her with my keys, my alarm code and my life. I'm sure she has smelled alcohol on my breath. I'm equally as sure she has never seen me like this before. And her reaction proves I'm right.

She opens her door and gasps at the sight of me rocking back and forth, holding on to her porch wall with my right hand. She catches me just before I sway too far to the left.

"Tracy. Oh my gosh. Tracy," she screams.

I cry out for help and blab in broken English. "I'm so drunk. Everybody is going to know." I glance around at our neighbors' doorways and gasp for quick breaths between my tears. "I can't find my keys. I can't get in my house," I wail.

Joan walks me the short distance to my front door and props me up against the patio wall. She quickly scoops the sprawled items back in my purse, except the keys she needs to push open my door. They had been in front of me the whole time.

She flips my right arm over her shoulder and cradles my body in her left while supporting my weight up the stairs and into the master bathroom.

The rest is quick flashes of memory. Snapshot: I'm crying. Snapshot: I hear my voice, but I don't know what I'm saying. Snapshot: I'm pulling off my shirt, then my bra. Snapshot: She's saying my name and she sounds scared and uncomfortable with my lack of modesty. More brown.

Is she still behind me? I don't know. At some point, there are no more voices, but my brain can't put together a decent timeline. I do know the shower water is running and all I have to do is take off my underwear. But I don't make it before I defecate. The runny stool streams down my leg and onto my socks.

Everything goes black.

March 21, 2017

"Are you okay?" Kerry's voice and face fill with apprehension as I approach her for our lunch date.

"Yeah. Why?" *It's not like she could have known what happened with Joan.*

"You passed out, and I didn't know what was going on," she says.

What the hell? This all started with one innocent beer on Friday night.

I can't believe what I'm hearing. A beer on Friday turned into a staggering stroll through the arts market on Saturday, bed wetting and a wasted day on Sunday, demonic nightmares and passing out at dinner on Monday.

"What does that even look like?" I ask.

"Two glasses of wine and dinner accompanied great conversation, lots of laughs, and then, out of the blue ..." She pauses. "Going. Going. Gone."

"What does that mean?" I'm freaking out wondering how many people saw this. *It was 6 o'clock in the evening for Pete's sake. What could everyone possibly be thinking?*

She goes on to say that I suddenly stopped talking, leaned into my sandwich, and slowly kept going until I laid my head down on the table and went to sleep.

"Just ...," she shakes her head trying to make sense of it. "Boom. You were there. Then you weren't." Kerry says she didn't know what to do. She didn't know what was happening.

"I wasn't sure if you were having a seizure or had a medical condition I didn't know about or what?" She holds her hands out and shifts her eyes back and forth on the floor, searching for answers to that night. "You seemed fine when you walked in. And you only had two glasses of wine. I was so scared."

March 26, 2017

That weekend was the beginning of the end. The start of a weeklong stretch of incoherency. I don't have any memories to share from the next and final weekend of intoxication because I was not conscious. I was upright. In motion. Just ... not there.

When I think back on it, I'm looking up at a stranger with my face. She's standing on the ledge of a tall building at dusk. Her eyes are blank. Empty. Dead. She's not there. Is she sleep walking? Is she going to fall? I can't tell. She is definitely not in control. Her brain is being held prisoner.

In an instant, I'm transported. Floating behind her. She's now standing in dark, rapidly flowing water. Motionless. Looking down at something. What is she looking at? As my levitating body nears her, I can see the bigger picture now. The water breaks at her ankles, gushes past her toes, and powers over a cliff into oblivion.

This final weekend is the moment of truth. I only have two choices. Lose myself in the watery abyss. Or quit.

I wanted to do the latter for my dad. And the fear of disappointing my mother makes me determined to get on the plane home for the funeral sober. But it won't come without paying the detox gods their due.

CHAPTER 3

THE MOUNTAIN IN FRONT IS ACTUALLY A MIRAGE

March 27, 2017

The last day I took a drink, I did not know at the time would be the last day I took a drink. I only knew I had flu-like symptoms and I needed to be on a plane in two days—the amount of time it typically took me to feel pretty spry after drying out. Seemed like a good place to stop. For now.

The severe vomiting started at some point a day or two before. It's hard to gauge and many times the days ran together. Waking to a clock read and a window glance could mean it's 7 a.m. at dawn or 7 p.m. at dusk. Followed by upright bolt and three frantic outbursts: What day is it? What day is it? What day is it? If the answer was Saturday or Sunday, I said out loud to no one, "Oh, thank God." And reached for the bottle beside my bed.

If the answer was Monday, I didn't even have to ask. Anxiety dry heaves told me, starting around 5 o'clock. I assume it's a sign about how I feel about my job. On this Monday, there is no way I can go in. And I'm scared. Really scared I will be too sick to get on the flight. So, I'll stick to the plan. No alcohol today.

Around 2 p.m., I hear the doorbell ring, grab a robe off the back of the bathroom door, and rush down the stairs. It only takes a second to do, but in 15 years of home ownership, I still think the mystery guest behind door number one will have time to lose interest in seeing me, walk back to their car and drive away.

I pull the curtain back to see Leah standing on my worn 'elcom' mat that once proudly read WELCOME. Submissive eyebrows top moist eyes looking back at me through the glass. I let go of the curtain, crack the door, and move a head and one shoulder out of the darkness.

"Are you okay?" She tries to peer past me.

"No." I open the door, back up and give her the international arm wave of welcome to my humble abode.

"No. I'm not okay." My voice cracks under the pressure of realizing I was about to expose a secret. The pleasure palace had crumbled. Crumbled like that old mat she stood on. Crumbled into the dungeon I was trapped in.

"What's wrong? I've been worried about you. You haven't been to work in days." She moves meekly through the doorway. Her eyes dart around the room. Trying to adjust from the sunshine of the outside world. Searching for the serial killer that had to be lurking around here somewhere in all this negative energy.

"Look at this place." Embarrassment tears flow. The dining room table is covered with my entire kitchen. The cupboards, refaced weeks ago, still haven't been reunited with their contents. The open floor plan exposes crap everywhere in the living room. Random items dropped off after excursions outside the dungeon.

"I don't know what to do. I'm so overwhelmed. I've dug myself a hole I can't get out of." I point to all the rooms. "I can't stop throwing up, and I don't have any food in the house. I'm tired and hungry and I'm freaking out."

"Okay, well. When do you fly home?"

"Wednesday."

She fiddles anxiously with her keys and scans the room looking for the answers written somewhere in the mess. What was really wrong with me? What could she do to magically make me better? Neither motherhood nor marathon training has prepared her for this moment.

"What can I do?" Her voice is desperate.

"I'm hungry." Mine is pleading.

"Okay. I'll go get you some food." She shifts in discomfort, still scanning my world spilled haphazardly on the ground around her. "When you get back from your dad's funeral, I'll come help you get this cleaned up."

She leaves swiftly. And never returns. A text arrives a few minutes later.

"I'm sorry I can't get you anything at the store. I have a meeting I have to get to at the beach. I'll see you when you get home," it reads.

My stomach growls. Restless spirit grumbles. How am I going to get food in this condition? I walk in the kitchen to the two dozen empty liquor bottles of every size shoved in the corner. I hadn't thrown any of them away since my dad asked me to quit drinking. The empties were a physical reminder I need to do that someday.

I grab an empty pint and turn it upside down on the tip of my tongue. The clear remnants slowly flow into a tiny droplet. The delicious sensation stimulates my receptors. I don't want to get drunk. I only want the vomiting to subside. I grab another and then another until I felt good enough to go get some food.

This ritual isn't new. I often did it on nights of regulation. Promising myself only X amount tonight sometimes led to licking the glass clean just to taste the poison one last time before falling asleep.

In a sort of divinely deranged way of thinking, I never once upended an empty without remembering a story an elder shared in church.

"You know how when you take communion, and there's always one more drop at the bottom?" He gestured his fingers around an imaginary cup. "And then you tap that drop out, but there is still one more drop." His voice shifts to disbelief. "To me, that's like God's grace. He continues to pour it out. Even when your think your cup is empty."

I shake my shoulders to brush off the guilt and put on my shoes. Twenty-five minutes later, I'm back next to the empties and add two more minis to it. Just enough to feed the monster. Not enough to get drunk. Twenty-five minutes later, the trash can overflows one last time with colorful labels. Red Smirnoff. Blue Amsterdam. White-capped mountain peaks on Pinnacle.

March 29, 2017

Two days later, I don't remember what I was thinking at the time, but I do know I am a very ceremony driven creature. Firsts and lasts are my jam. I make them memorable. I obviously did not believe this needed to be remembered. And besides, my entire being was not focused on that being my first day of sobriety as much as it was focused on it not being my last day on Earth. I knew if I could make it to today to get my butt to the airport, I would be home free.

Almost. First, I need to make it to work at least one day.

Dry heaves. Shakes. A worn path from the bed to the master bathroom toilet. The brain is saying I can do it. Get dressed. Get packed. Get going. The stomach is screaming its objection.

Somehow. Slowly. I make it. Dragging in only a few minutes late.

An unlocked door, lights on, fresh coffee on my desk means one thing.

Shoot. I throw my head back. Groan under my breath. *I really wanted the office to myself today.*

"Thanks for the coffee," I say. No response. A peek around the cubicle wall reveals intern Heather's chair is empty.

Thank God. I plop down. Arms freefall to the side. Eyes closed. *How long can I stay just like this? Why am I still so foggy?*

Heather interrupts my thoughts with a chipper salutation before getting right into it.

"Where have you been?" she asks.

"I've been sick. I think I have the flu."

She stares at me silently. Looks around my desk. "Have you eaten?"

"No."

"I'm going next door. Can I get you anything?"

"I don't think I can keep anything down."

She goes over the cafeteria's list. One. By. Irritating. One. Scrambled eggs? No. Toast? No. How about some crackers? No. Soup?

Oh my gosh. Stop!

Heather is the sweetest child. A senior at the University of North Florida, she scrambled to find an internship to be eligible to graduate. When I received the call from my professor and mentor, Paula Horvath, asking for help, I jumped. Heather has been a joy to be around. If for no other reason, fresh coffee on the desk every morning.

This morning, however. Not so much.

She steps into the hall. Whispers float through the cracked door. She returns with a barrage of questions.

What are my symptoms? When is the last time I threw up? Am I feverish? Shaky? Lightheaded? When is the last time I ate? She collects the data. Steps back in the hall.

What is up with these questions? Who is she talking to?

She bursts back in. I jump with paranoia. Grab at the pounding heart in my chest.

"You scared the crap out of me."

"My mom says you need to go to the doctor." Her young voice is frantic. "Right away."

I feel her standing within inches. I refuse to make eye contact. *Does she know? No. How could she.*

"I'm not going to the doctor." I laugh off the suggestion. Hoping she doesn't recognize it as a deflection.

Two hours, three phone calls home, several more rounds of questions. It feels like it will never end.

Am I in hell? What is happening here? I told her I think I have the flu. Why isn't that good enough?

Heather finally disappears. Twenty welcome minutes of silence follow. She comes back with a bag from the drugstore down the street.

"I talked to my mom, and she said these would be easy on your stomach." She pulls out a single-serve oatmeal cup, some kind of breakfast bar, crackers and a Gatorade. "If you're still vomiting in the air, you should go to the emergency room as soon as you land."

I'm too afraid to ask why.

***

Sleepy and queasy, I lean back in seat 47A, curl my legs up into 47B, and rest my head against the side of the plane.

Please, God. Don't let this seat be taken.

I stare out the window at the luggage handlers, working in quick succession right below me, but my mind is 1,795 miles away.

So far, I've kept the promise to my mom not to drink.

"Tracy. I'm having a hard-enough time with this. I can't deal with your dad's death and you being drunk at the same time," she told me.

I know drinking bothers her, but not that it causes distress. After the Gate River Run debacle, it was the least I could do.

Three days of detox vomiting has me sweaty and shaky. I pop a Xanax to calm the waves of rolling rapids through my entire body. There's no expectation for the Ambien chaser to work. It hasn't for four nights.

Christine is the inflight movie. It's the true story of a 1970s Florida reporter with an affection for community stories and an all-consuming longing to be liked and loved.

Christine Chubbuck's inability to connect with her mother, her news director, and an unrequited love-interest co-anchor has her making awkward, desperate life choices.

The cinematic characterization of the long-haired brunette strikes empathy and fear into my heart. Her story hits too close to mine. The actress beautifully embodies a woman with a spinning mind and an inner voice no one can hear crying out for help.

But I hear her. I cry for her since she seemingly is unable to do it for herself. I cry for her many times. When she buys the gun. When she makes a final attempt to be taken serious as a reporter and a potential girlfriend. And finally, when she sits at the news desk one last time.

Airing her final moments of life into thousands of homes through the magic of the camera lens, she speaks in a monotone voice, mocking the sensational news stories the station demands.

"In keeping with the WZRB policy, complete reports of local blood and guts," she says, "TV-30 presents what is believed to be a television first."

Christine brings the pistol swiftly to her temple and pulls the trigger.

The irony is not lost on me. I, in effect, am also pointing a gun to my head in front of an audience. My bullet is just moving a little slower.

The 8-hour trip provides much-needed meditation.

I'm ready to come clean and lean in to whisper my confession across the dimly lit living room to the woman I trust most in the world. My sister.

We arrived in Phoenix one hour apart. I met Nancy at the front door at midnight, and we quietly giggled, dragging her overstuffed luggage all the way to her bedroom.

Minutes later, sitting cross-legged on the loveseat across from her rocking in the chair, nobody is laughing.

"I'm going to tell you everything. But not her." I motion over to our snoring mother on the couch.

I share the worst parts, knowing I'm in a safe place. Her face is stone. Rocking slows with each revelation. Every vignette takes her further away from our carefree childhood and fun-filled juvenile delinquency and brings her closer to understanding the dire circumstances.

"It's the fifth time the doctor has told me if I don't do something, I'll get cirrhosis."

Her rocking stops.

I try to put a Band-Aid on her fear. "But I quit every year for a couple weeks, and when I retest, my enzymes are okay. So … I mean. That's good, right?"

She stares at me in silence. I imagine she's thinking back to our trip home two months ago. The first time all five of us had been in the same house in 30 years. It was a celebration, so all three kids drank, much to the chagrin of our parents.

The part she missed was the bottle I snuck into my closet to snag a chug from throughout the day, masking the color and smell in an endless cup of coffee.

I look at my fingers, nervously picking at my nails. *I've gone this far. I need to just say it. I can't do this anymore.*

"Lately, I can barely function."

"What do you mean?" She finally talks.

"Do you remember when I did the 904 Thin program? When I lost all that weight?"

"Yeah?"

"Well, when I did it, I opted not to drink at all. It was pointless," I say. "You can have drinks, but for me, it would have only been a tease. So, I didn't drink at all. For 45 days."

I lean forward, hoping my body language helps her comprehend how foreign that is in my world.

"Forty-five days I didn't drink. It's the longest I've ever gone for like, gosh I don't know, like 10, 15 years."

Her eyes bolt open in disbelief.

"My anxiety went away. I slept. The hot flashes stopped. And I kept eating healthy. Even after the 45 days. I felt great." I smile recalling those glorious months. "But then I drank."

The grin fades.

"Not a lot at first. Some wine. An occasional shot. It wasn't long before I was back at it. And so were all the symptoms. Only this time it was worse."

"Like what?"

"I mean, I feel like I'm going crazy." I tell her about the demonic nightmares, the hallucinations and the paralyzing depression.

"I'm constantly in my head." I tap both palms three times to either side of my brain. "It's like I can't shut it down. I can't take it anymore." I lean all the way to my lap and put my head in my hands.

Silence follows and when I finally look up, I'm not prepared for what I see. Tears barely held back by the red rims.

Our whole life, Nancy really only had two expressions: serious and a

Botox smile. In between she can do a sideways grin with a chuckle, reminiscent of our dad, but that was rare. Her resting face, conversation face, older sister giving orders face always expressionless. Until something humors her. Then the eyes light up and the corners of her mouth reach skyward. All other facial muscles secure their position.

Crying? I don't really recall her ever crying. She's always been tough as nails, holding true to the psychological first-born effect. That is until last year.

We lock eyes and I can't tell if I'm in trouble or what is about to happen.

"I'm going to tell you something." Her voice softens to a low plea. Her eyes never shift. "In one year and seven weeks, I lost my son and I lost my dad." She inhales deeply through her nose.

The police ruled Cody's fall from a North Dakota overpass a suicide. My sister believes he was startled by a passing vehicle. Either way, the results are the same. He's dead. And that day, part of my sister died on that highway with him.

"If I lose you, too. I won't survive." She swallows hard and clenches her jaw. "Because, right now?" She looks down and shakes her head slowly before meeting my eyes again. "I am barely hanging on." Her tears break free. Mom's soft snoring is the only sound.

Retired to our separate bedrooms, I lie awake most of the night. Hank's voice in my head.

"So many people love you. This whole city loves you. Why don't you love yourself?" she said.

I shook my head and mouthed the words, I don't know.

"You need to figure it out, Baby. Because there is something going on up here," she tapped my forehead, "that is making you drink."

She relayed the same 'I'll die without you' sentiments as Nancy.

But there hadn't been anything until now penetrating my entire world like my sister's love. I am on fire with a renewed will to live. I will do anything to make it happen. I don't care if I have to embarrass myself to do it. The unknowns—primarily my job and my community reputation—

no longer matter. All that matters is Nancy. She saved me. And now, I live to save her back.

April 1, 2017

I speak on behalf of my siblings at the funeral. We put our father to rest. Three days later, I board a plane to Jacksonville, conviction in tow to put my addiction to rest.

April 4, 2017

I got demoted today. You've never seen anyone happier to lose 35 percent of their annual income. I was already making plans on how to make my house and car payments while I go to treatment. And I think if I don't have a job, treatment is free, right? I'm not sure. The stress of figuring all this out has been overwhelming. But when I told my boss the truth, the craziest thing happened. I physically felt relief wash over me like a warm, cleansing rain. Cliché be damned. It's #truth.

This morning, I walked into her office. Sat in front of her. Fists clenched. Teeth clenched. Barely breathing. I figured I was getting fired for taking so many days off.

May as well be honest on my way out the door.

I thought about backing out. The mountain in front of me looked so big. So real.

Why bother? I'm getting fired. What's the point? I'll just be an embarrassing joke for them in their executive staff meetings.

I said it anyway. "I need help." No backstory. No explanation. No details.

I felt the air expel from her lungs and my lungs simultaneously. Her shoulders dropped and her head followed. The mountain crumbled. It turned to dust. It was a mirage the whole time. She got up and hugged me close. Tight.

She said she has to demote me. But she also said it doesn't have to be for good. I can earn my way back. She believes in me. And then HR gave me the best news of the day. Our health insurance covers treatment.

Everything is going to be okay.

April 5, 2017

A text comes in. It's Dawn. She's short. To the point. With an attachment.

Check this out Trac …

The link is a preview photo of our friend and former co-worker Tom. The Portland, Maine, headline reads: Police looking for missing WCSH meteorologist.

I read through the info. None of it makes sense. He went to an event a couple of hours from Portland to emcee a festival Saturday. No one has heard from him since. While I was delivering my father's eulogy, was Tom delivering his own?

No. That couldn't be. I'm sure he's fine. He probably ran away from home. Our brains hosted the same type of fantasies.

"Wouldn't it be great to dump this TV business and run off to the British Virgin Islands? Become a bartender like Tom Cruise in *Cocktail*?" He laughed off my question but agreed during one of our day-drinking episodes in 2012. Five years and one news station later, maybe he got sick of the new gig up north. Took me up on it. Forgot to send the memo.

April 6, 2017

Elvis Duran and the Morning Show are talking about relationships. Dysfunctional relationships. Perfect morning drive conversation for my current situation.

"Broke people can't fix broke people." Elvis offers a good point. But how do you know when someone is broken?

Jake and I are going to church together Sunday. Pro. Of course, we're not exactly back together. Con. I am grateful he introduced me to his church. It's been five years. Five long years since I darkened a church door. The warmth, the safety of God's grace again. It feels so good. Pro. He didn't mind that I kept a pint behind the seat to open right after services. And he didn't follow through when I asked for help with controlled drinking. Con. I can't deny the red flags.

I want to keep him around. I don't want to be alone. But at what cost? What am I really getting in return?

April 7, 2017

Tom is dead. Suicide. I am stunned. Numb.

I've talked to Dawn and Christina and Tera. We've all been in contact with him since he left the TV station we all worked at together. How did this happen? How did he do it? No one has answers. Everyone reports he seemed fine. According to the paper, the last thing he was doing was the thing he loved the most. Emceeing a party. A celebrity judge at a margarita mix-off, part of a festival at a ski resort.

This is exactly the kind of event we would have co-hosted together. Me, your official funologist. Him, the quirky weather guy with the pocket squares. The Tracy Dot Com and TJ Thunder Show. Never again.

How did this happen? All I know is they found him in harsh outdoor elements. What was he doing there? Did he take pills?

What happened, Tom? What was so bad you couldn't go on? Did you cry? Did you think you were alone? I was just one call away. My heart hurts so bad tonight. If only you had known I was getting help. I could have helped you. While you were falling apart, I was picking myself back up. I could have carried you, my brother. I wish you would have told me.

Oddly, I didn't cry. Not when the call came in. Not while I poured my heart out in my journal. Less than two weeks ago, I would have been a puddled mess. Binging to forget. I'm not sure what to make of this. I'm sad. Like I wrote, my heart *is* broken. So why no tears? Maybe like Tom's motivation, the answers will come. I need some rest. I'm emotionally drained.

April 13, 2017

By the time I plop down in the comfy chair at the Greenfield Center, I am equal parts frustrated, relieved and frazzled.

"So sorry I'm late, Dr. Jackson."

"Please, call me Brian. It's fine." He shuts the door to his office.

"Not in my book. I'm former military and make it a point to always be early."

"As long as you arrive safe, I never care if you're late." He sits down with a pad and pen in his lap.

"Well, I'm just happy to be here. It was tougher than I thought it would be."

"What do you mean?" He cocks his head. "Like, finding the place?"

"No." I pull out my phone to scroll through as some sort of futile reference to all the places called before Greenfield. "I mean, when I finally decided to ask for help, finding it was way harder than it should have to be."

"Where did you start?" He props his elbows on the chair arms and grips both ends of the pen in his fingers.

"Google. Then called the first place that popped up." He gives a knowing nod to the name of the facility. "They did an analysis over the phone."

"What did they recommend?"

"They said I needed inpatient treatment." I lift my hands off the desk and flip my palms up in surrender. "Which, you know, was fine because that's what all my friends told me I needed. But then they told me they didn't have any beds."

My incredulous look reveals a selfish ego, convinced I'm the only person in the largest land-mass city needing help at this moment in time.

"Then I asked my friends. Pointless. No one knew anything. Here are these people begging me to get help, but nobody knows how to do it. I asked them to post it on Facebook. You know, crowd source info to find the best recommendation. They said they would, but they didn't."

I shrug my shoulders.

"I get it though. Probably afraid the 'just asking for a friend' would send tongues wagging."

I slump back in the chair.

"Hank's always posting funny memes about drinking. I guess you can do that when you have nothing to hide. And Jake, he has his career to protect."

"Who are they?" Brian starts taking notes.

"Hank is one of my besties. Her name is Henrietta, but we call her Hank. She's pretty much the only one who knew how bad it was. She's been begging me for years to get help. I kept telling her I would. But I didn't."

I lean on the table between us and fidget with my fingernails.

"And then when Jake came around, I guess she finally felt like she had somebody else who would listen. He recommended Lakeview, but they don't take my insurance. So, I finally called the insurance company and they recommended you. They said ..."

"Wait. Back up. Who is Jake? A boyfriend?" He holds his pen ready.

"Um." I scrunch up my face. "Not really. I mean, he was. Sort of. I told him not to call me his girlfriend, but he ignored me. And that was fine. But then things got out of control."

I give him an overview of the train wreck, including the bedwetting incident.

"But we're still friends. He calls almost every day to make sure I'm getting help. And we still see each other at church. He got me to go back, so I have that to be grateful for."

Another shrug signals that's all I got on this subject.

"I asked about inpatient, but the insurance company said I have to come to your outpatient program first, which is fine. I have an important project at work, so I don't want to go until then anyway."

I smile at him to lighten the heavy topic.

"I figure I could roll here with you fine folk for a while until I can go."

Brian furrows his brow and cocks his head again.

"What makes you think you need to go to inpatient at all?"

I break down my daily habits and massive quantities of unhealthy liquid intake.

Looking down at his notes, he asks, "When was the last time you took a drink?"

"Hmm..." I purse my lips and look up at the ceiling. "A little over two weeks ago, I guess."

His head pops up. Mine pops down. Surprised, intense eyes lock mine.

"Did you go somewhere to detox?"

"No."

His eyes snap wider and his head juts forward.

"You detoxed? On your own?"

"Yeah. Why? Is that a bad thing?"

"Well, yeah."

Until now, I'm ignorant about people who have face planted to death as their body is trying to recalculate. Cracked heads on concrete. Temples to sharp corners. Falls down stairs. Silent hemorrhaging.

It's a miracle from God I fell forward on my staircase landing.

"You can stroke out during a detox," Brian says. "Or suffer a seizure."

Heather. Heather's overt concern makes sense. Did she know? "You need to go to the hospital right now." Did she believe a plane ride with no medical supervision was a death sentence?

He assures me I'm in the right place and is convinced I won't need to go away for help.

"At the end of the 10 weeks, I think you'll realize you don't need inpatient." He waves a hand in front of him. "Heck, you've already been through the hard part. If you had come up here and said your last drink was in the parking lot, well, that's what inpatient is for."

He says I've already proven by my 17 sober days I can pass by a bar and not stop. My responsibility moving forward would be to come for two and a half hours after work Monday–Thursday.

It dawns on me I would not have needed to confess to my boss. I could do this program and no one would have been the wiser.

But I'm glad I did. Now I can take the first step stumbling into sobriety. Just one step. Not worrying about the next.

Stumbling. An unsteady walk. A misstep. When the right leg gives out, the left snaps to attention, pushing forward in an attempt to steady the whole body. Then the right jumps back in, follows through, and so on and so on until we are stable again.

The brain doesn't have time to stop and wonder what the next step should be before taking the first. And neither should I. Just like stumbling feet, the rest will fall into place. But not before I take the first step.

Asking for help.

CHAPTER 4

WHERE ARE ALL THE PEOPLE WHO LOOK LIKE ME?

April 17, 2017

The goal. Avoid being the new, all eyes on me, zoo animal the first day of Intensive Outpatient Program—IOP.

I figure if I get there before everyone else, the slow procession of arrivals and introductions won't abolish the awkward, judgmental sizing-up process, but it will minimize it.

Direct plunges into cold, strange rooms is in my wheelhouse. Today I prefer to ease into the social waters.

You'd think a 30-minute jump would be enough. It's not. There's a name scribbled on line one of the otherwise blank sign-in sheets.

Aaron C. Damn overachiever.

After an exchange of pleasantries with the receptionist, I move from the waiting room into the meeting area to confront this clown who screwed up my well-laid plan.

Aaron is kicked back in a comfy chair that looks to be reserved for the doctor. It's contrasted by 16 informal lunchroom chairs arranged in a circle.

He's a blue-collar guy with a full beard and worn jeans. Handsome in the burly category, Aaron is a laundered, pressed kind of dirty. I'm sure he could clean up nice if motivated. I don't think he's motivated very often.

Less than impressed to see me, he gives a quick chin nod.

That's it? No 'Hi, I'm so-and-so'? No acknowledgement of how scared I am behind this façade? No reassurance everything is going to be okay, and I'm in the right place to change my life forever?

Posturing with a wide man spread and a loud voice, Aaron continues his conversation without skipping a beat. He's hollering a rundown of his daily manual labor to the receptionist while munching on a Subway sandwich. She's responding in muffled tones.

It's an opportunity for me to survey the lay of the land I will be calling home for 2 ½ hours every Monday through Thursday evening for the next 10 weeks.

There's a coffee nook against one wall. *Of course, there is.* I smirk at the thought. The caricature of what treatment looks like in my head always includes worn down faces and shaky hands gripping copious cups of joe. On the wall above is a list of rules: No interrupting. No crosstalk. All conversations are confidential. Etc… Next to it is a color-coded poster of a brain on alcohol. A flea market motivational plaque with the Serenity Prayer hangs on an opposite wall post in between a line of windows overlooking the top of a parking garage.

Extra chairs and random art line a third wall. Across the room a white board with a blue marker list of names filed in chronological order down the left side. Monday – Ken 3, Robert 4, Tuesday – Gwen 2, OPEN, Wednesday – Jim 2, OPEN, Thursday – Dionne 1, Elizabeth 5, Monday (17th) – OPEN, Aaron 4

I take a seat by the window, a safe five-chair distance from Aaron C., and file through the black binder Brian gave me at our first meeting last week. There's nothing new in it. Only a desire to look busy and avoid eye contact with my fellow inmates.

They stream in one at a time, greeting each other with bromance hand slaps and jovial Whassup?s.

Didn't you guys just see each other? Sheesh. Could that much have changed in four days?

Falling in line with Aaron C.'s social skills, none of the all-male cast acknowledges my existence.

Has no one in this group read "How to Win Friends and Influence People"? And am I the only girl?

Both questions are answered with the next arrival. A fiery red head gets a round of synced alto voices welcoming her. "Elizabeth!"

I immediately like her as much as they do. I can tell she's read the book as she sits down near me.

"Hi, I'm Elizabeth."

She reaches across the empty chair between us and opens her fresh-lipsticked mouth to reveal a bleached-white toothy grin. Her auburn locks are twisted so professionally, I can't tell if she is naturally curly or dropped by the Dry Bar this morning for a blowout. Her sparkling black dress is a sharp contrast to the denim-filled room, and the stiletto heels punctuate her femininity when she crosses her legs, grips a knee, and gently rocks a leg back and forth.

More seats get filled, including a guy and girl who appear to be a couple, a couple more dudes, and a woman who looks extremely troubled.

"Okay, take your seats." Brian enters the room and takes a seat on a plain, old lunchroom chair against the white board. Not very fitting for the king in my opinion. He deserves a comfy chair to listen to our sob stories. "Everybody say hello to Tracy. She's new." The group responds haphazardly.

"Alright. Let's go around the room, tell Tracy a little bit about yourself, why you're here and how your weekend was."

They each take a turn in order around the circle. I'm equal parts surprised by how similar we are in lifestyle as how different we are in our addictions. There's a doctor, a nurse, a lawyer, two business owners, a student, a parolee, an unemployed 40-something living with his mother, a housewife and several blue and white-collar employees ranging in age from 19 to 59.

Some are here by choice, others court-ordered, and many via the friends and family intervention program that I am a proud card-carrying member. I assume everyone is here for alcohol the same way I always assume everyone is a Christian, falsely. There are Christians, Catholics, Jews, Agnostics and Atheists. They have alcohol addiction. Heroin addiction. Cocaine, Xanax, marijuana, oxycodone, hydrocodone, benzos, and a gross combination of any or all of the above.

The clear-skinned, clear-eyed innocent faces look like they've never touched a drug or drop of alcohol a day in their life. Others as if they came out of the womb jonesing for the next mood adjuster. And one guy in the corner looks like he's still using.

He's a late arrival, disrupting the whole flow of introductions with his nervous chatter about why he's tardy. I surmise by the group reaction this is a nightly ritual. Same excuses different day. He plops into the chair next to the person who has the floor and flips his long, sweaty hair away from his face and over his shoulder.

Before she can vocalize anything more out of her open mouth, the troubled woman, who had barely gotten her name and addiction out before he barged in, is interrupted for a second time. Loud grunt. Crinkling sandwich wrapper. Pop of a soda can. Slurp from said can. Heavy sigh.

A man in golf shorts sits with his arms crossed, glaring. He's clearly unamused by this ongoing lack of self-awareness.

Brian darts his eyes around the room. His jaw shifts. He swallows hard, but his voice is soft. "Go on, Dionne."

My heart aches for her on her third attempt.

Aaron C. had just shared how great his weekend with his kids turned out. His ex-wife even let them stay an extra night as a reward for his progress. Jim got word his job is going to let him return after his next drug test, assuming it comes back clean.

"But it will," he said and smiled confidently. Andy went to church for the first time since getting clean. And Amber cleared her phone, blocking numbers of known drug dealers from her past life. *I guess a lot did happen in just a few days. No wonder they were so excited to see each other.*

Dionne, however, hasn't been quite so lucky.

"I had a crappy weekend," she says. She hasn't lifted her eyes from the floor in front of her since she got here. "I'm still obsessing."

"Yeah, I know what you mean," the long-haired late guy says.

Oh, dear Lord. Tardyman has more to say.

He talks with his mouth full and drops his sandwich in his lap to wipe his brow with a jacket sleeve.

Why is he so sweaty? Did he jog here?

His right leg shakes up and down while he talks. "About a month ago, I was going to a ..." More than one in the crowd releases a groan.

"Miles." Brian puts his hand out in a stop signal. "Let her finish. You'll have your turn."

"Oh. Yeah, yeah, yeah." He waves her on. "Go ahead. Go ahead. Sorry."

"I'm still craving it. Thinking about it. Dreaming about it." Dionne takes a long pause. Eyes never shifting from the ground. Brian gives her some time so as not to step on a thought. Silence.

"Does anyone know how long a normal craving lasts?" he asks. Somebody offers 15 minutes. Brian points in the speaker's direction. "Yes." He looks back at Dionne and waits.

She shrugs her shoulders. "That's it." I get the feeling her cravings are not normal.

And it is nobody's business.

Brian gives her a few more seconds. "Okay," he says. He shifts his body from her direction straight on and raises his voice to direct the group. "Is anyone else having dreams about using?" Nobody raises their hand. "It's okay if you are. But as addicts, we need to be diligent about what our bodies are telling us. Dreams are one of the symptoms leading to a relapse. So, if you're having them, tell me, tell your sponsor, meditate, go to a meeting."

I don't understand half of what he says. I opt to keep my mouth shut for now.

Miles is the last to talk. He crumples up his dinner bag and smiles a sideways grin. I can't tell if he's embarrassed or excited to share his life's misgivings. He reveals a strong grouping of the drugs listed above, including alcohol. I don't trust anything coming out of his mouth. He's either lying or blowing up the truth for dramatic effect.

His stories of near-death encounters with pimps and drug dealers and cops and the Boogie Man have a lot of holes. He supposedly has a wife in prison, but he offers up without being asked that he can't say why she's there.

"My lawyer doesn't want me to talk about it."

He lives with his widowed mother, who used her retirement savings to cover his bail bond and lawyer fees for a crime still under investigation, but he has full custody of the kids.

His right leg bounces up and down and his eyes dart all around the room, never making eye contact with anyone except me. I imagine he's trying to read my poker face. Wondering if I'm buying what he's selling. I don't flinch.

"Tracy?" Brian ignores the litany of fairytales that just happened. "Do you want to share with the group why you're here."

"My name is Tracy Collins and I am a tragic binge drinker." I sit upright, expecting this admission to be emotionally draining. "I drank every night to black out and pass out."

There. I said it. I lean back in my seat and drape my right foot over my left knee. Hearing all of their stories made me unusually comfortable in this room full of strangers. I'm not unique. And for the first time in my life, that is a bonus.

I tell them an abbreviated version about my dad. "My dad never told me he loved me. On March 1st, he called to tell me he was proud of me. He talked to me about my drinking. And he told me he loved me." Sighs. "Two weeks later, he died." Gasps. "And now, here I am. Hanging out with you fine folk." I sweep the circle with my hand. "Hoping for a new way of life."

At 7:02, Brian releases us for a break. We all stand and the whole room bolts for the door except Elizabeth, Jim, Brian and me.

"Where'd everybody go? I thought the bathrooms were right there?" I ask and point to the side hallway.

"They all smoke," Brian says. "Well, most of them. Tonight's alumni, so some of them go downstairs to catch up."

"Alumni?"

"Yeah." Elizabeth jumps in. She's been listening to Jim whine about how his wife is still suspicious of him. *'Even after four whole months of sobriety!'* I think she's looking for an excuse to get out of the conversation. "After you graduate, you can come back every Monday for alumni meeting in the other room."

"And Elizabeth will be in there next Monday," Brian says. They both smile and she nods her head.

"You're graduating?" *Darn. You're the only one I gel with.*

"Yep. Doing my step five tonight."

"What is step five?"

"It's the last step you do on the night you graduate," Brian says. "It's your life story as it relates to the disease." I shift my eyes to the white board behind him. He and Elizabeth do the same.

"Oh. Yeah. Last week's schedule." She points to her name. "I was supposed to do it on Thursday, but …"

"But I wasn't here on Wednesday," Jim says. "She let me have her spot for step two."

"And Aaron's going to do his step four tomorrow." She smiles and gives me a reassuring look. "We work together like that."

After 15 minutes, the group meanders back two to three at a time. Nobody seems to be in any hurry. It annoys me.

Don't you know Elizabeth is about to graduate, people?

Miles brings up the rear, figuratively blowing some smoke up the very disinterested butt in front of him.

Good God. He sure has a lot to talk about for someone who has been sitting around playing Xbox in his mom's basement for the last three months.

Elizabeth starts with her name, date and location of birth. She runs through some basic 'growing up Elizabeth' details and gets to her first memory of use. Alcohol is her drug of choice.

I knew I liked her.

When she talks about her teenage boys, her face lights up. When she shares her crazy drinking story, she's able to laugh at herself. She's a professional with a good paying gig. A victim of affairs of the heart. Fiercely devoted. Repeatedly taken advantage of.

She's sassy and strong, and I think she may be my sister from another mister with a ginger gene. Her downfall, and subsequent rebound, revolved around a relationship. One she knowingly admits will continue to be her Achilles heel after she leaves the group. She's scared. And vulnerable. And smart enough to know it.

"Do you have a sponsor yet?" Brian asks. She doesn't. "Do you go to meetings?" No. But she plans to go.

Brian pulls out a gold coin with a butterfly on one side and a motivational phrase on the other.

"This coin signifies your transformation in the program. We'll pass it around the room and everyone will put some positive energy in it to send you off."

The coin makes its way towards me with comments of adoration.

"I appreciate your guts to ask tough questions," Aaron C. says.

"You've got a good head on your shoulders, kid. I know you'll make it," Jim says.

These are followed with, 'You are one of the strongest women I know.' 'I hope we stay in touch.' 'In this coin, I place peace. May you continue to have it.' And so on. And so on. Until the coin is placed in my palm.

I look at the butterfly. *What do I say? I don't know her.* Flip it to the sentiment. *You have really pretty hair? I enjoy the makeup palette you selected today? It really compliments your skin tone?*

Brian senses my discomfort and says, "Tracy, you can just share something you related to in Elizabeth's story."

"Oh." My face lights up with relief. "Well, that's easy." I turn to my left and give Elizabeth the same toothy grin she greeted me with nearly three hours ago. "Elizabeth, your story is my story. Ya know, except for the kid thing." I roll my eyes and she laughs. "In fact, could you just come back in 10 weeks and re-read it?" I point at the papers in her hand and throw out a phrase I've heard in the movies. "Thanks for sharing."

We stand up, gather hands, and recite the Serenity Prayer from the wall.

"God, grant me the serenity to accept the things I cannot change, the courage to change the things I can, and the wisdom to know the difference." The hands I'm connected to start bouncing up and down as everyone says in unison with excitement, "Keep coming back, it works if you work it. So, work it, you're worth it."

I wait patiently while Elizabeth accepts her parting hugs. When the room is clearing, she walks over to me.

"So? Whadya think?" She reaches out and playfully slaps my crossed hands.

"It was good. I think I'll come back. I hear it works if I work it." I open my mouth and feign a giggle.

"You're funny." She laughs at my cheap joke. "I like the 'tragic binge drinker.'" She raises her hands and puts air quotes around the last three words.

"Alcoholic just sounds so …" I purse my lips and think about it for a second. "Boring. I was going for broke every day of my life." She nods in agreement. "I added the word tragic after hearing an author talk about being a 'tragic alcoholic' on NPR's Fresh Air with Terry Gross." It was my turn to use the air quotes. "She asked him why 'tragic alcoholic' versus 'alcoholic.'"

"What'd he say?"

"It somehow sounded more …" my eyes widen, "severe." Verbal strike on the last syllable. Just the way the author would have like it. "So people would stand up and take note. Not ask him stupid questions like, 'Can't you have just one?' or 'You don't drink? Like ever?'

"You want to exchange numbers?" Elizabeth asks.

It occurs to me it was a thin, thin thread of God allowing me to meet Elizabeth. Without that one meeting shift in schedule, our paths would have never crossed. I've known her less than three hours, but it feels like a lifetime. Her sheer being makes me feel normal.

That night, I lay my head on my pillow and thank God for one more day of sobriety. And hope.

"Thank you, God. I finally have hope."

April 18, 2017

The rollcall is much faster tonight. There are no newcomers and not much to report since we parted ways 21 hours earlier.

Halfway through, a pretty girl with straight brown hair walks in. I don't recognize her, but everyone greets her with enthusiasm. Embarrassed by the attention her tardiness caused, she offers a flat reply and avoids eye contact.

"Hey." She pulls her shoulder strap bag off over her head and takes an empty seat closest to the door, dropping the bag quietly next to her.

Then, just like clockwork, her polar opposite bursts through the door, sweaty and frazzled. Miles is loudly blasting off something from his man-my-life-is-so-dramatic repertoire, but I'm not paying attention. I'm too busy not minding my own business wondering where a few of the missing faces are tonight.

Brian waits for Miles to take a breath, then answers my burning question.

"So, you may have noticed Dionne is not here." We all shake our heads. "She has decided to check into an inpatient facility."

"Good," a guy to my right says. I don't recognize him from yesterday either. "I was an inpatient years ago. I can completely relate to everything she was saying." He leans his right forearm on his leg and cocks a hand on his left hip. "It's like that's all your mind can think about, you know what I mean?" The room nods in response. "It sucks."

"What happens in inpatient treatment?" I ask. "Hi, I'm Tracy, by the way."

"Oh, hey. Andy." He stretches out his hand.

"Yeah, you guys didn't meet yesterday," Brian says. "Andy, why don't you tell her a little bit about yourself and go ahead and answer her question."

Andy is handsome with tanned skin and bold Native American features. He looks to be mid-30s, and his mouth barely moves when he talks. Or even when he laughs, really. His eyes do the work. Like my sister's. He's dressed in jeans, work boots and a plain white V-neck T. Moments earlier, he says, he had a work shirt covering it.

"But," he shrugs one shoulder and scrunches his face. "I'm not really interested in advertising they have a drug addict working for them." He chuckles and I join in a half beat behind, looking around for confirmation this is okay. His demeanor switches gears with the topic.

"No, but seriously, to answer your question. Inpatient is great." He points to a few others in the room, including the shy, tardy girl. She nods in agreement. "Instead of being out in the real world, desperately trying to pass the time until we come here each night, you're kept busy all-day long."

"Doing what?"

He again points to the girl, signaling it's okay to jump in anytime. "You go to meetings." He waves his hand in a circle. "Like this."

"Yeah, and you go to classes." The shy girl finally speaks. "I'm Gwen." She puts one hand on her chest and gives an uncomfortable, close-mouthed grin and eye roll.

I mirror her smile and give a quick wave. Anymore, and I'm afraid I'll scare her into silence.

"The classes are, like …" She looks at the ceiling and starts counting them off on her hand from memory. "Coping skills, Big Book study, 12-step study."

"Twelve steps?" I ask. "Like the steps we do in here?"

"Well, sort of." Brian chimes in. "We do five steps, and their based off the same principles, but the assignments are different."

"And then we also did things like yoga, meditation," Gwen says. Still counting on her fingers, she throws both hands out. "Stuff like that. The point is without it, I wouldn't have stopped using."

"Nope." Andy shakes his head and leans forward. "Me either." Both elbows on his knees. Fingers clasped. "It was too tempting. I could last a couple of days, but that was it."

"Why don't you tell Tracy why you're here," Brian says. He looks at Gwen. She's staring back in time. Still nodding from Andy's last comment. "Gwen?"

"Oh. Me?"

She returns from la-la-land and gives me a rundown of her self-inflicted misfortune.

A drinking and driving hit-and-run in her hometown of Austin, Texas, coupled with discovery of benzos and other drugs, landed her in the county jail. The court agreed to release her into the custody of her mother in Jacksonville and ultimately an in-patient treatment facility. After 45 days, she went to stay with her mom again in a nearby high rise down by the river. Attending IOP keeps her on track.

"I still have to go home to Austin for court dates," she says. "And I have to carry this around with me everywhere." She pulls a black box out that looks like an oversized ear thermometer.

"What is it?" I walk over to get a closer look.

"It's a home breathalyzer. I call it my breath baby." She laughs at her own joke. "You know, like, 'I'd love to go to the movies, but I left my baby at home, and it's time for her feeding.' Get it? Because I have to blow into it every four hours."

"Every four hours?" I'm shocked as my mind runs down what it would be like to have to stop what I'm doing in my busy life every four hours. "Even at night when you're sleeping?"

"Yep." I hand her baby back to her and she puts it away. "I set an alarm. Every night. And every morning."

I curl my mouth in disgust and walk back to my seat. I hate alarms. They're the devil.

That night I think about Gwen's predicament. She's so young and pretty. Her big doe eyes and full, peach-stained lips on her plump cherub face don't look like the features of a pill-popping, booze-guzzling

56

alcoholic addict.

But there's no denying the car accident—the one no one got hurt in— the one that's going to cost as much as her a college education in fines, fees, restitution and treatment co-pays—there is no denying the car accident ultimately saved her life.

Her little frame couldn't take much more of the abuse she was putting it through. And even if it would, she was destined to kill herself or somebody else as a serial blackout driver.

She can't see it now. It's still fresh and she's still broken. But that's what we're all in treatment for. To get stronger together. To help each other live long enough to figure out why God spared us.

April 19, 2017

Tonight's topic is relapse. I already have an emotional problem with it. *Never drink again? Like never? Never ever?* I raise my hand and confess my difficulty comprehending this concept.

"There's a clear vision in my head of what retirement looks like." I bounce my open palms around the crystal ball on my shoulders doubling as my skull. "And it involves future me, in front of my future beach house, sipping margaritas at noon." I don't even like margaritas. No clue why I said that.

Brian coughs a chuckle and holds his hand out for me to whoa this thought pony. "Okay, hold up." He shakes his head and sits up. "Let's not worry about 20 years from now. Let's take this one day at a time."

"One day at a time?" Groan. "It sounds so cliché."

He ignores my complaint and asks if anyone else wants to share. Andy starts talking about his relapse. Or should I say, relapses. I was mistaken thinking he came straight here from inpatient. He's had several missteps to straighten out. I can relate. I've lived it, too. On many levels. The only difference is, I didn't go to rehab in between.

Benders.

Per Urban Dictionary: The status of being bent for more than a day. Usually results in loss of memory, money, strange tattoos, and other things you'll have a hell of a time explaining.

Per Tracy Dot Com Dictionary: Enjoyable, mischievous weeks of too much fun too many days in a row. Nobody got caught. Nobody got hurt. Nobody had to check into rehab.

Downward Spirals.

Urban Dictionary: Commonly used to describe depression and/or drug abuse, but can be applied to anything that starts out bad and just gets worse and worse and worse ... until the person crashes, and maybe finds their way back to happiness.

TDC Dictionary: Same.

Benders were borne out of excitement. Spirals out of negativity. Benders were fun, easy to come out of. Spirals usually—check that—*always* occurred after a break up or unexpected death. Escaping their grip was brutal and typically required a series of days with flu-like symptoms.

After a bender, I looked back fondly but ready to get on with the rest of my life. After a spiral, I negotiated my future. Swearing repeatedly, I would recognize the signs next time and ask for help rather than hibernate on Smirnoff Island. As we both know by now, I didn't.

"This last time, it was my divorce that did me in," Andy says and shakes his head. "I knew it was coming." His furrowed brows raise up towards his hairline. "Heck, it was my idea we hurry up and get the paperwork turned in." He laughs and throws imaginary die out of his right hand. "I told her, 'Git 'er done. Let's close this chapter and move on. Raise our kids in peace.'" He lowers his head and wipes his eyes before any tears can fall. "I don't know why she didn't have me sign the last time I picked them up." His shoulders shake once as he tries to laugh away his embarrassment. His voice is muffled. His face is fully flanked in both hands as he makes a ceremonial final swipe to rid himself of all emotion. "I knew the divorce was coming." One final red-eyed shake of the head. "I still wasn't prepared when the courier showed up on my doorstep."

We all sit in reflective silence, taking in his spent energy.

I feel his pain. Life threw me sucker punches back-to-back-to-back. It was Muhammad Ali clockwork. Every six months. Just as sure as Andy expected to see divorce papers, I was sure, one day, we all die. But the courier of death showed up unexpectedly on my doorstop last year with news of my nephew and again this year with my dad. One-two-punch to the gut with a stiff uppercut broken romance sandwiched right in between.

Each time, I did what he did. Spiral. Each time, he opted for more rehabilitation. I opted to lie my way through it.

After the meeting, I sat in the car. Keys in my lap. Finally, the CRV's engine fires up. Breaks the silence of the parking garage. The noise is quickly covered by Melissa Ross's welcoming voice. "Next up, we have Phillip on the Southside. Hey, Phillip. What's your question?" The show is a repeat from this morning. I never get to hear it live. And tonight, I won't get to enjoy it secondhand either. There's more pressing business in need of immediate attention.

As soon as the Bluetooth confirmation message replaces the digital radio/time/temp information, I reach for the phone cradled in the car mount and press the home button. Ding ding.

"Siri, call Pat."

Ding ding. "Calling Pat."

Pat is a sober friend. A sober friend who understands intimately the pitfalls of relapse. She's 68 and got sober the first time in 1974, right before her first child was born.

"I didn't want my children raised in a house of alcohol," she once told me. "Like I was."

Her wiry, long grey hair gives away her hippy roots. I imagine she was the 'cool mom' of her sons' friends. In spite of her teetotaling ways. And she was successful at it. She raised two fine young men on the working-class side of Boston. Put them through college. Sent them down the yellow brick road. All without a single substance tainting her purified blood.

"Twenty-seven." She pumped her fist violently the day she told me her history. "Twenty-seven yee-ahs and I threw it ah-ll away." Her accent and mannerisms are a *Saturday Night Live* Bostonian caricature. But there was nothing funny about her message. One day, she picked up a drink, and spent the next decade in the bottom of a bottle. But why? I had to know.

She picks up the phone on the second ring. A seven-year comeback kid.

"So, remember the time you told me about your relapse?" She does. "Well, I didn't want to pry at the time, but we were talking about relapsing tonight, and I said I figured by the time I retire, I should be cleared for cocktail hour?"

"Oh, gawd, Tracy." She shouts. Not the angry kind. The New England kind.

"Well, I don't understand why it is that …"

"Do you wanna know why I drank after 27 yee-ahs? What landed my sweet behind in that bah stool at 51 years old and kept me there until I was almost ret-ah-yud?" Her loud voice bounces off the windows.

I reach to lower the volume and put the car in drive.

"Because I was stupid." Her reasoning is little too elementary, but she backs it up with clinical logic.

"I have a disease raging inside of me. And just because I don't drink for 27 yee-ahs, doesn't stop the disease from progressing inside of me."

I can hear her finger tapping against something near her mouth.

"The day I picked up a bee-ah?" she says. "I picked up 17 right behind it." She pauses for my reaction, but I'm holding my breath.

"True stahry." Pause. "Like I nevah stopped."

Hollow sounds of spinning tires fill the space on my end. A hand slap of the knee on hers.

"I'll leave you with this, kid," she says. "If somebody had told me, 'Pick up that drink and you won't be able to stop for 10 years,' I would have nevah done it." A final knee slap. "Nevah."

April 20, 2017

I can't take my eyes off of Gwen. I'm strangely drawn to her in a big sister kind of way. Even though she's young enough to be my daughter. Her sad eyes rarely make contact with anyone looking back at her, and she only speaks when spoken to. She's always lost in thought and looks extremely uncomfortable, shifting in her chair and wringing her hands, when called upon to speak.

Every night before break, somebody is assigned to do a step. And every night after the break, the same. The progression is one step every two weeks until graduation. But since we all started at staggering times, the stages vary.

Andy shared last night; however, Gwen mysteriously disappeared after the break and missed it. Hmm. Odd. She and Andy are tight. Why would she miss supporting her friend while he's exposing a deep part of himself? A taboo topic at that. Religion. Spirituality. Higher Power. Deep stuff.

Her absence wasn't missed by Brian either. He decides to address it before we go around the room.

"Gwen," he says, breaking her concentration. When the good doctor calls your name, it never feels like your being sent down to the principal's office. Only concern for your well-being. "We missed you last night after the break."

"Yeah." She stretches her arms, gives him an awkward grin and rolls her eyes. "My mom couldn't come get me last night and the last bus leaves right after the break. I'll have to take it again tonight."

Brian looks around the room. Shifting his jaw. Waiting for someone, anyone to jump in.

"Can anybody help Gwen out?"

I excitedly offer up my services. So does another woman, as well as several men. We all do a vocal battle to see who gets custody of Gwen. A couple of the men are pretty assertive. This seems inappropriate to me, and Brian confirms it is, in fact, deemed bad form in Sobrietyville.

"It would be best if you rode with another woman." He shrugs one shoulder at the suggestion. "But it's your choice."

"You can take her tonight," the other woman says. "I've got a meeting after this." She looks over at Gwen. "If you ever decide you want to go to a meeting after this, I can take you home after that."

"Yeah. Good segue," Brian says. "Let's go around the room and talk about what we did last night and then share what our plans are for staying sober this weekend." He points his pen around the room. "So, for example, if you're going to a meeting or spending time with family and friends. Any ideas that will help each other come up with alternative ways to spend your time." He raises his hand at the elbow. "Who's all going to a meeting this weekend?"

Three people raise their hands, including the couple and Jim.

"What meeting are you talking about?" I ask Brian. My eyes bounce around the room to everyone offering up their opinion.

"A.A.," the woman says.

"Not necessarily," Jim says.

"Well ..." A third person chimes in.

"Hold up. Hold up." Brian sets down his pen and holds up both hands, waving the audience into submission. "We always encourage finding a 12-step based program outside of treatment, as well as a sponsor. Someone who has some time in the program to guide you and keep you accountable in your journey after you graduate."

I had been to an Alcoholics Anonymous meeting once. I share an abbreviated version of my debacle with the group.

"I made a pact with a friend to go after yet another two-week long brutal bender."

Some look confused. Others nod knowingly. I expand the backstory to clear it up.

"My friend and I, a co-worker, we formed the Daytime Drinking Club. We met up at the Ale House at least once a month after wrapping the noon show. Whoever got there first snagged our usual stools on the patio and gave bartender Nik the order." I drop my voice an octave to mimic his announcer voice. "Two Blue Moons. Two shots of Captain

Morgan. Make 'em a double, Nik."

The DDC only had two members. And the first rule of the DDC was don't talk about the DDC. We didn't want any more members. Our secret was safe with each other. But our secret was out of control.

"That week, we met up three times and commiserated about broken hearts and unsuccessful attempts to drown the misery in sauce," I say. "So, under the cover of daylight and sporting shades as a cloak of invisibility, we met up on a Saturday morning and snuck into an A.A. meeting."

I cringe reminiscing about what it was like.

"I was immediately mortified as I realized they were going around the room, boldly announcing their first names."

Then came the moment I felt thrown under the bus.

"I followed in line and did what everyone else did. I said, 'Hi, I'm Tracy. Alcoholic.' But my friend?" I pause for the rhetorical question. "He said, 'Hi. Just happy to be here.'"

Mouths drop. I'm feeling justified in my betrayal.

"I looked over at him like, 'What the heck, dude?'" I laugh remembering his response. "He wouldn't look at me. I stared him down hard, too. But he strategically waited until the roll call moved a safe distance down the line. That's when he turned to give me a clownish grin."

I smile at the memory. Turns out the DDC president didn't need to profess alcoholism. He used that trip to get himself in check. Slowed way down. I, on the other hand, did not recognize how bad I needed it. Mostly because I didn't see anyone who looked like me.

"I told him, 'I'm going to get a drink,' after the meeting," I hold up my left wrist and tap it with a finger. "He looked at his watch and was like, 'It's 10 o'clock!' I said, 'It's midnight in Australia.' I put on my shades. Did an about face. And I was out."

Afterwards, we never talked about that day again. The DDC voted to cut back to quarterly conferences.

"You need to visit another group. They're all different. Different personalities. Different expectations."

Others in the crowd nod approval.

"They don't all make you introduce yourself. Slip in the back. Keep your mouth shut. Or don't. The choice is yours."

"There's 650 meetings a week in our area," Brian says. "I'm sure you'll find one you like."

"A.A. is the one most people are familiar with. But there's all kinds," Jim says. "I prefer Celebrate Recovery."

"What's that?"

"It uses the same principles and traditions as A.A., but it incorporates Christian beliefs," he says.

"I'm looking into Smart Recovery," someone adds.

I look to the corner the voice came from. "What's that?"

"No God involved. I'm non-believer," he says.

Jim guffaws at the thought.

"A.A. has meetings for agnostics," he says.

"Yeah, I'm just not into it. Smart Recovery teaches how to rely on yourself for the decisions you make."

Another snort from Jim. Confrontation makes me uncomfortable. I jump in to play peacemaker.

"To each his own."

CHAPTER 5

ONE DAY AT A TIME & OTHER CLICHÉS I'M LEARNING ARE TRUE

May 2, 2017

Step one. It's my turn to take off my guilt-drenched covering and stand emotionally naked at the front of the class.

I've spent two weeks listening to others share at their varied progression in the steps. It's an odd process as an observer. Some hold back. Give lame answers. Guarded stories. Others break wide open. Toe-curling tales. Shame-filled body language.

What I've noticed is, while the information is embarrassing, and rightly so, for the person sharing, I feel no judgement. The nods that roll around the circled chairs are a non-verbal "I've been there, brother." Encouragement to keep the speaker on track. To know he or she is not the only person on the planet who has committed the four-page list of Q&A sins in his or her trembling hands.

Typically, two people share per night. Multiplied by the four nights per week times two weeks of treatment. That equals 16 people, the entire class give or take so far, I've told in response to their stories, "Meh. No biggie. Hold your head up. We've all been there. I don't even know why you were so nervous to share those stories."

How strange it is now to be in the hot seat. I look around at all the faces. I'm used to studying their reactions unnoticed. Now all eyes are on me. I take a deep breath.

"You know," I say, "I couldn't figure out why you guys are so nervous when you're doing your steps." I rub the back of my neck and fidget with the papers in hand. "This is harder than I thought it would be."

Heads bob in agreement. Others chuckle.

Deep breath. Loud nose exhale.

Am I a happy person? I wouldn't say I am a completely "happy" person, but I am grateful for no longer being a sad person. I'm trying to find my new purpose in life. I know it exists. God is not finished with me yet. Otherwise, I would be dead.

Has my drinking caused problems in my life? Thirty grand per year with demotion. One week of vacation per year with self-induced illness. I've missed many events (too drunk to attend). I've destroyed every romantic relationship and worried family and friends who believe I will die.

Am I weak in emotions, physical health, or spiritual pursuits? I cried all the time—happy or sad. I had a suspicious liver sonogram. I turned away from Jesus out of shame.

Have I ever tried to stop drinking? Did any of these things help? I tried quitting for a month each year. I tried only drinking on weekends. I tried only drinking beer and wine. All of it worked for a brief period of time. Sometimes slowly, other times immediately, I went right back to excessive use.

Is it difficult to admit alcohol has defeated me? Not at all. I am all in. I have let everyone know I am in recovery because admission will keep me accountable.

What makes me happy? I'm not really sure right now. I feel like I'm in limbo trying to rediscover myself. I'm trying new things to figure that out.

Four pages and 22 questions later, the group takes turns giving feedback on everything they heard. The responses are unique based on personal experiences. They are similar in camaraderie. Platoon soldiers. Stuck in the same foxhole. Fighting the same war.

"It is so surreal to hear other people talk about their life mistakes and realize how alike we all are," I say. The toxic truth purged from my system has an overwhelming affect. This internal calm is foreign to me.

"We all believe we are terminally unique when we get here," Brian says. "Automatically thinking nobody could ever understand your problems or compare to the severity of what you did in your addiction is normal."

He knows what he's talking about. Before Brian got his Doctorate in Addictive Disorders, he sat in his own drum circle at Betty Ford Clinic for alcohol and Xanax addiction. This street cred is invaluable when mixed with a degree. Observations are not analysis produced by plugging in a client's check list. They're a visceral reaction to having lived the check list.

Brian is always the last to give feedback after every step. It's equal parts positive reinforcement and equal parts clinical for education purposes.

"You said your friends and family believe you will die," he says. "It also sounds like you were under the impression that would happen with a faulty liver."

I nod.

"What are other ways our disease can kill us?" He looks around the room.

Random answers come from people with more time in this room than me. Heart attack. Stroke. Alcohol poisoning. Fatal fall.

Oh. That's right. He told me about a lot of those during our first meeting.

"We know how many people die from cirrhosis because it can be directly linked," Brian says. "But there's no accurate report of many of the other deaths as a result of chronic use."

I knew it. I knew my body was dying. Those weird sensations during the final stage. Arms. Legs. Veins. Muscles. Brain. Inexplicable in medical terms. Hard to verbalize. Very real though. Very real.

"I can't tell you how relieved I am to find people who speak the same language," I say. "Finally. Someone who gets me. I don't feel lost anymore." I raise my arms above my head and wave them back and forth. "Like I've been lost alone at sea. And the rescue chopper finally spotted me."

Not everyone in my life has been as fortunate.

May 4, 2017

My obsession over Tom's death has been a month-long, daily Google search. Frantic for answers. Desperate to make sense of his senseless death.

It could not have ended worse than it did today.

My beautiful friend, who wanted nothing more than to be liked. Who fixated on ratings. Headstrong to be No. 1. Willing and relishing in community service to make it happen. All of that for nothing. Overshadowed by rancid headlines about sexual assault. He finally made it to national news. Never the way he intended.

According to the police report, after a day of drinking, a woman lies down for a nap. She wakes up naked in bed with Tom. A friend walks in and confronts them. The woman says she doesn't remember what happened. Tom gets dressed and leaves. She goes to the hospital. Charges are filed. Police try to reach him. He gets wind. Buys a razor. Drives to remote location. Cuts his wrists. Walks into the freezing woods. Dies of hypothermia.

Class B 17-A 253.2.D—Having sex with someone who is unconscious or incapable of consenting.

I weep at the words. Confusion swirls my brain. How could this happen? How did Tom get to these people's house? The man I know is not a predator. I take the information I've been given and try to play out in my head the series of events.

Celebrity judging the Margarita contest. He's funny. He's charming. He gets invited to a house party of strangers. He's flirty. He misreads signals. And then he makes a move.

The scene violently throws me back to my own teenage nightmare.

After a full night of drinking and smoking and laughing the evening away, I went into the host's bedroom to take a nap while everyone else kept the party going. I woke in a fog, on my side, slowly aware my pants were down. A friend's boyfriend pushing against me from behind. I cringed at his hot breath on my neck. My body tensed as I heard his girlfriend open the door.

"Pretend you're asleep." Zero panic in his voice. He rolled over.

I froze. Felt her get in. She moved quietly. Trying not to disturb what she believed were two sleeping people in her bed. My mind raced trying to make sense of it.

Where is Colette? We had come to the party together. Why is someone I know and trust trying to have sex with me? He was talking when I woke up. Did he think I was conscious the whole time? He's supposed to be my friend. Why was he doing this?

I wanted so badly to jump up and run out of the room. My muscles did not respond. Fear shut down my brain. I woke again to the sounds of snoring. Moving centimeters at a time, I crept out from under the covers. Pulled up my pants. Packed my shame. Silently escaped into the living room.

I walked over to the couch and shook a sleeping Colette awake. Her eyes popped open and met mine. Rounded and hollowed out with fear.

I quickly put my pointer finger to my lips then pointed to the door.

"What's wrong?" Her frightened face mimics mine. She's scared though confused as to why.

On the way home, we sat in silence. For a long time.

"Do you want to talk about it?" she asked.

I opened my mouth. Nothing came out for several miles. *How do you explain something you don't fully understand?* I told her what happened. We never spoke of it again.

Now, a quarter of a century later, I'm trying to make sense of it all over. Then apply it to Tom.

Was my mind in a pass out or was my body responding to his touch in a blackout? I do not know. I never spoke to that guy again. I'll likely die not understanding what he was thinking.

Because of the out Tom chose, I'll never know what he was thinking either.

I'm frustrated. I'm angry. I had no right to be touched. I also had no right to take my brain off the grid. If one or both parties in either of these scenarios had not been drinking, none of it would have happened. None of it. Not mine. Not his. That should be enough to scare anyone reading this to second guess drunken sex with a stranger. Ever.

Alcohol. Spirits. In Tom's case, an evil, deadly spirit. It caught him before I could share my recovery story with the only person who took me by the hand and tried to help.

Survivor's guilt tears burn my cheeks. For Tom. And for Colette. She drowned in the Pacific Ocean under suspicious circumstances two years prior.

Why them? Why not me?

May 8, 2017

I hate Mondays. Always have. I suffer eternally from the Monday Blues. Fun withdrawals. The better the weekend, the worse the symptoms. But this first day of this work week is different. Ten minutes in and I am only now slowly taking mental note of my timeline location on the traditional labor calendar.

What day is it? Is it Monday?

Until recently, my mornings always started the same. The internal rooster woke the mind hamster who alerted the stomach butterflies it was time to churn the ulcer juices.

At a minimum of 30 minutes before the alarm went off, I would lie in bed unsuccessfully fighting back dry heaves. Hoping. Praying. *God, please stop time. Please. Give me just a few more minutes.*

Unanswered prayers forced me to stumble in and face a grotesque reflection in the bathroom mirror. Tangled hair from a night of tossing. Mascara wiped into a smudge after a nightly appearance from tears-of-the-forgotten-cause. A dumbfounded look, empty eyes staring back, reminiscent of a teenage friend who lost half his braincells in a motorcycle accident.

On a good day, I got through the toothbrushing without spewing colorless, odorless liquid in between the molar and the incisor scrubs. On an excellent day, I made it through the entire shower without doing the same.

But on every day, the shakes and fermenting stomach convulsions continued until the Xanax kicked in.

Fortunately, I'm a woman. Thirty-five minutes later, I'm a new person.

Tah-da! There is nothing hairspray and makeup can't fix.

The internal dialogue today, however, is a sharp contrast.

Is it Monday? Oh my gosh, it is.

I look down at the slowed lathering my unshaking hand is creating over an unagitated belly. I recall brushing my teeth without fanfare. I didn't even bother to glance at my reflection.

No train wreck to see here, folks. Move along.

Lathering stops. Right forearm leans against the cold tile. I take in all the sensations. The sound of warm water beating on my head. The sight of waterfalls flowing down and off the ends of my long dark hair. The clean smell of Pantene and Irish Spring melding.

No anxiety. I have no anxiety. Then the real truth hits me. Oh my gosh, I am. Never. Going to feel anxiety again. Not from detox anyway.

"Thank you, God." I close my eyes and lean my head against a propped arm. "Oh, thank you. Thank you. Thank you."

I take a grateful moment to bask in God's grace. My unhurried mind meditates to rushing water.

May 10, 2017

Frustration. Doubt. Fear.

"Why don't I feel happy?" Slam. Open palms on both knees. "I haven't had a drink for almost six weeks. When is euphoria going to kick in?"

I sounded more like a whining fifth grader than a woman on the cusp of 50. I cross my arms dramatically and look up at the circle of blank faces staring back at me.

It's the same look I give the men in the room when they bitch about their wives.

"Why doesn't she trust me? I've been sober for 12 seconds. I do so much for this relationship. Can't she see how hard I've worked? I should just drink. That'll show her."

It's annoying. Decades of abuse and expected forgiveness in weeks. I mask my self-righteous internal eyeroll with the same fake apathy they are reciprocating me with now.

Eyes to the floor. Nobody has the answer. That's worse. Then, out of my peripheral, from across the room, I see Sage Saul uncross his arms and lean his weight forward. I look over to see his propped back chair drop down on all fours.

"Well." He tugs one leg at a time on his golf shorts, adjusting the fabric underneath for the recent shift in his seat. Rubs his hands on his bare knees, rocking back and forth in unison when he speaks. "When you were taking breaks from drinking all those times, you were probably feelin' pretty good weren't ya?"

Saul stops rocking in the forward position and scratches his right calf while I answer. Then he goes back to the knee rub ritual.

"And when you were doin' that diet thing …"

"904 Thin."

"Yeah, that. You said it's the longest amount of time you ever went without drinking. I bet you were on top of the world."

"I was." I nod eagerly.

"Yep." He pauses. Scratches his calf. He has the attention of the entire room. We are all hanging on his every word. Some leaning in at the neck. Others with the entire torso.

It's always like that when Saul talks. Gwen nicknamed him Sage Saul because of his addict wisdom and the calm way he chooses to deliver the message. He's the junkie whisperer.

I'm convinced he's not a patient. In my overactive creative mind, he went to Monkey on Your Back University—or MYBU to the locals— and is participating in an episode of *Undercover Boss* to make sure his facility is being run right.

In reality, years of alcohol, cocaine and opiate abuse, followed 26 years of clean living and church leadership and inmate mentoring, followed by a decade of disappearing down the rabbit hole again brought him back to our island of misfit toys. By the time our paths crossed, he had been in the 10-week program for six months.

He doesn't want to leave, and no one wants him to leave. When the spotlight is turned on any of us for our turn to share a step in the program, we pray Saul is at the session to help through the vulnerability. He is always the last one to comment before Brian gives his final analysis of our growth. The crowd-elected executive officer to Brian's commanding officer.

So, it didn't surprise me when he waited to see if anybody else wanted to pitch in two cents before giving his words of encouragement.

"See, when you were quitting before, you weren't quitting for good," he says. "And your mind knew it. Your brain is smart."

He taps his right temple.

"It's saying, 'Okay, we'll quit for a while. We'll quit so we can get a clean bill of health from the doctor on the liver enzymes. Okay, 45 days is a long time. But we'll quit so we can get in shape and lose weight. That's alright.'"

Saul tips his hands back and forth like a scale of justice.

"But the whole time, it's looking forward to the end. Counting down the days like it's Christmas."

It was true. Within three days, after the blahs wore off, I would feel heavenly. Empowered. Energetic. Logically, deductive reasoning told me if I removed alcohol from the life, I could feel this way all the time. But the obsessive bargaining I did in the interim drove me crazy. The deal always ended the same. Me agreeing I would start drinking like a normal person. Brain – 1. Tracy – 0.

Saul assures me, I will find that joyous place again. It's just going to take longer. I thank him and somebody else raises their hand to share. I pay no attention. I'm lost in my self-analysis.

It makes sense. It's like that fight you have with your boyfriend. You know the one. Where you storm out, slam the door, knowing full well you'll make up in a few days. It's not the end. So you strut around glowing in the temporary power you hold. Refusing to be the first to call and apologize. And then he does call. And you cave almost immediately. And then you reunite and have mad, passionate, makeup sex. And you live happily ever after.

Until. Until you don't. And that's it. And you know it.

That's where I am with my lover, Alcohol. We are through. And I know it. And I am deep in the mourning process. But if I believe that, then I also have to believe Saul is right. Just like the love I had to move on from, I can move on from this, too. Eventually.

And just like any true love, a piece of it will always be with me. I'm sure there will be mental scenes. Fond flashbacks of the good times. Wondering why we couldn't make it. I'll see alcohol in pictures with other girls, having a good time, and I'll pine for the love we once had.

A country artist singing about raising whiskey for a toast. A crooner whispering about the sexy savorings of sweet sangria. And for a second and a half, I'll ponder, "Why not me. Why can't I be the one to make it work with alcohol."

But I can't. Alcohol is not my true love. It is a liar. It is an abuser. And it is a cheater. Like many relationships, I morphed my world to make ours fit for cohabitation. I changed my core values to accommodate the addiction. It happened so slowly, so methodically, inch by tiny inch, I didn't even realize it was happening until the fog cleared. I dozed off on a raft near shore and woke up in the middle of a hurricane, lost at sea.

No. This was not meant to be a forever relationship. The sooner I deal with the truth, the sooner I can move on with my life and find the euphoria I crave as my reward.

I realize I missed an entire conversation about relationships when I hear the tail end. Something to do with guys going to strip clubs and what we choose to feel is socially acceptable now versus when we were using. Gwen is piping in.

"Yeah," she says, wincing and scanning ceiling tiles. "In the single world, that does *not* look good on your resume." She shakes her head and directs her attention back to the group. "In my passive aggressive world … it does."

Everyone laughs at her self-deprecating humor.

May 19, 2017

Tommy and Elvis Duran. Nothing in common, these two.

Tommy is a 6'4" buff heterosexual black football coach. Elvis is 5'6" homosexual white radio personality who used a gastric sleeve procedure to cut his weight in half.

Nothing in common. At first glance.

But internally, they march to the beat of the same bongo. They both have the heart of a lion. And they use the power to help others. Check that. To empower others.

Tommy does it on a daily basis with kids and adults with barriers to education, employment, and self-worth. Elvis does it on a global level with his New York City syndicated radio program, Elvis Duran and the Morning Show.

His voice carriers a daily 4-hour message of positivity, being good to one another, doing the right thing. With a whole lotta dirty innuendo, pranks and shenanigans mixed in for good ratings. I'm addicted to the show because it is my dream job. Good-hearted banter with a fearless naughty side.

This morning, for example, he gave me some positive news that I thought was a prank. In response to a segment one of the producers questioned in the lineup, Elvis said, "Of course we're doing that. We always do it on Friday."

I couldn't believe my ears. *It's Friday? Is it the weekend already? Do I have tomorrow off?* I quickly calculate the days in my head. *Holy cannoli. It is Friday.*

Auto is my pilot for the rest of the ride in to work. Self-awareness invigorates my body in the same, although polar opposite, way anxiety once lived.

"Thank you, God. Thank you for this freedom." I glance quickly port to starboard, hoping none of the other commuters saw me talking to myself.

It is Friday. No better, no worse, than any day before it or after it. All days this past week have been equally fulfilling and joyous. Each day brings something new and exciting.

Wow. I finally know what they mean by "Live in the now."

It was just over a month ago I was dreading Mondays, physically reacting to the loathing I had for the day. Tuesday was a wash. On Wednesday, I started to smile, belting out the Geico phrase the talking camel made popular: "It's hump daaaay! Hey, Mike. Mike, Mike, Mike. Know what day it is? It's hump day." Thursday my mood was stabilized.

And then there was Friday. The finish line. Mere hours from my first of many drinks in the days to follow. That was once what I called freedom. Not anymore.

Pulling into my parking spot, I hop out of the car and take a few skips across the street before realizing this may look a little childish and slow it down. But I still swish my pony tail from side to side as I approach the front door.

As he does every morning for no other reason than to be a gentleman, Tommy swings open the front door. He works in the first office, so I rarely see him throughout the day. But I love that his is typically the first toothy grin to greet me and today is no different.

"Happy Friday," he says as I glide by. His voice is an octave higher, signaling his pride in singing my signature phrase to me before I can to him.

I stop quick at the door jam and snap my face back to him.

"Tommy," I say. "Every day is Friday in the Dot Com Empire."

Tommy drops his chin and giggles. He lets gravity take the door and walks away shaking his head.

"You so crazy."

Oh, Tommy. If you only knew how right you are.

CHAPTER 6

MY PROBLEM IS MY GIFT — DID NOT SEE THAT COMING

I am thankful for this disease because without it,
I wouldn't have stumbled across my strengths.

~ Quote on the board at IOP

May 21, 2017

A doctor on NPR, touting the benefits of positivity as medicine, cites an 8 year old who authored *My Book for Kids with Cansur*.

The misspelling retained for authenticity, Jason Gaes penned his thoughts through chemo and radiation treatments to calm the fears of other children going through the same. Emphasizing the reality of survival.

"If God wanted me to be a basketball player, He would have made me seven feet tall," the doctor quotes Jason. "Instead, He gave me cancer so I could write a book to help other kids."

From the mouth of babes. A message of hope.

It's been seven weeks since I took my last drink. I feel like God has saved me for a reason. I don't know what it is yet. Oddly, I'm okay with that. It's weird because my type A personality doesn't typically allow the peace I'm feeling.

Competitive. Ambitious. Impatient. That's my comfort zone.

Serene? Happy? Content? That's what I'm feeling.

In 1981, I should have died. The sound of shattering glass and ripping metal. The smell of burning rubber. That feeling of discombobulated spinning. It never leaves. Neither does the anonymous prophecy that followed.

It was a sign of the times. A 17-year-old teenage girl could walk into a liquor store and walk out with a fifth of regret.

At only 13 years old, my plan to spend the night in her unsupervised home got disrupted by a revelation. On the verge of becoming a legal adult, my friend discovered her best friend recently became the new object of her ex-boyfriend's affection. Traumatic news at any age.

I shivered with repulsion as we sucked down the vodka mixed with Tang. We got in the car to go catch them together at the drive-in. Weaving in and out. Row after row of cars next to speakers on metal sticks. No luck. Leaving the scene empty handed, anger spewing from her lips, she gunned the gas pedal.

Police estimated she was going 120 mph and attempted to switch lanes to avoid a motorcycle on a slight curve. I remember her arms. Frantic. Correcting. Back and forth. Overcorrecting. Back and forth.

I squeezed my eyes shut. Covered my face. Crunched my body into a ball. Waited for the impact. I remember hearing glass shatter. Then eerie silence. I opened my eyes. I looked across my body in the back seat. I saw empty, smoke-filled asphalt in front of me through a hole in the car where a door had been just seconds prior. I had no idea how I got in the back, but I remember thinking we rolled the car. I surmised later an angel must have flipped me over the front seat to safety.

I didn't have a scratch on me. She was dead.

When the car lost control, my passenger side was headed directly toward a tree behind a chain link fence guarding the fairgrounds. But when the car hit the curb, the velocity of the speed flipped the death trap into a 180-degree spin 10-feet into the air. It slammed into the tree, ripping off both driver's side doors. The sudden impact caused a toy car effect, pushing the 3,000-pound piece of metal back the 180 degrees, two lanes over from where it started.

In the weeks following the accident, I received calls and letters, but the one that stuck with me my entire life was the anonymous sender who wrote this sentiment: I know it is so hard to lose someone, but just know God saved you because he has a purpose for your life.

I took the message seriously. Through my military career. Through using my communications degree to spread good news. Through everyday engagements. Encouraging others to be the best they can be.

Today, I have a renewed belief that, once again, God pushed me through a near-death experience for a purpose. I am ready. I am more than willing to keep all of my senses open to His word.

More than that, I'm patient. He can take as long as He wants. I am genuinely giddy living in the present moment.

May 22, 2017

Step two. Time to get real. Identify the craziness. Women have more than one child because they forget the pain. The goal today is put the pain, at least the top 10 painful memories, down in permanent ink. Never forget. Never go back.

"A little bit of sobriety can be dangerous," Brian says. "You start feeling good. Physically. Life starts to go smoothly. Relationships start to heal."

I see where this is going. The thought has crossed my mind. Maybe I can control my drinking. A glass of wine at dinner. Couple of beers at the football game. Why do my friends get to drink and I don't? It's not fair.

"The further we get away from our mistakes, the easier it is to justify them. Believe we've changed," he says.

I pull out my list of indiscretions. Ready to air the dirt. Eternalize them in my heart. Handwritten reminders of where I never want to be again.

"So. The first thing I want to do is read a love letter to alcohol I wrote," I say. My face flushes. It's not part of the assignment. Not everyone in the room is going to get it. This is a safe place. Doesn't mean I won't feel judged. Feel awkward.

Dear Alcohol,

I love you. I love you so much. So much that I will change my plans to be with you. So much that if you are not invited to the party, I will stay home to be with you. I'll pick you up on the way home from work. Let you run errands with me. Keep you close in the glove box to and from events. You are my ride or die bestie. My shotgun rider. In the front seat with me during all of my free time. You will never take a backseat. I would die for you. I almost did.

Sincerely,

My former self

"It sounds crazy," I say. "But the more ridiculous the better." *Sweet. Somebody is nodding. I don't feel so dumb.* "Because it's all true. Every sentence is true." I look around to gauge the crowd. "And it sounds re-dunk-you-lous." I punch each syllable. "So, why would I ever want to go back to that?" It's a question that doesn't need an answer.

"Moving on," I say. "This is what I wrote for examples of the unhappiest, insane scenarios that would never happen to a person that isn't powerless over alcohol."

I read off a couple that are pretty status quo based on what I've heard others share: Once I start, I can't stop. Taking naps to try and sober up for obligations. Difficulty connecting emotionally. Thirst for validation. Desperately needing to be liked.

"Learning we are emotionally stunted at the age we pick up makes so much sense to me," I say. "As an adult, I knew I wasn't having normal reactions to breakups. I couldn't even end relationships I knew were unhealthy for fear of being alone. Now I am thrilled to be single. Freedom to do what I want every single minute of my life is a beautiful thing."

I kick up my feet and throw out my hands in unison. Opening my mouth in a wide grin, I stick out my tongue and make a winded sound like I'm grateful to finally breathe out after holding my breath for two minutes straight. The group laughs at the outburst.

"Okay, here is the one that is so insane because it requires so much planning." I read from my notes, trying not to sound monotone. "I was in a long-distance relationship and flew a lot. I manipulated every step from start to finish to keep a buzz going. I hid four minis in the car and sipped on two to the airport, saving two for the trip home. The airport bar is conveniently located next to my gate. C-4. While watching out the window for the incoming flight, I'd order a tall beer.

A shot on the side is only $3 extra."

I look at the crowd and impromptu. "And because I'm always up for a good bargain ..." I grin. They laugh. I keep reading.

"To save time, I paid and tipped immediately. When the plane pulled up to the jetway, I would ask for a Styrofoam coffee cup with a lid and dump in the beer. This gave me something to sip during boarding and takeoff until the flight attendants, or as I like to call them—bartenders, came around to take my order."

I run my middle finger across my forehead and flick it away, pretending it is coated in sweat.

"Draining," I say. "No wonder I'm so active now. I've got a lot more free time on my hands." Chuckle. "And my mind."

Next on the list: Binge – Ambien – Xanax – Repeat.

"I was mixing a depressant with a sedative with a muscle relaxant and wondering why I was on a daily dose of anti-depressants. Wondering why I could no longer find meaning for life."

I tell them I no longer need the Ambien or the Xanax. It's not a required share, but I feel like it's necessary for anyone in our little makeshift dysfunctional family who is looking for hope to hear.

"I want to preface this next one by saying, I do not remember the last time I had a tan." I raise my right hand in a swear-to-tell-the-truth motion. "Spoiler alert. Isolation while dog sitting. It's a bitch." We all laugh. I keep reading.

"I agreed to care for Hank's dogs over a long weekend. First and foremost, I love her dogs. Almost equally, I love being tan. However, my tendency to stay inside in the dark had gotten so bad, my doctor said I was low in Vitamin D. Trying to break the cycle of no UV rays on the skin, I fantasized about walking the dogs on the beach. Laying out every day. Partying every night. The ocean is one block away. Jax Beach bars just as close. I never made it to either. Not once. I could hear the nightlife. Smell the ocean. Feel the salt air. I participated in none of it.

"The ocean was right there." I raise my voice and point my finger aggressively at the door. "Right across the street."

Another thrust of the finger. "That's crazy, right?"

All yeas. No nays.

"Okay. This is the last one." *Home free. Feeling good. Healthy catharsis.* "I was on my way home from Nashville, talking to my then-boyfriend, Robb, on the phone while I walked through the airport. The gate I always fly out of is on the same concourse as Tootsies." I stop reading. "You guys 've heard of Tootsies, right?"

Most nod. A few look confused.

"It's this bar in Nashville, and it's world famous. They have a satellite bar in the airport." I ditch the script and opt to tell the story from memory. "Anyway, so I'm walking down the concourse, talking to Robb. I'm drunk. We've been drinking all day. And I hear a guy singing "Talladega" by Eric Church. Do you guys know that song?"

No surprise, the same crew who didn't know Tootsies don't know "Talladega." Or Eric Church.

"I hate that song." Laughter tells me I'm not the only one. "I just think it sounds so ridiculous. So, I'm walking down the concourse, talking to Robb, and I interrupt myself to belt out, 'Talladega.'" I give it the same gusto I gave it that day. Obnoxious. Over modulated. Over twanged with Southern hostility.

In the wake of my friends' laughter, I feel an unexpected burst of self-condemnation.

How could I do that? I'm disgusting. When I included this memory, I did it to show how rude I could be in my disease. A contrast to my usual happy-go-lucky personality. The mortification feels fresh. My mood shifts. Body language follows.

"Wow," I say. Defeated. Slumped. "I remember the disgust in Robb's voice when he asked me what I was doing." I look up at a guy in the room who plays music. Give him a nod. "I get it now."

I pick at my fingernails. I don't want to go on. I know I have to. It's an unspoken agreement. They've spent the last five weeks living their lives wide open. Sharing shame. Trusting me. I owe the same respect.

"Musicians don't play at Tootsies in the airport because it's a cash cow." My voice is shaking. Angry. "They do it because they're chasing a dream. It's their lifelong dream." I can feel the tears forming. "They're doing it with hopes that a music producer, or a big star, or a movie executive passing by to catch a flight will hear them. Sign them. Pull them out of obscurity. Push them on a big stage."

Oh my gosh! What is happening to me? I can't believe how much this is affecting me. Grown men have cried every time they are doing step two. It seemed weird. I could not figure out why. Now I know. The armchair psychologist in me recognizes it as a breakthrough. Although I still don't know how it works. Tears flow. Andy hands over a tissue.

"I'm not a dream stealer." Vocal cords shake. Lips start curling. The way they do right before an ugly cry. I breathe in deep to hold back tears and swab the right eye. "That's not who I am." Repeat on the left eye. "I'm a people builder. I live to be the positive voice in the room. I'm the one who goes out of my way to give you a compliment because I know you've been hearing negative all day. You guys know that, right?"

Empathetic eyes stare back at me.

"I was voted Best Righteous Crusader. Twice. By *Folio Weekly* readers. For all the work I do in the community." I blow my nose. "And I don't know what I did. Maybe nothing. But what if that guy heard me." I digress with an outraged guffaw. "Heard me? Of course, he heard me. I was so loud. So obnoxious."

I belt out "Talladega" one more time to make the point. *What an idiot.*

"What if he heard me and he thought I was making fun of him? What if his own insecurities were so bad on that particular night, that when he heard me—not knowing I hate that song—thought I hated his voice. Thought that I was saying, 'You suck!'"

I drop my head in my hands.

"What if he gave up on his dream that night because of my actions." I shake my cradled head. "I'm such a jerk. I never want to do that again."

"You won't." Andy reaches out and rubs my back.

May 24, 2017

First eye appointment in six years today. Didn't even let the optometrist's assistant get the question out. I screamed NONE when she asked, "Any tobacco or alcohol use?" I caught her off guard. It was awesome. I can't wait to share it at group tonight.

"It's a funny milestone," I say. "But a serious fear. When the year started, dementia and blindness terrified me. Do you remember Brian? When I told you about my memory lapses at our first meeting?"

"Yep." Brian nods.

"Blurriness, even with glasses, made it difficult to read in bed," I say. "It's more than the expected double vision. Words shook back and forth at a lightning speed." I shake an imaginary book in front of my face. "An invisible film covered my eyeballs like Vaseline. It was as if my optic nerve transmitter went to sleep before the rest of my body each night."

A couple admit to the same experiences.

"The memory lapses though." I shake my head. "They terrified me. I had a grandmother who died with Alzheimer's. It was devastating. Will that be me? My older friends say being forgetful is common for my age."

This would be a really good time for someone to say I don't look my age. I pause to give them a chance. Crickets.

"Incomparable scenarios played out every day. I left conversations not remembering what we talked about minutes later. I started to write everything down at work. Paranoia hunted me. I kept wondering how long I could maintain before someone noticed?"

"Wet brain," someone says.

"Yeah, that's what I was thinking," Gwen says.

When I get home, I Google it. Frightening results. Wet brain symptoms mimic dementia.

- Staggering, irregular gait, and other muscular incoordination
- Confabulation, remembering events that never happened
- Inability to form new memories
- Loss of memory, this can be severe
- Visual and auditory hallucinations

- Vision changes, including double vision, eyelid drooping, and abnormal eye movements

Other than the staggering, my life was on point to make this a reality. True wet brain is permanent. I am so grateful it never got that far. Just like Brian promised in our first meeting, my memory is restored. Vision is normal. Night terrors have ceased. The music in my closet is quiet.

May 29, 2017

Awake again at 3 a.m.

According to Dr. Wayne Dyer, everyone does this. That's the time our higher power wants to talk to us. The silent middle of our sleep cycle. Free from the noise of life. Since learning this information, I've noticed, it's true. Test this theory yourself. Next time someone says they woke up last night and couldn't get back to sleep, ask what time. The results will freak you out.

This morning, God and I are having a conversation about my next great adventure. Brain waves are consumed with clues. Ideas swirl around gray matter. He keeps revealing to me conversations with my sister.

Convinced I was coming home jobless after the funeral, Nancy randomly threw out ideas. Like, super random and out of context.

"Uber driver." She casually mumbled over breakfast. "Public speaker." Interrupts a conversation about best options for covering grey hair. "Author. TV. Public Relations. Commercials." Her faith in me was way stronger than my self-esteem at the time.

"You're talented," she said. "Use those talents. You'll figure it out."

I also can't help but recognize the miracle of my existence.

With no family near and a no real regular connection with another human being, I could have guzzled into oblivion behind closed doors. And if I lost my job before that happened? Joan would have smelled my decaying body next door before anyone noticed I was missing. True story.

A spiritual awakening rushes through me. Revelations of pain. Isolation. God reveals to me multiple rooms with hidden exits. Crying women, reaching to the ceiling. Begging for help. They can't find the way out.

"I have to help them," I say to myself. "I will help them," I tell Him.

Sleep is impossible. I am in awe. It is nothing short of a miracle. In eight weeks, I went from urine-soaked nightmares and anxiety-filled angst with a side of despair to being on fire for throwing out lifelines and spreading hope.

I have no idea how I'm going to do it, but I know it will be done. The details are God's job. Believing is mine.

May 30, 2017

Step three. Write a letter to your Higher Power.

This is an interesting fork in the road for a few friends. I've watched the men and women who walked in agnostics and atheists get to this point at varying stages.

Some still don't believe but agree to describe their wants, needs and fears. A few are opening to the idea there is, at the very least, something out there bigger than themselves. One even admits to feeling a shift towards the possibility.

"It's a miracle," she says. "That's the only way to explain the fact I'm still here."

For me, it's a no brainer.

"I love Jesus," I say. "I don't know how to describe it to anyone who doesn't believe. It's always been this way. I don't know why I know it. I just do. Does that make sense?"

Even non-believers who don't understand the dogma understand the sensation and nod in unison.

Tonight is supposed to be about my decision to turn my will over to God, but I'm not going to miss an opportunity to bring someone with me.

"Russell Brand has a great video on YouTube about Higher Power." I point across the room. "Miles has seen it."

He nods reluctantly. Caught off guard.

"Yeah. It was pretty good. Pretty much dead on." His smile fades into concern. "With a lot of F-bombs though. Not for religious zealots. Definitely relatable to someone grappling with the Higher Power concept."

"If you're struggling with the idea, he keeps it really simple," I say. "He points to objects around the room and says things like, 'I didn't create this. Or this.'" I point randomly to mimic him. My voice getting louder with every example. "'I didn't create the sun. Etcetera.' He says, if you can at least admit there are things you can't explain that obviously something or someone greater than you did, it only makes sense there is some kind of Higher Power."

I fidget with the papers in my hand and apologize for getting so worked up. I'm not actually sorry for the passion, but I can see I'm making some folks uncomfortable. Taking ownership seems like the right thing to do before I start reading the letter.

Dear Lord,

I cannot believe I finally made it to this place in my life. It is something I have prayed about for decades—the strength to completely turn my back on alcohol.

I have always known in my heart you have something way bigger for me to accomplish. And I knew it would only come after I completely turned my will over to you.

I want to know what it is you would like me to do. But one thing life has taught me—it is *always* in your time.

I have been inspired by the positive influences in my life since March 27th, and I feel like I keep getting a clearer focus of my future in serving you.

My needs are few. You have always fulfilled your promise to take care of me.

My fear is that I will let my guard down. Blindly led in the wrong direction. I know the enemy is always waiting. Please continue to protect me, and help keep my eyes wide open.

Sincerely,

Tracy

The next page is a series of seven questions, also revolving around honesty, open-mindedness and willingness. The most important on my inventory is number five. It's about how faith helps me with making decisions.

"I have started to pray about everything," I say. "As a result, I can hear God's voice again. I'm sure that sounds crazy to some of you."

Ugh. Why do I always worry what everyone else is thinking? Who cares if they don't know what I'm talking about. Or think it's Christian mumbo jumbo. Knock it off. Speak with conviction.

"I used to know God's voice. I'm starting to hear it again. So, I've been very diligent about praying each morning. Thanking Him for another day of sobriety. Consulting Him throughout the day on decisions. Being still to listen for His response. Then finishing the day with grateful prayer."

I start to put my sheets away.

"Oh." I pose an afterthought. "And I know I'm growing in this program because I make my bed every morning and floss my teeth every night."

June 7, 2017

Greenfield Program Director Diane McQueen is filling in for Brian tonight. She's mid-sentence when the door busts open.

A tall, lanky young woman stomps in and swings the door closed behind her. The only empty seat is pushed up against a table in the corner facing a wall. Without looking around to see if there is another available, she makes a beeline for it.

Diane's eyes follow her across the room. She finishes her thought just as the intruder's butt slams into the seat. Arms crossed. Facing the wall.

Her back is to Diane. I'm positioned to see her profile. Her eyes shift from the wall to the table to the floor then back.

Isn't she going to turn the chair around? What the heck is she doing?

I'm humored by the mimed faces engaged in a silent circus of confused chaos around the room. Diane is not excluded. She looks at me, furrows her brow and points.

"Who is that?" She mouths the words.

I shrug my shoulders and mouth back that I don't know.

"Hi. Are you supposed to be here?" Diane asks.

That's hilarious. I think it's pretty obvious by her bizarre behavior, she definitely needs to be here.

No response.

"Excuse me." Diane repeats herself. "Hi."

The millennial turns her head in my direction to cue Diane that she's listening.

"Are you supposed to be here?"

She nods.

"Brian told you to be here tonight?"

Another nod.

"Okay. Well, why don't you turn your chair around and join the group."

Andy and I move our seats apart to give her a spot. She scoots the fold-out seat into the space.

"Do you want to introduce yourself?" Diane asks.

Silent Bob shakes her head.

"We were just going around the room. Telling about our day. Go ahead." She points to the man on her left.

We all give the newcomer our elevator speeches about how we got here, and then share the peaks and the pits of our day.

The woman stares at the center floor tile, occasionally looking up when she hears something that interests her. When everyone is finished,

Diane circles back.

"Now that you've heard everyone else, would you like to share anything?"

Her face softens from angry to shy. She's naturally beautiful. No makeup. Light brown hair in a messy bun. Jean shorts and laced-up ropers reveal long legs. A cut-off T shows off her tan abs. She grabs either side of a plaid shirt coverup and wraps it around herself with crossed arms. She shakes her head again. This time, Diane gets a slight smile out of her.

That night, I call Gwen to tell her all about our odd, new friend. She had to work and missed it.

The next night, Gwen and I give her a ride home after the meeting. We share our battle bruises and our medals of honor in recovery. She shares that her name is Kylie.

"What are you going to do this weekend?" I ask her.

"I don't know. Maybe paint? I used to love to make art. I haven't done it in a long time."

I watch her walk up the driveway towards a mother-in-law suite behind a historic Riverside home.

"I will be shocked if we see her on Monday," I say to Gwen.

CHAPTER 7

STUMBLING INTO EMOTIONAL MATURITY

June 9, 2017

No relationships for one year. Suddenly those lucky bastards complaining about their spouses look like they have it all. Not really sure if I'm emotionally mature enough to pull this off. I've been told you stop growing emotionally when you start drinking. Which would explain why I'm strangely drawn to those Mickey Mouse single-sided Valentine's Day cards.

U.S. News & World Report did a VD story—that's Valentine's Day, not venereal disease—this year about the subject. A psychologist said the challenges of staying clean were stressful enough.

"It will be easy for many to find replacement addictions, such as a love addiction to replace the high the drug or alcohol provided," said Indiana University Health drug addiction counselor Anne Lewis. "Many people enjoy the honeymoon phase of relationships, feeling euphoria from the new love, making it more challenging to address issues that underlie the addiction."

Anne, you are singing my song, sister. But first I need to close the circle on my past life. I am fraught with need for a fairy tale ending on every chapter of my life. I book a flight to Nashville. Music City is the home of my Valentine. Robb.

If I'm going to embrace this new life of abstinence, his is the last kiss I want on my lips to start the journey.

6:50 p.m. I arrive at gate C-4. No need to be early. My mind and my coffee mug are free from poor life choices. Before the wheels touch down on the tarmac, I spend 90 minutes reliving our relationship that started February 14, 2014.

It was early morning Valentine's Day, when I sent the text.

Valentine's Day is CRAP!

I hit send. Dale and Hank responded lightning fast in agreement.

Yeah! Screw VD!

Let's be each other's Valentines. St. Augustine?

Hours later we are booked at the Howard Johnson and on our way to our nation's oldest city. I decorate mine and Hank's room with flowers, candles, nosh eats and a full bar while she picks up our local friend, Steve, and Dale settles into his room next door.

After an impromptu cocktail party under the glow of a neon NO VACANCY sign, the four of us stumbled through several hours of barhopping. I can't say if it was the brutal morning show hours earlier that day or the brutal attack on our makeshift hotel lounge earlier that evening, but at 10 o'clock, a coquina crusted wall came hard and fast and I was done. I excused myself back to the hotel and quickly fell asleep watching Winter Olympics.

The dreamy sounds of skis rushing through powder packed snow came to an abrupt halt. I wake to two drunky monkeys. Hank on the left. Dale on the right. I look up at two arguing faces over my bed.

"Tell her, Dale, tell her!" A night of boozing elevated Hank's voice an octave. She points aimlessly in the direction of my face. I pull the covers over my T-shirt and up to my chin.

"Tell her what?" He throws his hands out to the side.

My eyes bounce back and forth from her demands to his inability to comprehend them.

"Tell her," she says.

"What?" he says.

"Tell her how good looking this guy is."

"I'm a dude. I'm not telling her how good looking a guy is"

Hank finally acknowledges I'm in the room and looks down at me.

"Tracy. We met this guy who is so perfect for you." She splays her hands apart and pours syrup on her words. "He is good looking times 10. He's good looking on steroids. He's good looking like … like … He's your lobster."

They both look down. Patiently waiting for any sign I may be about to jump on her excitement train.

"I'm sorry." I blink a couple of times. "What … is going on?"

"I saw an old friend. He was playing at the bar we went to after you left," she says. "His best friend is going to be your new boyfriend." She's practically jumping out of her skin.

"Okay." I lean up on both elbows. "You do know Dale and I used to date, right? This is kind of awkward." I look up at Dale.

"Oh, I don't care." He blows me off with a swipe of the left hand.

"Exactly." Hank points to him, then back at me. "So, to recap. My friend's best friend is going to be your new boyfriend, and they're coming over for an after party." She gets a giant grin and shakes her hands violently. "Isn't that great?" She looks to Dale for confirmation. "Dale, isn't that great?"

"I don't know." He throws both hands in the air and heads for the door. "I'm going to my room."

"Just wait." She squeals with delight. "He's totally your type."

My type? What does that even mean? Seriously. I can't wait to see what this clown looks like.

Being the eternal optimist and always up for a good party, I don't argue. Instead I ask, "Can they pick up McDonald's?"

Thirty minutes later, there's a knock on the door. I start bouncing cross-legged on the bed and clapping like it's Christmas morning.

"Yeah. McDonald's is here."

Then "he" walks through the door. A giant grin rolls across my face. Bounce. Bounce. Bounce. Clap. Clap. Clap.

"Yeeaah." Feverish head nod in Hank's direction. "McDonald's is here."

We let them stay over. Nothing scandalous or even worth writing about happened that night. But Robb did kiss me. And it truly was a magical night in St. Augustine indeed. The next morning, we all woke up a little hung over to the clanging of the tourist trolley bell. Our room was right next to the Senator Tree, a famous stop on the tour.

An hour later, we stood hemming and hawing under its long branches.

"Okay, well, it was nice to meet you." I squirmed like a fifth grader with my fingers locked behind my butt.

"Nice to meet you, too." He snorted a laugh and turned to open the passenger door of the truck.

I started to walk away but snapped back aggressively. *What the heck. I've got nothing to lose here.* "Why don't we exchange numbers." He doesn't say anything fast enough for my nervous chatter to start. "You're single. I'm single. It was Rob Thomas' birthday when we met last night." He looks confused. More nervous chatter. "I'm a huge Matchbox 20 fan, so Valentine's Day is Rob's birthday, so ..." I throw up one hand in surrender, roll my eyes and outwardly laugh at my own dorkiness. "Talk about signs."

"Okay, cool."

"I mean I live in Jacksonville. You live in Nashville. So, we got the whole 'ville thing going on. And then there's ..."

"No. I meant cool. Yes. Give me your number." He shakes his head and pulls out his phone.

For the next two and a half years, we took turns flying back and forth on what I called our Best of Both Worlds Tour. My sleepy beach town and his sprawling treed hills kept us too busy to care about the strikes against us.

Strike 1: Our age difference. He is 18 years younger. When asked, "How old is she?" by a curious friend, he texted back out loud for my benefit, "Didn't ask. Don't care."

Strike 2: Location, location, location. Door to door 595 miles. Fortunately for us, Southwest crunched the travel time down to 75 minutes and made it financially affordable with Wanna Get Away? fares.

Robb did something no man had been able to do in a long time. He held my interest. A modern-day Renaissance man who can listen to a song and pound it out in perfect rhythm on the drums. Watch a YouTube video and strum a new tune on guitar. He is equally as comfortable in nature primitive camping with no running water or electricity as he is in the hot tub of an oceanfront hotel suite. He pursued music in lieu of a degree, but his private Christian academics and a fierce lust for books and NPR allows him the privilege to hold his own in any conversation.

He walks with musician swagger. Flows like water, really. His take on life always caught me off-guard and made me think or cracked me up. He once told me a stoned guy at a party looked at him and said, "Dude. Your face looks like an alien." After visualizing an alien, slanted eyes and small mouth, I busted up laughing. "Oh my gosh, he's right." Those sharp alien features framed by Keith Urban hair gives him a model's edge. I would watch with intrigue when he walked into a room as all eyes followed behind.

There was nothing about him that didn't do something for me. Except the ongoing lonely feeling that he didn't feel the same way.

Strike 3: My alcoholism. The first two were manageable. The third struck me out of the game.

The sun is starting to set when I see the Chrysler convertible with the ratty top and broken bumper ramble up the departures ramp. It's been our pick-up area of choice for three years. Less traffic than arrivals.

And now, here we were again. Blown away and barely breathing.

Robb fidgets with the broken door handle and finally pulls his long, graceful, sexy body out of the carriage. His smile. My butterflies. His swift moves to meet me at the trunk and embrace. Deep breath in. Lips press hard and long. Shaky breath out. Eleven months of heartbreak melts away. Replaced by the giddy feeling the night he walked through my door.

This time was like all the others. My arms-folded grip around his neck. His musky scent romancing my nostrils. One hand grasping a hand full of his thick, shaggy hair. But this time there would be no strategy for tragedy. Only restitution for everything I cost this relationship.

We left the airport and went straight to a local Japanese restaurant. Sitting table side at the hibachi grill, I laugh at myself for wondering if he picked it because he knew I like new experiences or because I couldn't make a scene while dining with complete strangers.

Fortunately, the four others at the table are all the way on the other side of the grill. We're close enough to laugh in unison at the chef's corny jokes. Far enough away to have intimate conversation throughout the meal.

"I know I've told you a thousand times how sorry I am." I look at the remnants of the steak, shrimp and rice on his plate. I don't have the guts yet to make the required 90-degree turn for eye contact. The nerves in his right foot tap the non-existent bass drum in time with the chopsticks in his hand.

"But I wanted to come here. Tell you in person." I turn the rest of the way to look at him. He doesn't look back. "I am here. And I am sober. And you deserve for me to apologize to you in person. I am truly sorry for all of the crazy crap I did when we were together." I look back at the rice.

His foot stops tapping. The chopsticks go down. His entire upper body rocks with his nodding head.

"That's deep," he says. He reaches down to stroke my leg. Our eyes meet. "Thank you."

I sigh with relief. Hands on his arm. Head on his shoulder. And then …

"I remember the first time I visited you in Florida," he says. "You got so drunk and started cussing out that bartender."

My head snaps off his shoulder.

Seriously? Right now, after this beautiful moment. And the very first incident? You want to start right at the beginning?

"I told you, you should run," I say. "Run. No, wait." I give the timeout sign. "Drive. Drive as far as you can until you run out of gas." I point to an imaginary point A to point B. "Then get out of the car and run."

We both crack up.

It could have been a long night if he wanted to hash out every misstep since then. But he didn't. The rest of the night and weekend went great.

He never said it, but I'm pretty sure he was surprised when I didn't do my Saturday evening halfway mark freak-out. Tears always flowed at this point when I realized our time was almost over. But I was too busy enjoying the moment. Living in the now.

Sunday night, I gripped him one last time. Hard. No tears. Only smiles.

I'm ready to start this journey alone. Without feeling lonely.

June 12, 2017

Kylie bounces into IOP wearing a fresh crop top over shorts, a long-sleeved plaid shirt wrapped around her waist, and new-to-her Roper boots.

"I got them at a thrift store." She spins a tanned leg on her tippy toes to show them off.

Wow. What a difference five days of sobriety makes.

Slanted, bloodshot eyes transformed to big, beautiful blue peepers. A giddy smile closes to sip from her Jesus Loves Strippers coffee mug. Something the boys really got a kick out of. She's chatty. Engaged. Open. An unrecognizable double of the woman who sat in her seat four days ago.

Did I look that much different when I first walked in? I visualize my drunk selfie video after the bed wetting incident. *Yeah. Maybe. Maybe I didn't cover it up as much as I convinced myself.*

June 13, 2017

Step four. Dig into your behavior. Courageously face what is really going on in your life. Take a look at the moral implications of your actions.

Character defects. The word "defects" by itself hurts. Flaws. Imperfections. Attach it to your moral compass and it flat out stings.

Using journalistic instincts, I kept track of what day anyone senior to me in the program had to do step four. I observed their angst leading up to the day. Tense shoulders. Curled toes. Sweaty palms. All signs that the next victim had been working on the homework.

I suffered the same fate this past week.

However, right before class on the day of the big reveal, each patient met with Brian for a private session and came out looking like they had been granted a reprieve on a life-term prison sentence.

Something weird must happen during those hours behind closed doors.

Today, I uncovered the secret.

All that crud. Built up. Thick. Festering. A cesspool of character defects.

Writing it down is like allowing a master plumber to push two augers into the hole of my soul.

The first with rotating thick blades. Cutting away at the roots of years and years of bad decisions. A hole I kept pouring sin into. Trying to fill up. Always left unsatisfied. An empty abyss.

The second snakes through with strong scrubbing bristles to polish the space. Providing a clean place for God to reside.

Sharing my writings with Brian flushes the sludge. Words come out of my mouth. Shame toxins spew from my belly. The knots relax. With each scar revealed, he provides a logical explanation of poor decision making from the past. Useful suggestions for the future.

We cover in depth false pride, being phony, selfishness, impatience, self-pity, intolerance, resentments, guilt, fear and more.

It almost seems too good to be true. Exposing without prejudice every secret, every flaw in a safe environment. Stripping out the lies without fear of judgement. I walk out of Brian's office feeling like my sins of the past are erased. A clean slate to start my new life.

That familiar I-know-something-you-don't-know grin lights up my face when I enter the group meeting room.

Bobbing smiles returned from those who have done it.

"Shindig's gettin' real, yo."

Laughter breaks out at my assessment of this step's requirements.

"I like to say tragedy plus time equals humor. But I'm recognizing jokes are my way of deflecting." I chuckle. The reaction justifies my self-analysis. "This one was hard."

The information discussed behind closed doors is strictly for the patient. A guide to begin to learn to know herself. For the purpose of class time, the crowd shouts out positive character assets about the person doing step four.

Brian tries unsuccessfully to keep up with the shouts. Scribbling on the board as fast as he can with a dry erase marker.

"Slow down." He shouts then laughs, knowing we do this to him on purpose every time.

My list, per this room of friends, includes sociable, witty, loving, willing, empathetic, dedicated, resourceful, accepting, happy, grateful, humble, admits mistakes, clear thinker, gets things done, honest, sober.

When they finish, I take a photo of the white board. Visual edification to drown out the devil's lies. My past is not my future.

June 15, 2017

I am emotionally stunted.

Do you remember "Shake Your Booty"? It took me well into my 20s to realize KC and The Sunshine Band didn't mean pick up your bootie-socked feet and shake the little pom-pom on the anklet while you dance. This is worse than that.

I grew up slower. Peter Pan style. Waited three years out of high school to join the Navy. Didn't go to college until I was 30. Kept the sorority party rocking until I'm knocking on the door of a half a century old. I can't process disappointment properly. I date men who are emotionally unavailable. FOMO (Fear of Missing Out) transforms to difficulty making decisions.

I learned in treatment, this is normal. Multiple studies show emotional growth stops at the moment the drug of choice is picked up.

Having a sponsor is not a suggestion in my case. It is a requirement. If I'm going to stay sober, I have to check in daily. My child brain is not trustworthy.

That's a tough fit though for someone who doesn't like to connect. Keeps everyone at arm's length. Won't get a pet because that would require an attachment.

In spite of all that, I did it today. A woman I know agreed to keep me accountable and walk through the 12 steps with me. She's celebrating being sober as many years as she was drunk.

I'll get to do that, too. When I'm 88.

June 16, 2017

I swing through the grocery store. Rotisserie chicken salad, fresh buns and chips from the deli. Cherry pie made fresh in the bakery. Hand-spun ice cream in frozen foods. Total: $14.31.

Fourteen bucks. Sheesh. This is one meal. I should have gone out to eat.

I approach the exit. My eyes lift off the receipt and connect with the product display I missed on the way in. A lovely two-foot tower of stacked boxes filled with crisp whites and full-bodied reds. The sign reads: Today's Special $13.99. I look back at my receipt.

Oh. Good one, God. Good one.

June 19, 2017

First day of the last week of IOP. Legs bounce with excitement. I'm busting at the seams for my turn to share.

"I feel like I've got my brain back." I grab the cranium with open palms. "No. More than that. Like I've won my soul back." Cupped hands against the chest.

No one is allowed to say anything during a share. Their anxious faces silently yell, *You've got our attention.*

I tell them the story about how I had a meeting with my boss and the advertisers. The man pitching the idea for our next commercial is new. He painted a picture with words. Used key phrases. Branding terminology. Stock imagery.

"I was bored," I say. "And frankly, a little confused. I know our non-profit helps people get work. But what does that mean?" I point at the day laborer. "Does that mean you?" At the waitress. "You?" At Brian. "You? Sure, we've got listings that could include even you, Brian. But the majority of the people coming to us need a second chance. Or even a first chance."

I shift my seat and shift gears.

"Then I started thinking about the employers. What motivates them to use our services? Who are they looking for?"

I share how I zoned out the presenter. Scribbled on the pad in front of me.

"Before he finished, I had a storyboard and script for a 30-second commercial." I grin from ear-to-ear. "A simple, straight-forward message to people looking for entry-level jobs and employers looking to fill them."

A golf clap round of applause breaks out.

"I couldn't believe it." My voice shakes with emotion. "For the first time since … Well. I honestly can't remember when. I raised my hand proudly and confidently." A re-enactment palm goes up in the air. "And I asked if I could share my idea."

A murmur of congratulations washes through.

"And they liked it," I say. "They genuinely like it. Like, you know how sometimes people politely brush you off with confirmation?"

Heads nod.

"This was not that. When I looked around the room, I realized by the looks on each one of their faces, this was something new. Really different from what we've been doing."

I sit back in my chair. Content. Spent.

"I don't know if anyone else has had this happen yet," I say. "But when I got back to my office, I was so overcome with emotion and thanked God for restoring my brain power. My creativity. It's who I am at the core. I'm back." I pump my fists in the air. "I. Am. Back."

Maybe I'll get the demotion reversed? Get my money back? My boss said she fully expected me to earn my way back. This is a pretty good start.

June 22, 2017

It's 11:28 a.m., and I want living proof, a sharp contrast to my drunk video, that things have, indeed, changed.

Holding the iPhone in my left hand, I punch the video program into selfie mode. It's hard to get a good glow under fluorescent lighting, so I move the camera around my face until I'm satisfied with the production value.

"I am super excited because I am about to graduate from IOP. There have been so many changes during that time just a few short weeks ago, um." I take a second to collect my thoughts. "That I can't wait to share with everyone."

Sitting at my desk, I replay the message to make sure I'm happy with it. Bright-eyed. Bushy-tailed. Love it. Then I embrace the daunting task of looking back at the March video. Swollen face. Puffy eyes. Hard to believe it's the same woman three months and three days earlier.

***

It's not just graduation night. It's Beta test night.

I'm ready to share what I've been working on. What I've been on fire over. The project I've alluded to during my share time the past couple of weeks with the voice of a giddy school girl. In television, that's called a tease, I tell the class each time.

Before the break, Kylie does her step one. She looks like a completely different person.

"I didn't think you were coming back over that first weekend." Now seems like a good time to come clean.

"Are you serious?"

"Yeah. That's what I told her that night we dropped you off." I point to a nodding Gwen. "Boy, did you prove me wrong. I knew you were a pretty girl. Sober? Your beauty radiates from the inside out. I love you, sister. And I am so proud of you."

This past week, getting ready for tonight, a moment of clarity hit me. The women divinely placed in my path during this time were huge influencers.

Kylie. Watching her daily transformation gave me a brutal, beautiful outsider's view of what drugs and alcohol can strip from us. And what we can do to take back our lives if we are willing to surrender.

Gwen. So young. So wise beyond her years. She didn't speak much. When she did, all ears perked. She once described my relationships as "dating alcohol, not men." Excellent assessment of my decision-making skills.

Elizabeth. It was a thin thread of God we met. I needed her in that one and only first meeting. Until Elizabeth, the only alcoholics I saw were red-faced men. Rode hard and put up wet women. I needed a college-educated professional in heels to say, "I'm an alcoholic," before I could believe I was one, too.

I share my revelations with the class.

"I had a preconceived idea of what an alcoholic looked like before I got in here and realized how much all of us are the same," I say. "I felt alone, you guys. So alone." I shake my pointer finger at the door. "How many people are out there feeling the same way we are because they don't have anyone in their social circle who has gotten help?"

I explain that, through several meaningful prayer sessions, God laid out for me the knowledge there were many out there like us. Waiting. Hiding in plain sight. Praying for a way out.

"I believe all they need is to see someone they can relate to." I shake my head. Stare at the floor. Speak in soft, firm tones. "I have a goal. I am going to do everything in my power to rip away the stigma and the shame associated with this disease."

I look up to wide eyes and baited breath.

"No one should be ashamed to be in here." Shake of the head. "We didn't know." Shrug of the shoulders. "I didn't know. I didn't know what was wrong with me. I didn't know why I was making the same bad decisions. And I sure didn't know how to fix it. I didn't even know what the first step should be."

No one makes a sound. If a pin drops, I will hear it.

"Now I do," I say. "Tonight, there is someone like me. Someone is lying in bed. Reaching up to the ceiling. Tears streaming down her face. Sweat pools staining her sheets. She is begging God for help. All she needs is to hear one person she can relate to say, 'Follow me.' And I am on fire." I slam my fist on my knee. "On fire to go find her."

June 23, 2017

I'm spending today's lunch break with a group of sober friends. Patiently waiting for my turn to share graduation news. Phone vibrates. Screen reads MOM. *I'll call her back.* Phone vibrates again. This time, my cousin. *Back-to-back calls from Phoenix? That's weird.* I excuse myself and walk outside.

"Aunt Doris died," my cousin Heidi says.

I slump back against the brick building. Equal parts surprise at the news and my reaction. No tears. No desire to drink. Only peaceful pause.

Doris was one of my favorite people on the planet. I could tell her anything. No judgement. She loved me unconditionally and I her. She lived life on her own terms. The timing almost seems orchestrated.

I went through a really bad break up almost exactly four years ago to the date. Doris told me, "Don't bury yourself in the bottom of a bottle over it." The comment stuck with me all these years. I smile at the memory.

"I graduated yesterday." I can hear Heidi clap on the other end. "She lived long enough to see me get sober."

Time to get out there and help other people experience these transformational moments.

CHAPTER 8
A NEW PURPOSE & A NEWER ADDICTION

July 22, 2017

The wooden door of a 1950s block home opens to reveal a tiny literary oracle.

Is she even five feet?

Nervous the author/editor can read my face, and thus my mind, I smile and give a quick salutation.

Lynn Skapyak Harlin is a small package with a huge reputation. Famous in writing circles. Beloved in breast cancer awareness groups. She edited former First Coast News anchor Donna Deegan's chronicles of her multiple fights against the disease. The books, *The Good Fight* and *Through Rose Colored Glasses*, proved to be as successful as Donna's battles.

I knew about the books. I know Donna. But I had never heard of the editor. Apparently, I am the only one.

Everyone I spoke to with tracks in the written word chuckled at the mention of her name. More than once told, "You better have thick skin. She's good. She's tough. But she's good."

My friend Pepper put Lynn on my radar when I revealed plans to share my story. Warned of her iron fist and glass jaw, I'm not surprised by this sweet little grandma face framed in grey hippy hair pulled back in a loose tail. I am concerned about when the tough love is coming.

"How is Pepper?" Lynn signals to follow her to the kitchen.

The ghostly smell of a thousand extinguished Marlboro Lights arrest my lungs.

Reminds me of home. This place would be Daddy Dot Com approved.

"She's good," I say.

"Coffee?"

"Yes. Thanks."

I take a beat to read the mug: I know what my problem is. WHAT'S YOURS?

She's too smart for this to be a coincidence. I like her sass.

We head back to a room fitted with two desks and a reading nook. She takes a seat in the nook surrounded by floor to ceiling shelves filled with books. A three-foot floor lamp lights up half her face. I sit across from her, an ottoman in between, and gleefully pass over the 24 pages I've already written.

During our initial call, I told her I would come see her when I finished. She insisted I come right away. Before I screw it up any more.

"Stop. Do not write anymore until we meet. You people in television are used to *telling* us stories," she said. "I need to teach you how to *show* the story. It will be easier to instruct you now than have to fix it at the end."

Passing over the three-ring binder, I'm convinced she will be delighted and amazed by my writing skills. I throw out a couple of book titles I've been kicking around.

"Whoa." She waves me off. "Let's write the book first, okay?"

Over the next 60 minutes, my ego winces. Writhes. She points out example after example of telling, not showing.

"This isn't a book. It's a bunch of random thoughts and bullet points." She flips the binder closed and pushes it towards me on the ottoman.

"You don't want to keep it?" I ask.

"No." She makes a face like she smelled something foul then lights a cigarette to cover the stench. "You don't have anything there worth editing."

How can she say that? I think it's got some good points.

Although I don't know enough to understand what or why she is saying this, I trust the crowd sourcing that has brought me here.

"Can I take your class?" I ask.

Lynn's Shantyboat Writers Workshop has a life of its own. It's not just a quirky name for Lynn's coveted class. It literally takes place every couple of months on her cherished shanty boat. A floating classroom she and husband Jim found in Jessup, Ga., during one of their first dates.

"We'll see," she says. "Now, I do want you to know." She takes a drag off her cigarette and starts to talk again before the smoke comes out. "I believe you have a good story here." She pats the binder. "It's an important story. One worth telling if it will help others."

Lynn goes on to share her own battle with the bottle. A cross she bore three decades ago turned out to be the love connection that brought her and Jim together in an A.A. meeting. Neither attend now.

I'm equal parts shocked and excited by the revelation and all of the onion layers that go with it.

"My doctor suggested I stay active in some type of 12-step group four times per week," I say.

In a do-as-I-say-not-as-I-do motherly way, she tells me it's important advice. As well as not following in her footsteps of trying to find my true love a couple months into sobriety.

"I have this clear vision of what God wants me to do with this project." Holding an open palm sideways to my face, I drop it, pointing to her. "I have to stay on track. At this age, trying to fold all the complexity of someone else's life into mine." Fingers on both hands crooked and spread, I fold them together like cogs on a wheel. "Would throw a wrench into all these plans stirring in my heart."

"Good," she says. "It makes me happy when a woman realizes she doesn't need anyone in her life to complete it."

I hug her goodbye. Something about her embrace tells me this will be more than a professional relationship.

July 25, 2017

We don't get sober overnight. There are stepping stones. People strategically, divinely positioned in our path to guide us towards the light when all we see is darkness. In my case, there was one in particular who stuck with me. A woman who assisted in changing the trajectory of my story. Even though we never met.

Her daughter Brenda is a friend. A really good friend. We barely see each other lately. When we do, it's work related. Still, we share secrets with each other. Very personal parts of our lives saved for the inner circle.

One day last year, she opened up about something which had a huge impact on my decision to ask for help.

It was a hot June afternoon. I sat in Brenda's office waiting for her to come upstairs from her studio. We had a meeting that day to go over some video my company hired her to do.

When I got there, one of her producers told me she would be right up, and we wasted the few minutes catching up on the latest in our personal and professional lives.

The door finally opened. I knew something was off. She rushed passed me with a forced smile and a quick, "Hi. I'll be right with you."

Her eyes were red. Her demeanor frazzled. After a quick bathroom break, she was back.

I asked her what was wrong. She wouldn't open up right away. Business first, always.

Eventually, after the clouds parted enough, we went to lunch. She was able to tell me she had hung up from a very disappointing conversation just before I arrived. A bid rejection on a high-paying gig. She couldn't bring herself to come upstairs right away.

"We're friends," I said. "You don't have to put on a mask for me. I'd be honored to love you through it."

"You're so sweet." That's always her reply when I do something nice for her. It seems so simple but means so much every time she says it. Mostly because I'm in love with her Jersey accent. I could listen to her read the phonebook and find it adorable. She will never get too old for me to say she is so darn cute.

She admitted the work barricade du jour was just another layer to add on to everything else she was going through. Most notably, the first anniversary of her mother passing.

I never met her mom. I was, however, deeply emotionally struck by her heartfelt share. The painful sorrow that comes with loving an alcoholic. While she talked, I visualized every woe-filled memory as if I lived it myself.

"She ruined every great moment in my life. *Every* great moment." She took air in and let out a labored breath. I sat silent. "My mom was drunk at my graduation." A sniffle and a hard swallow. "She was drunk at my wedding." She stared past me. Searching the outside street for the answer. "She … You name it, she was drunk."

She took a few minutes to wipe away tears and compose.

"But I loved her," she said. "And she loved me."

Of that, I did not doubt. Late last year, Brenda posted a beautiful photo montage of her mom with terms of endearment.

Today would have been my mother's 66th birthday. In June, she lost a 35-year battle with alcoholism. Those who remember her remember a smart, beautiful, stylish, and generous woman with an incredible sense of humor. Few truly understood the pain she was in for so long. While I may never understand that pain myself, I am lucky enough to know she loved me very much. I will miss her forever.

Her characteristics hit really close to home.

"During the last years of her life, she didn't go anywhere," Brenda said.

Isolation?

"Nowhere? But, like, how did she get food?"

How did she get alcohol? That's what I really want to know. How did she get alcohol?

"I would do most of it for her. The grocery shopping and errands and stuff. In the last years, it was like I was the parent and she was the child." She stopped to reflect. "I guess it was like that most of my life, really."

"What about the alcohol? Did she go buy it in the morning before she started drinking?"

"No. She had people for that."

"What does that mean?"

I ran out of liquor in Nashville once while Robb was at work. I called an Uber driver to take me to the store. I couldn't wait two hours for him to get home. Needed to keep the buzz going. Coincidentally, it was the same weekend he broke up with me.

"Like she ordered a Lyft or an Uber or something?"

"No," Brenda said. "Worse. She had a cab driver who would pick it up for her and leave it on the back porch."

"People do that?"

"Sure," she said. "Alcoholics find all kinds of ways to get people to do what they want."

"How did she die?"

What I'm really asking is, tell me how I am going to die, Brenda. Because, so far, your mother's story is my story. I have ruined weddings and graduations and special occasions. The guest of honor may not have called me mom, but they definitely wished they hadn't called me at all.

And that isolation you talk about is going to happen approximately 25 minutes after our meeting. The only difference is I will stop by the liquor store and the grocery store myself.

"I called her every morning on my way to work," she said.

Oh. There is one more difference in our story. There will be no loving daughter calling me tomorrow to make sure I'm alive. And as long as it doesn't happen on a work day, there won't be any phone calls.

"When she didn't answer..." Brenda looked down at her half-eaten plate, hands in her lap. She silently shifted her gaze off to the right. I could tell she was reliving the scene right in front of me. Her eyes welled up.

"I called Kip and told him, 'She's dead. I know it. She's dead.'" Tears cascaded down rosebud cheeks.

"When I got there, I found her on the floor in the hallway." She started to sob. "She died alone. My beautiful mother died all alone, just like I knew she would."

She tried to pull herself together. I cautioned her not to. It's good to let it out. Besides, there wasn't anyone near us in the restaurant to disturb these raw emotions.

It was cleansing for Brenda. For the memory of her mother. For the storm raging inside of me.

I asked Brenda to lunch today to let her know what a huge impact her mother's story had on me that day last year. We sit outside on the patio of the Mediterranean corner café. In spite of the normally brutal Florida summer temperatures, it is surprisingly cool under the sprawling oak tree.

"I went to treatment," I say. Looking in Brenda's eyes, I take a bite of my food, chew slowly, and wait for the response I want.

"I knew it," she says.

That wasn't the response I wanted. 'What? No! Not you?' would have worked magic on my ego.

"I knew it. I knew it." She pounds a fork on the table with each beat. Her face lights up with satisfaction. Mine, not so much.

"Why? How? Was I that bad?"

"What? No." She shakes both hands back and forth. "No. No. I hadn't heard from you in a long time and something about your posts on Facebook was different, and, I don't know." A hand brushes in my direction. "I just knew something was going on."

She shakes her smiling face and puts a fork in her salad.

"Why did you decide to go?"

I look down at my food. I can't look at her when I confess. I don't know how she is going to react. My goal is not to dredge up old pain. You never know how people will respond to new revelations.

"Well." I pause. "Partly because of the story you told me about your mom."

113

She doesn't say anything. I slowly raise my eyes to see hers. I wouldn't say her eyes were misty, but I could tell it affected her.

My teeth clench. *She's probably thinking, Really? How? How did the pain of watching the woman I love slowly kill herself help anyone?*

"Do you remember that conversation?" I ask.

She nods. Eyes wet.

"That evening, I sat on the couch, staring out the sliding glass door at an imaginary man—my future cab driver—setting a handle of Smirnoff on the patio," I say. "A twenty and a hefty tip waiting for him under a mat just inside the broken metal door."

I describe how the bright sunlight in contrast to my darkened living room would make it impossible for him to see me watching him. Impatiently waiting for him to get out of earshot, so I can pull back the glass barrier separating me from my addiction.

"I pondered how long it might take," I say. "Months? Years? Before this fantasy becomes my reality like it did for your mom?"

For the past year, the story haunted me. I wondered what she did all day.

Did she lay in bed and watch TV for hours on end like I do? Did she contemplate what could have been if she only had enough conviction to put down the bottle? Was her mind continuously berating her for mistakes she cannot change, then lying to her about productive tomorrows that will never come? And then telling her no one would miss her if she disappeared?

Yes. Her story haunted me. I didn't want to see it to the end. So, in effect, I guess she inspired me. This woman, whose name I don't even know.

I need to remember to ask Brenda today.

"Is it okay if we talk about this?" The last time we did was the first time we did. I didn't want to cause her any more pain.

"Yes, of course."

"When we sat in the restaurant last year, and you told me about your mother," I say. "The whole time, all I could think was, 'Oh, my gosh. That's me. That's my story.'"

"Really?"

"I was numb. No life inside. No fight left in me."

"I honestly had no idea."

"Visualization becomes realization and your mother's memory stuck with me," I say. "Guiding me to realizations of where I didn't want to end up. I could find pieces of her in every misstep. She stayed by my side. Reminding me there were plenty of Brenda's in my life. People who cared for me even if I didn't care for myself."

She puts her fork down and stares at me.

"I want you to know," I reach out for her hand. "Your mother didn't die in vain, Brenda. I'm going to share this story, my story and hers, to others who need to hear it. We are going to save people."

She glances away deep in thought with welled-up eyes just like she did during our first conversation. This time, there's a light in the dark brown pools. She nods in understanding.

"Yeah. I guess you're right." She wipes away the wetness before it can fall. "I never thought of it that way. That someone else could be saved by all of this pain."

I sit silent. Giving her a chance to process her thoughts.

"My friend Hilary commented on my post about my mom. It was perfect. Let me think. What was it?" Brenda draws her hair behind her right ear then covers her mouth to think. "It was something like, "Losing you is hard. But the hardest part is the loss of hope."

"You mean, the loss of hope she would eventually get sober?"

"Exactly. I loved her so much. I think every child of an alcoholic holds out hope that one day they will get help. Once they're gone?" She purses her lips. Shakes her head. "That's it."

We wrap up our lunch and hug our goodbyes. I turn away from her then quickly turn back.

"Oh! I forgot to ask," I say. "What was her name?"

"Her name?" She smiles at the question. "Her name is Susan."

July 26, 2017

I put together a report for my boss today. Fabulous results. Since I took over a flagship donation project four years ago, the number of participants doubled and donation dollar value tripled. I've got my fingers crossed. I hope this means I'm one step closer to getting my money back.

July 27, 2017

I have a new addiction. Sugar. And it is painful. Google turns up a couple of logical explanations.

My body is missing the daily sugar intake. One shot glass at a time. The new pain in my joints and muscles is probably inflammation from binging on fructose, glucose and sucrose. Or, it could be an ongoing problem masked in a cloudy brain for who knows how long.

There's also something called transfer addiction. Some people take up smoking. Others drink copious cups of coffee. Then there's me. Copious cups of coffee with multiple packets of sugar.

I'm hoping Dr. Rafael Foss can provide some answers. He's the founder of 904 Thin. The program I lost 21 pounds on last year. I ask him to meet me for, what else, copious cups of coffee.

I've got a secret to share. And it's not just the sugar I sneak in my cup before he arrives.

"Hey Doc." I stand to hug him. He sits across from me empty handed.

"No coffee for me." He flashes his million-dollar smile. "I'm only here to catch up with you. How have you been?"

"Funny you should ask. I wanted to meet with you because I need to come clean."

Rafael cocks his head. Confusion rolls across his face in perfect time with the wheels spinning in his head.

"I'm just going to throw it out there. I'm an alcoholic."

Eyes pop open. Almost as wide has his mouth.

I believe I heard the sound of your wheels squealing to a halt, Doc.

"I've had a lot of ah-ha moments since going to treatment." Head and torso rock in nervous affirmation. "One of them is I need to thank you for your part in saving my life."

Confusion melts into disbelief. Furrowed brow. Shaking head.

"What? No. I didn't do anything. What did I do?"

"I did your program because I had so many things going wrong in my life." I count them down on each finger. "Anxiety. Sleeplessness. Night sweats. Depression. Weight gain. I thought I was going through early menopause."

"Yep. I hear that a lot." He nods.

"I figured if I could take one thing, my weight, and focus on that, maybe I could start to address the other problems."

I give him a quick overview of my annual 30-day liver toxins sabbatical.

"I wondered if there was a correlation to mental health," I say. "I didn't drink on your program."

"Yeah, but you could have," he says.

The comment is a common one for non-alcoholics. Having a glass of wine with dinner, as in one glass of wine, is pointless. Futile. Insanity, really.

"It's easier for me to have none than one. So, I had none for 45 days. I emerged from the experience feeling like a brand new person. No anxiety. No sleeplessness. No night sweats. I said to myself, 'If these symptoms come back, I may have to admit there is one common denominator.'"

"Wow." He sinks back against the chair. "I am ... I'm blown away. I did not expect this conversation."

I tell him about my recent love affair with sugar and subsequent weight gain.

He ribs a friendly scolding for not allowing him to treat me through the process to avoid this situation. Then explains all of my many questions with one PhD word. Neuroplasticity.

Neuroplasticity is the ability of the brain to form and reorganize synaptic connections.

"Your body has receptors," he says. "When a receptor is damaged, it craves unhealthy things. And some of those things are sugar and alcohol. In fact, alcohol turns into sugar. So, when you heal those receptors." He holds his fingers up into what I can only imagine is an outline of a receptor. "Your body will stop craving those unhealthy things. That's what's good about the program. It balances those receptors and puts your body in balance so you don't have those cravings. If you keep yourself in check, you'll keep yourself healthy for the rest of your life."

"So that's why my body craved alcohol. Craves sugar. And when I'm doing 904 Thin, craves healthy fruit?" I ask.

"Basically, anything your body gets," he says, "your body is going to want more of. You can apply it to anything. Good habit. Bad habit. That's how our neurosynapses form. Every time you do an activity, it forms neurosynapse. Eventually, you don't even have to think about it."

I feel like I've gotten there with alcohol. No. I take it back. I do allow myself a few romanticized moments. That block of time when you think getting back together with an ex is a good idea? It's like that.

It happened a couple of weeks ago at a concert when country crooner Cole Swindell sang about raising a whiskey toast.

"Aw. I want to raise a glass." I turn to my friend and hairstylist Kimberly. Raised an imaginary highball. "To our brothers in Iraq." Then I remembered that remorseless selfie video. "No." I scrunched my nose. "Never mind."

Flight of fancy permanently grounded.

CHAPTER 9

A CROWN, A CAUSE AND A POT O' GOLD

August 1, 2017

Miss USA 2006 Tara Conner is celebrating 10 years of sobriety.

I'm sure when she won the crown, Addiction Advocate by Example was not her dedicated platform of choice. Getting busted for cocaine use changed that.

In a TEDx Talk you can find online, she describes treatment as finding the pot of gold.

Sweet. Someone who is speaking my language. No shame in her game. Only a desire to go share her story in the hopes it will help someone else feel safe enough to speak up. Ask for help.

"There are currently 20 million Americans struggling with addiction. Far more than those diagnosed with cancer," she says. "And only 10 percent of those will receive treatment."

She says she doesn't mind sharing her dirty laundry with whomever will listen, and I'm starting to think she had me at hello.

"I challenge those who are in long-term recovery. All of the families whose lives have been recreated through recovery." Her voice pleads with passion. "Join together and recover out loud." She softens with empathy. "Then maybe, we can take the shame away from those who are in the shadows, and encourage them to step into the light. I know I will."

I know I will, too.

It's thanks to people like Tara that I have been able to forge through moments of self-doubt. The venomous self-talk seeking to derail the mission I am convinced is divine. A gentle reminder the enemy lives to trip me up. Take me off course. Keep the ripple effect from reaching the next person I'm intended to help.

I may not have the long-term qualification, but I definitely have the shameless part down.

August 4, 2017

I'm seeing why not everyone shares my agreement of living life in the light. I told a longtime acquaintance about my newfound freedom today. It didn't go as planned.

His first reaction was approval. A "good for you" head nod.

I told him I was looking forward to volunteering at his school again this year. Reading to the fifth graders.

"Call me," I said.

"Right. Yeah. That'll be great." His words were positive. His body language said he won't be calling.

I wonder if Miss America ever gets this reaction?

August 6, 2017

It's time to put my money where my faith is. After another inspirational sermon today, I pull up the online giving app and enter 10 percent of my income. Payable every two weeks on Fridays.

Even though the struggle continues with reduced income after the demotion, I believe God will provide. He's never let me miss a house payment in 25 years. I don't think he's going to start now.

I don't have a budget game plan yet for the decision. I've learned action first creates the momentum. I'll figure it out. Always do.

I step out on faith and push CONFIRM on the app.

August 7, 2017

The sting from my conversation with the principal Friday smarts my heart and my brain.

When I was a morning show personality, one of my duties was a segment called Cool Schools. None of the other reporters liked to do it. I loved it. Every Friday I went live from a different school.

"Coming up after the break, these kids are excited to show you what makes this school so cool." I had to scream to be heard while Chris Mills panned to hundreds of glee-filled, squealing faces. Excited to tell moms and dads, grandmas and grandpas, "I was on TV!"

I spent time with them in between live shots. Identifying the class clown. The misunderstood child who likely got 'talks too much' on his or her report card. I knew I had the right kid when a nervous teacher or principal pulled me aside to say, "Oh, no. I don't think you want to have her on air with you."

I'd look over at Chris. He'd give me his knowing look. I'd mouth back, "Perfect." He would nod. We'd give each other a wide-grin, silent giggle. Lights. Camera. Action.

For years since, I've wanted to join a mentorship program. Figuring I had something to give to some confused teen who doesn't fit in. Alcohol always held me back. Fear of being exposed as the fraud I was.

Leah enters my office to do our Monday morning catch-up session. The timing could not be more on point.

As part of her many duties, she runs Take Stock in Children, a college-success non-profit. In its simplest form, a high school student who has the intelligence but not the funding to get postsecondary education is matched with a mentor. If the mentor meets with the student one hour per week during the school year, the graduate receives college funds.

Before she can open her mouth, I blurt out my intentions.

"I want to sign up for Take Stock."

"Oh." She stops in her tracks. Eyes wide with this out-of-the-blue revelation. "Great."

"Can I request a student at Douglas Anderson School of the Arts though?"

"Sure. We can do that."

TSIC tries to match mentors with mentees who have similar interests. I know any student from this school will be a good match.

I multitask filling out the online form while she fills me in on her latest boating adventure with her boyfriend. Before she can walk out, the good deed is done.

August 9, 2017

"I can't believe how much I'm accomplishing."

"Like what?" Mom asks.

I've been calling my mom on a regular basis since my dad died. Gone are the days of Momma Dot Com guilt shaming me with 'guess you forgot my number' texts.

I never understood people who said things like, "I talk to my mom every day."

About what? I thought.

Now I get it. I look forward to talking to her. When I have good news, she is the one I want to share it with. Nancy, too.

"When I think of something, I do it." Surprise resonates across the phone. "I don't just go, 'Oh, yeah. That's a good idea. I should do that sometime.' I do it. Right away."

"Like what?"

"Like, I signed up to be a mentor to a high schooler. I started tithing at church."

"Oh, wow."

"I met with that lady who will be my editor." Suddenly, I remember the best part. "Oh. And she said I can take her class next month. I'm super excited."

"Oh, honey. Congratulations. I'm so proud of you."

The words catch me off guard.

You're proud of me?

The last time my mom saw me drunk, I said to her, "Why don't you ever say, 'I'm proud of you.' That's what I need to hear." To which she pushed my body and my breath away from her, clearly annoyed, and said, "No, you don't."

Brian was right. If we are patient, and do the next right thing every day, the people who love us the most will come around.

August 10, 2017

The smell hits me as soon as I open the Soul Food Bistro door.

Mmmm ... fried chicken and collard greens.

I search the restaurant for Kerry's pink and purple coiffed hair.

She's hard to miss, not only because of her fun follicles, but also because she's 5'11". I spot her in a purple European Street Café T-shirt and pajama bottoms. Standard uniform when she doesn't wander outside a 15-mile radius from her Riverside home. And sometimes when she does.

We grab our grub, push our cafeteria trays and ourselves into a corner booth to catch up. Mid-sentence Kerry spots defamed Congresswoman Corrine Brown. She's out on bond, staving off jail food for soul food until her appeal.

"Check it out." She juts her chin in Corrine's direction. "I gotta get a selfie."

I look over my right shoulder and catch the back of the Congresswoman's head.

"Darn. She's going to the other side. I thought she was coming our way." Kerry looks back at me then glances again. Back at me. Back at Corrine. "I'm sorry. I can't focus until I get this accomplished."

She holds her phone apprehensively in front of her in the camera position. She's in hunter mode. Silently. Patiently. Waiting for the perfect time to twist in her seat, put the iPhone in front of her face, snap a shot with Ms. Brown in the background.

C'mon Corrine. Make a decision already. She paces back and forth, stopping to fumble through her purse. *I think she's on to us. What is she doing?*

I'm getting impatient.

"Don't you have a bunch with her already?" I ask.

Kerry's snarky. She can insult you to your face and all you can do is laugh. Her delivery is spot on. The only person to ever deny the Official Selfie Queen of Jacksonville is former Mayor Alvin Brown. He wasn't wooed by her charm. It took on a social media life of its own known as Selfiegate, with its own hashtag and everything. Until he acquiesced.

Corrine disappears around the restaurant divider and Kerry is all mine.

"How's the party planning going?" she asks.

"Great. You want to hear the details."

"Of course." She waves her hand out in front of her with permission. "Proceed."

I pull out my notes.

"We've got the location but not a DJ. We're going to have a costume contest and a dance contest."

"A costume contest? What's the theme?"

"80s music."

"Woohoo!" Her face lights up. Kerry is the only person I know who loves 80s music more than me. Tears for Fears and Hall & Oats are still her favorite bands. "Let me think. What should my costume be?"

"You should be the lead singer from Missing Persons."

"She's blonde."

"Yeah, but she has pink and purple streaks in her hair. You could just put on a 3/4 cap wig and carry the album around your neck like a billboard for reference." We laugh at the visual.

"How are you going to tell everybody about the drinking thing?"

"I've got a whole presentation ..."

"Of course, you do." She throws her hands up and slaps them back on the table. "You're Tracy Dot Com."

"I want to keep it light. You know, like ..."

Kerry raises a hand. Pointer finger extended.

"Like, '*Hey everybody ... I'm a drunk!*'" She mimics my high-pitched voice. "'*Bet you didn't see that coming ... Cheers!*'" A mimed toast follows.

"Oh my gosh. You need to get someone to take a picture of the crowd's face. They'll be saying, 'Party Girl USA?'" She cocks her head to the right then left to converse with imaginary guests. "'Party Girl Dot Com?'" Her head shifts again. "'She's an alcoholic? Huh. Didn't see that one coming.'"

We lose our composure. The table behind her turns to find out what's so funny,

She changes the subject.

"Who's your boyfriend now? I can't keep track. With me it's easy. Nobody. As in, 'Wow, Kerry and Nobody have been together a really long time."

"I don't have a boyfriend," I say. "I don't want one. I am so on fire for this mission of letting people know that it is okay to ask for help, but it is a lot of work. To have someone walk into my life now with all of their problems and idiosyncrasies, likes and dislikes." I intertwine the knuckles on both hands like a cog. "And to try and meld all that crap with my crap right now? That would be too much work and distract me from this."

I point down to my notes and Kerry nods in agreement.

"I always thought I had to be with someone," I say. "That I was a better me when I'm part of a team. I've been that way my whole life. I assumed it was a character defect I was born with. Tracy, the chronic co-dependent."

Kerry's nods quicken with my intensity.

"I realized I had been drinking *so* long—and that was the source of the neediness—but I had been doing it *so* long, it's all I remember. I just assumed that's who I am. It turns out it wasn't a trait or a defect of my authentic self. It is ... *so* ... freeing not to have to have someone to put my happiness on."

"Do you crave alcohol?"

"Heck yeah, I craved it. I couldn't get off work fast enough to get my first shot. It's all I thought about all day long." I take a bite of chicken and shake my head through the chews. "Even when I was trying to convince myself I was okay by not drinking during the week. On Monday, I was so down in the dumps and called it the Monday Blues."

"Ugh." Kerry throws her head back. "I do that. Except it starts on Sunday."

"Me, too. And then my mood would elevate each day throughout the week. By Friday, I was on a high. Couldn't wait to get off work and get to the liquor store."

A busser comes by. Noticing our silverware lying unused on the table, she asks to take our plates. We refuse. We're talking so much, our plates are still half full.

"I was reading this book last night ... my editor recommended I read memoirs by women with addiction to help me write. Anyway, this book I'm reading talked about how even when she wasn't drinking to be good, she still obsessed about it all week. I totally got it.

"A co-worker said to me last week, 'Happy Friday.'" I tapped my pointer finger on the table. "I said, 'Tommy—in my world—every day is Friday.' And I meant it."

I lean back in my seat.

"I was driving to work, listening to the radio and Elvis Duran said, 'We do this every Friday on our show.' I literally said to myself, 'Is today Friday?' Because I genuinely enjoy every single day. I have something worthwhile to do every single day. So, it doesn't matter if I have to be to work tomorrow or not."

We pack up and Kerry grabs a giant slice of Red Velvet cake to go. It's going to be her last for a while.

August 12, 2017

I pick up Kerry at 9:23 a.m. We head to Fleming Island to meet Dr. Foss. Kerry has decided to do the 904 Thin program. I've decided to support her by re-committing to Phase II of the plan.

My decision isn't altruistic. I need to shed the 10 pounds I gained from my near-death, post-Dad-dying bottle binge and the subsequent 4-month sugarfest that followed when I quit.

"This lady with 30 years sobriety told me she was picking up a white chip to signify her desire to quit ice cream."

Kerry chuckles, so I assume she gets the joke.

"I told her I was just thinking the night before how I was going to start a group for non-alcoholics and apply 12-steps and a sponsor," I say. "I have two friends who are constantly battling and it all stems from something that happened years ago that they never talked about. Every day I am reminded the 12 steps relate to all areas of life."

I tell her I can easily explain it with the first step: We admitted that we were powerless over alcohol—that our lives had become unmanageable.

"If you replace the word 'alcohol' with anything—resentment, food, the inability to say I'm sorry—you can change your world."

"That's pretty deep," she says.

"I've heard Celebrate Recovery is like that." I shrug my shoulders. "I'm not sure. I haven't checked it out yet. I'm going to. I want to attend all kinds of meetings to educate myself. Not just on what I need. Everything. So, if someone asks me a question, I have an answer. Or know who to ask."

"Correction," Kerry says. "Seriously deep."

"I feel like I'm in college. I go to all these different meetings, and every time somebody says something that I learn from. How to live in the present. Why my sobriety depends on continuing to work the 12 steps and have a sponsor in my entire life. How to forgive people who could cause a resentment."

"Speaking of," she says. "Are you worried about what people are going to think after you 'come out.'" She uses air quotes.

I switch the music station to NPR and glance at my phone to see how much private time we have before we arrive.

I tell her I'm not worried. I have to focus on me. I don't have the luxury of worrying about anyone else's issues with my decision.

"I get it. It's like me and my depression. People always say to me," her voice raises an octave, "'Just get up. Go to the gym. Go do *something*.'"

She brings it back down. "They don't understand. I *can't* get up."

I pull into the parking spot. Kerry stares straight ahead. Neither of us reach for the door.

"It's like with cancer," she says. "People don't say, 'Stop having cancer!' My mental illness is a disease. Your alcoholism is a disease. It doesn't define who we are as people." Her voice rises in intensity. "We can't stop. We need help. It's like that with you." She turns to face me. "People will probably say, 'Just slow down. Have some water in between drinks. Stop at only a couple.' They don't get it. They don't see us behind closed doors."

"Yep. I remember this example so clearly," I say. "Nikos Westmoreland and I were having a lovefest backstage at a fashion show. We were waiting for our turn to go on stage and I couldn't stop hugging him. He always looks like he walked off the cover of a GQ magazine and smells like the inspiration for all the cologne inserts."

"Ah. True dat." Kerry breathes deep through her nose imagining it.

"I was telling him I wished we spent more time together. Then he said, and I'll never forget this, 'Yeah, I was thinking about you this weekend, but you're always so busy. You know so many people.'"

I shut the car off. The radio goes silent. My body shifts to face her.

"Do you know what I was doing that weekend? That exact weekend he was telling me about? The reason I remember it so well years later?"

She shakes her head in anticipation.

"Friday. Liquor store. Giant bottle of Pinnacle. Publix. Groceries. Home. Shades closed. Didn't step foot out of my house until Monday morning."

Anticipation turns to empathy. She stares at the floorboard. Head shakes lower and slower this time.

"That was my new normal. If I got a call to do something spontaneous over the weekend, I couldn't go. If I was awake, I had a buzz. Or if I found out several hours before, I would take an Ambien and force myself into sleep to try and sober up so I could go."

"Oh my gosh! That's so dangerous," she says.

"I used to look at that bottle and wonder, at what point is one more too many?"

August 13, 2017

The commercial I pitched came in today for approval. It is fantastic. If I do say so myself. Credit, of course, to the production team.

Better yet. The woman in charge of my paycheck loves it.

I am trying to be patient with God's timing. But I really, really, really hope she gives me my money back soon. Realistically, it will probably be at the end of the year. I need to make a conscious effort to wake up and go to sleep grateful I still have a job.

August 18, 2017

Facebook Post: I will take today in my arms and love it. I will love all it offers; it is a friend bearing gifts galore. #livinginthepresent

August 21, 2017

The first solar eclipse since 1979 dominates social media with hilarious memes. The funniest from John Phillips, who's third child is threatening to be born on the same day.

If his name is familiar, you probably enjoy a good episode of "Nancy Grace" every once in a while. The civil trial lawyer frequently trades jabs with the sassy blonde attorney on CNN. A shameless self-promoter and marketing genius, he is the best advocate for families in distress— most notably the family of Jordan Davis, the black teenager shot for playing his music too loud at a gas station.

Always on the cutting edge of helping people by helping people, John secured several boxes of eclipse glasses and gave them out for a donation to PinkLawyers.com, a non-profit committed to helping fight breast cancer. People all over Jacksonville were preparing to protect their peeps thanks to the Law Offices of John M. Phillips. And he wasn't even going to get to see it.

"While the rest of you are looking at the sun, waiting on the moon," John posted. "I'll be looking at a moon, waiting on my son."

Giggle. Hit LIKE. Set my phone on the console and head to a meeting.

The drive takes me under an overpass I never overlook. I can't. It's a memory I can't shake. I've traveled the path a thousand times. But for the last 500, I shiver over a mistake that almost cost me my freedom. And more important, a child's life.

It was Spring 2013. Yet another failed relationship had me spiraling to the abyss. Long work days. Longer drunk nights. But still giving my all to the community whenever she called.

The craziness started when I woke up and realized I forgot to ask the host what time he wanted me at the event. During the week, the space is a parking lot under the I-95 overpass, swarming with business suits and sensible heels. On Saturday, it's the Riverside Arts Market, swarming with vendors, shoppers and an occasional fruit fly. On this particular Saturday, the festival was going to honor city leaders who supported the ongoing efforts of saving the St. Johns River. I was asked to introduce each of them to the stage, which is an outdoor concrete raised elevation. Behind it, our beautiful river flows swiftly and famously for its south to north direction.

Following my own "if you're not five minutes early, you're 10 minutes late" rule, I arrived under the bridge before RAM opened its non-existent doors at 10 a.m. Parking was a breeze at that early hour. Getting there, not so much.

I had opted for deodorant and perfume as opposed to a shower. Spearmint gum in lieu of a toothbrush. Since it was outside on a beautiful, mild morning, a Scunci hair tie was my hair dresser, drug store sunglasses my makeup artist, and crumpled up athletic gear from the day before my fashion stylist.

It's all I could muster after hitting snooze on the alarm three times. I remember thinking, *What's happened to me?* I used to jump out of bed for these opportunities to serve. Now, I was waking to my inside voice screaming, *Why the hell did I say I would do this stupid event?*

But, hey, I was here. The sooner I got it over with, the sooner I could go home and drink.

"Where's the host?" I asked a volunteer. I scanned the empty stage wondering why there wasn't at least some sound equipment in place yet.

"He should be here shortly," she said. "You can hang out anywhere though. We won't be starting that part of the presentation until noon."

Noon? Noon? What? I glanced at my phone for the time. 9:58. Rubbing my forehead in distress, out of the corner of my shades, I caught the volunteer watching. I composed myself, tossed her a thumbs-up and a smile, and quickly walked back to my car.

Like a dog in Pavlov's Theory, I had conditioned myself to know that when the alarm bell rang, I had X amount of time before I would be rewarded. A floating target based on the day's agenda. Once the allotted time passed, salivating cravings started.

Being told the target got moved two hours did not set well. Both hands on the steering wheel. Tap, tap, tap with a forefinger.

This isn't a job. I don't work for these people. Tap, tap, tap. I could tell them I thought it was at 10, and I'm sorry, but I have another gig at noon. A glance to the mirror. A scowl at the reflection. Dangit. I can't lie.

It was one of the few redeeming qualities I still held to fiercely. Although looking back, a lie would have been harmless compared to the choice I made.

I fired up my ride and headed for home, calculating the time in my head. Twenty minutes to the house, twenty minutes back. That leaves a little over an hour to get back. Idle hands are the devil's workshop and my workbench was waiting for me in the dark corner of the kitchen.

I poured a shot. Stared at the clear liquid. Contemplated out loud. "Who all is going to be there?" I rubbed both eyes. Back and forth. Back and forth. "Let me think. Let me think. Let me think."

I settled on the belief that no one there really knew who I was. Moments earlier, ego had whispered there was no way the show could go on without me.

How will they ever be able to have such an entertaining presentation without Tracy Dot Com's quick wit and candid humor. If you weren't there, the show would run late from everyone stopping to ask, "Where's Tracy? I was so looking forward to meeting her. She's the reason I came."

Now, the monster negotiator inside convinced otherwise.

None of those people know who you are. No big deal. One shot. I can't. I know I shouldn't. It's a festival. It's noon. Everyone will have a beer in hand. It's not like you're going to stand out if they smell you. I picked it up. I set it down. The negotiating continued until it wore me down. You brush your teeth. Chew some gum. It's not like one shot gets you drunk.

Down the hatch. No big deal. Just two ounces. Except alcohol to the monster is like spinach to Popeye.

Just one more. You've got time. Another glance to the phone. 10:32. You can take a power nap. Sleep in your clothes. Walk right out the door. Ten minutes to spare. I promise.

Less than an hour later, the alarm snapped me out of slumber. I snatched my keys and my phone and ran out the door. I must have looked at the clock on the dashboard at least four times a minute, begging it to go slower. 11:42. I had to get there on time. 11:45. In the arts industry, it's referred to as a call time. 11:49. I had given myself a call time of five minutes early, but now I wished I had a buffer. 11:50.

"Come on." I screamed at every red light. 11:51. A call time is when you must be on set. 11:52. Not when you should be in the parking lot, which I almost was. 11:53. On set. 11:54.

I stopped in front of the entrance. I had one minute to pull across two lanes of traffic, park and run to the stage. I could feel my heart pounding.

"Come on." I screamed at the oncoming traffic whizzing by, blocking me from my goal. I pounded the steering wheel and then spotted an opening to make a break through. My eyes glued to the headlights of the final barrier. I put my hands in position to flip the wheel for a sharp left.

"Yes." I punched the gas just as the metal scooted by and readjusted my focus to the destination. That's when I saw her.

She had to be about 7 years old and on the lower spectrum of the growth chart. I still can picture her pretty brown hair bouncing in time with her steps. The steps that had gotten her two feet in front of her mother and one foot into the parking entrance.

SCREEEEETCH. Disc brakes to the rubber to the road. The car shook back and forth from the sudden halt in kinetic energy. Time stood still. Everything stopped.

Her tiny skull snapped to attention with the squeal. Her mother impulsively leapt forward to grab her. Our eyes met. The sound of blood violently pulsating in and out of my heart was the only sound.

I put my hand on my chest and mouthed, "I'm so sorry. I'm so sorry. I'm so sorry."

Deep in my head, not once implementing offensive driving skills to scan the sidewalk for the hundreds of festival goers who showed up while I napped. It was unforgiveable. Or nearly so, anyway.

Recalling that memory still labors my breathing as if it is happening in real time.

John's law office has a catchy phone number. 444-4444. His tag line is a play off the Star Wars lingo: May the 4's be with you.

It's cute. We all laugh about it in social circles. However, I spent many nights speaking into existence, "Please don't let me get a DUI. Please don't let me get a DUI ever in my life." It's funny now to think it worked. But it definitely was not a joke when I was praying.

It was a given I could call John if it happened. But that afternoon, under that bridge. I knew I would have been on my own.

You see, John is a victim's advocate. You can see him standing strong next to Jordan Davis' parents in the documentary *3 ½ Minutes*. His name appeared under Best Righteous Crusader right next to his name under Best Lawyer in *Folio Weekly*'s reader poll for his tireless work on that case. He lives his life, his mission, to fight for the people who are wronged.

And that day. That day the person being wronged would not have been me. He would have been best serving his God, his community and his conscious standing across the aisle from me in court. I am eternally grateful it never came to that.

I will never give myself the luxury of forgetting that day. I'll use the memory as fuel to keep fighting like hell to pull others from the same fate.

I'm not in it alone. Gratefully, the Greenfield peeps are equally fired up, agreeing to participate in this book. What started as an idea for a nonprofit is molding into a plan with a purpose.

The proposed name is The Crushed Velvet Project after my college blog of the same name. The title, an homage to my ability to get behind VIP crushed velvet ropes with a media badge, now conjures visions of a giant empty vodka bottle crushing the runway red carpet beneath accomplished feet.

Haven't figured out how to create the 501(c)(3) for the foundation yet, but I'm blessed to be surrounded by people a lot smarter than me. Hank says she can get it done by the end of the year. For now, I can get the business side going with an LLC, printing educational materials and offering to speak. Long-term goals include scholarships for out-patient treatment once the nonprofit requirements are complete.

Details need to be flushed out, but the only way to stay on target is through action. Chipping away at whatever I can.

Don't judge each day by the harvest that you reap,
but by the seeds that you plant.
– Robert Louis Stevenson

CHAPTER 10

BLINDSIDED, BROKEN & BEING A BLESSING

August 25, 2017

I hit send on the IRS site after my first cup of coffee. It's official. The Crushed Velvet Project is an LLC with an EIN tax number. Check.

Update car insurance on Uber driver apps. Check.

This project isn't going to pay for itself and I'm not even bringing in enough to get by after my demotion.

The boss calls to say our conference call with First Coast News is cancelled. Our CEO has called an emergency meeting with the executive staff.

That can't be good. Maybe they're worried about the hurricane. Matthew cost us hundreds of thousands of dollars. And it cost me hundreds of thousands of brain cells at the weekend-long hurricane party. No, that doesn't make sense. Hurricane Harvey is headed to Texas.

Walking past the board room on the way to the copier, my curiosity is too much. I lean in to listen.

Sounds like transportation changes. Yeah, I'm safe.

I haven't felt paranoid since my awakening. Until the next call from the boss comes in. Summoning me to her office. I've learned her inflection.

I turn the corner and through the cracked door see her sitting upright. Talking to someone across her desk. Two steps closer and our Chief of Human Resources comes into view.

Crap!

When HR walks down the hall of the executive offices, people like to yell in jest, "Dead man walking!" I have a feeling it's not so funny today.

"Can you close the door, please." A seat has been set off to the side for my arrival.

Maybe they're going to tell me I get my money back. My prestige back. My dignity back.

"We're making cuts and your position has been eliminated effective immediately."

Or... maybe not.

She asks me a series of questions about upcoming projects.

I guess I could say, "Figure it out yourself. I'm outta here." But I don't. I give her the information and tell her she can call me anytime. I beg them not to erase my computer.

There is so much on there that will affect future projects. As Chief Operating Officer, my boss wears so many hats. And she's been so good to me. The thought of her wasting precious minutes to find something on the computer of a schizophrenic creative mind is not fair to her.

"Are you sure I can call you?" she asks.

"Of course, you can. You saved my life."

We both start to tear up and stand simultaneously to hug goodbye.

"I'm forever grateful for not being fired. For having insurance to go to treatment. I don't know what I would have done without it."

My own words make me even more determined to make The Crushed Velvet Project a success.

Oh my gosh. What would I have done? I have no roommate. No one to rely on. No idea who to ask for direction. I cannot for a moment imagine what life would have been like if I lost my job before I got sober.

I shiver at the thought.

HR walks me to my office to collect my belongings. She helps me carry the stuff out to the car and collects my gas card. She tries to make friendly conversation on the way.

"So, you said you're flying out today?"

"Yes, I'm giving my aunt's eulogy tomorrow."

Her smile fades.

***

On the way home, I call my mom.

"Do you think you would have gotten laid off if you hadn't been demoted?"

What a stupid question. What the heck does it matter?

I can't be mad at her. She means well. She doesn't know how *not* to go to the dark side. Her pessimism is part of her DNA. The question would have set me off another time in my life.

Right now, I don't have the luxury of time to worry about it. My mind is scrolling through solutions.

"I'm sorry. That was just dumb. I shouldn't have said it. I'm sorry. You know I'll help you if need money," Mom says.

"It's okay. I'll be fine. I'll figure it out." I'm not really as sure as I sound, but my faith is in overdrive.

God didn't take me this far to let me fail. Dangit! Why didn't I start Uber driving when it was all extra money. GRRRR. Stupid Big Bang Theory. Drawing me in with nightly re-runs and endless excuses.

It's funny how you never have time for the things you need to do until you have to do them for survival.

***

I get home and scratch out the word RESUME in child's handwriting with a red Sharpee. My Facebook selfie reads: Been 20 years since I've had to do a resume. #thingsimgratefulfor #didntmakethecut Excited to see what great adventure God has planned for me next!

Half of me believes what I'm saying. The other half is hoping to speak it into existence.

***

I call my sponsor right before I board the plane. She asks me to go deeper with my feelings when I reply with a one-word answer: Apathetic.

"I don't feel anything right now." Fully aware I have answered the question exactly the same with five more words, she responds by saying nothing. Patiently waiting for more. "I'm not worried. I'm excited for the next chapter of my life. I have no idea what that is."

I look around the airport and wave my hand at all the travelers backed up three deep to get on our flight.

"It's like I'm in an airport about to go on a surprise vacation. I have no idea where God has booked this flight to, but I'm excited."

"Good girl," she says. "That's the attitude. But you don't have any resentments?"

"No. I'm grateful for the five months I had after I came clean with them."

My attitude changes when a text comes in as I plop down in seat 13A. Second of its kind from concerned friends: Do you get severance?

It's a question I never thought to ask while we were sitting in the dungeon of doom.

I started at CSX in 1997 and was wooed away to the Wonderland of multimedia journalism in 2005 after two years of begging by my internship mentor Rich Ray at The Florida Times-Union. Six years of over-the-top, feel-good reporting—the crazier the better—in print, online, radio and television as Tracy Dot Com caught the attention of Action News Director Mike McCormick. He sweet talked me into working for him with the phrase, "I'm a big fan of you, Tracy Dot Com. I want your positivity on my morning show every morning." From there, only the big bucks and grandiose title of Vice President of Public Affairs of a popular nonprofit could get my ego to release the pseudo name.

I had never decided where I was going next. Fate decided for me. My hard work paid off in dividends. Now, the debt was being recalled.

I can't believe I'm starting from scratch. No money in my pocket thanks to a kitchen remodel. Why did I do that stupid remodel? Severance pay? I've heard of it. I even got it when I opted to leave the Times-Union during job cuts. My offer to leave on my own saved someone else's job, and I got a little jingle in my pocket to visit my family before starting at the station. Win-win.

I text back: Don't think I get severance?

The three thought bubbles bounce on the screen as she types: How much time did they give you? Two weeks?

Me: No. It's effective immediately. I had to clear out my desk. I'm on the plane now.

Her: Wait ... WHAT? They didn't give you any money and kicked you out the door with no notice? Dude?!?

Me: I didn't know that was a thing. Should I ask about it?

Her: Yeah, you should ask about it!

She adds an anger emoji for effect.

I fire off a text to my newly former boss and HR: Do I get severance pay?

HR responds: Unfortunately, due to the financial circumstances there are no severances with this reduction in force.

My previously peaceful mind starts reeling.

Due to 'financial circumstances?' I'm sure my couple of thousand dollars is really going to mess up your $35 million budget. When she asked me for info on my donation project, I should have said, "Forget you. Figure it out yourself." I'm too nice. I'm everybody's doormat. I increased that program by hundreds of thousands of dollars, and I don't even get a gift card to McDonald's on my way out the door? I can't believe I made it a point to hug the CEO and thank him for everything. He did these cuts with no notice because he has to make budget to get his big fat bonus. In fact, I hope Folio Weekly finds out and the Brickbats & Bouquets column reads: Brickbats to the organization for unceremoniously laying off Tracy Dot Com.

I send my sponsor a message letting her in on my evil, resentful thought process.

In her ever-ongoing wisdom, she shoots back a praying hands emoji. Then types: Pray the resentment prayer, "God give all my former co-workers everything in life I would want for myself." More praying hands follow.

I heed her advice and the voices start to quiet.

My boss blessed me with way more than I deserve over the past four years. She's been my protector when I didn't deserve her grace. I need to be grateful for that company. They help so many people who don't have the support I do to get back on their feet. And yes, the executive staff gets a nice bonus. But they work countless hours to make sure only 10 percent is spent on admin costs. They deserve a reward for that.

I look at the text again and soak in for the first time the word 'severances,' as in plural packages. As in, 'this isn't all about you, sweetheart. The entire company isn't revolving around your existence or lack thereof.'

I'm ashamed of my thoughts.

I am so wrapped up in myself, I didn't even stop to think I wasn't the only one getting laid off today. I'm sure there is at least one person in worse financial shape. Three offers for positions came in before the plane left Jacksonville thanks to my sassy Facebook post. Is that happening for everyone? Be honest. Probably not. What a jerk.

I heard it over and over again in meetings. People whining 'woe is me' before realizing it was their own ego that put them into stinkin' thinkin'.

It was crappy to leave me with no lunch money. But who am I to not do the next right thing.

We land in Minneapolis early and I immediately text info on two other projects I remembered after I left my boss, *er*, ex-boss' office. I genuinely want to make the transition easy on her. I know it's the little tasks that eat away the clock.

Though part of me secretly hopes it's not *so* easy. Ego be damned. I want to be missed. At least a little.

***

That night I read my journaled thoughts out loud to Mom and Nancy.

Nancy sits solemn on the guest bed we will be sharing tonight. She looks worried.

Mom looks like a warrior.

"Of all my children, you are the one I worry about the least when it comes to work," she says. "You've been hustling to make a buck since you were 10 years old."

It's true. When I was 10, I wasn't old enough to get a paper route. My brother got one instead and hired me to help him. Babysitting started at 12. By 15, I was applying to a variety of local businesses.

I guess I have never really not worked. I mull over what this means logically. *God's had a good track record by me for 49 years. Why would he let me fail now? Doesn't make sense. Yeah. I'm going to be okay.*

Each evening as we wrapped up treatment, the Greenfield Center crew wrapped arms in a big circle and repeated the Serenity Prayer. I knew the prayer. I think I may have given my grandparents the prayer on a plaque as a gift one time. It's presence mysteriously near me all my life. Yet I don't think I grasped the meaning until today.

Nancy softly snores next to me. I pull the sheets up to my armpits. Breathe a sigh of relief the day is over. Recite the words in my head.

God, grant me the serenity to accept the things I cannot change, the courage to change the things I can, and the wisdom to know the difference.

Peace washes over me. I don't know how I'm going to be alright. I only know that I am. I truly am excited to see what great adventure God has planned for me next.

For now it will have to be Uber and Lyft. Sista's gotta pay the bills.

September 1, 2017

Mark it in the books. My first Uber fare. She needs a round trip ride to and from ... wait for it ... the liquor store! Ding ding ding. We have a winner. That, my friends, is how you know God has a sense of humor.

It's 3:30 on a Friday afternoon. Perfectly respectable time to get the party started in my former world.

The 30-year-old emerges from her Sante Fe style home in sweats and a T-shirt and immediately starts in with the excuses when the car door opens.

"I've been working from home today," she says. "I hate it when everyone piles work on me when I do that. Like I'm just sitting around doing nothing." She throws her hands up to feign exhaust.

It's a lie I told myself, and others, too.

I get so much more done when I work from home. I just keep going and going and knocking stuff out.

It was true. But the 'shiny object' syndrome kicked in overdrive, disguising busy work as hard work to my daily declining brain.

"I'm not supposed to drive for six months," she says. "I started having seizures and I can't get custody of my son until it's under control. I'm on medication, so we'll see."

I'm no doctor, but ...

"I probably shouldn't be drinking."

She answers the unasked question. Now ... I'm waiting for her to ...

"But I only have one or two a night."

BAM! There it is.

Her nervous chatter becomes babble in my head as my attention drifts to the day I took an Uber to the liquor store from Robb's house. I ran out while he was at work and couldn't wait two hours for him to get home.

Two hours to get home. Then he'll want to unwind, all the time I'll be screaming at him in my head, 'C'mon! Hurry up.' I'll just save us both some time and get a ride there.

I wonder what I said to that guy who drove me the short distance and back?

She politely pulls me out of my head and shows me on my phone how to tell the Uber app we've arrived so it will bring up the return route. I have a feeling she's done this before.

September 3, 2017

I tap my feet and fingers in time to the Austin Park song in my head. There is no coverage in the Douglas Anderson School of the Arts for surfing the 'nets to pass the time.

Kristen sits across from me in the guidance counselor's office. We make awkward conversation. I don't know if Leah told her I lost my job. If she does know, she's not saying.

A tiny-framed black girl walks in. Shoulders hunched. Books press against her chest.

She looks shy. Are there shy people in the arts?

"Tracy, this is Phaaryl," Kristen says.

"Hi. I'm so excited to meet you."

Am I fawning? I'm definitely fawning. She's so cute. I want to bundle her up and take her home with me.

"Oh." Phaaryl laughs nervously, embarrassed by the attention and obvious compliment. "Yeah. You, too."

Kristen leaves and I spend the next 30 minutes finding out only the basics. Her major is film. She loves Disney and Universal. Tuesdays at 11:26 will be our weekly meeting. Time passes quickly. We say our goodbyes and split in the hallway.

Reaching for the door to the back stairwell, I stop and holler down the hall to her.

"Hey, did your sister get a mentor yet?"

She shakes her head and keeps walking.

Liz was going to sponsor her twin sister, Daaryl. They would have been a match made in heaven. Not only do all three of them share a birthday, Daaryl is an actress (I think actor is the PC way to say it nowadays). Liz loves the stage as much as I do. She was bummed when she had to pull out. Her travel schedule will not give one inch for a weekly meeting on the other side of town.

That night I post on Facebook: ATTN Actor Peeps! Looking for someone to mentor a DA student. She's the twin of my mentee. Only one lunchbreak a week required to fulfill the commitment.

Elizabeth, who I convinced to also become a mentor, pipes in to confirm it is a gratifying, worthwhile task. In spite of the fact, we both have only one sample to base our opinion. Her validation is real though. She connected immediately with her mentee as well.

I garner lots of interest. Friends nominating friends. Sadly, no one responds.

September 10, 2017

The giant billboard calls to me. There's no avoiding it. They posted it at my turn. On my street. Following me home every day of my life. Or until the campaign runs out.

Steel Reserve Beer—Now in Flavors. Five cans, 6-feet tall, lined up high above my head.

CURIOUS IS CALLING the slogan reads. It's not advertising. It's reality.

I imagine what each color tastes like. Purple for blackberry. Pink for punch. Blue for blue raspberry. Green for watermelon. Orange for pineapple. The graphic-induced drips of sweaty condensation look delish.

"I'll never know what you taste like," I say. Sigh.

At Alumni, we go around the room. I share my new found, never to be tasted obsession.

"Steel Beer has flavors." I talk like a woman who hasn't had a sip of water in the desert for a month. "Doesn't that sound refreshing?"

I get the laughter I'm pleading for.

"Why?" I shake my fist at the heavens. "Why are you doing this to me, Steel Beer company? I shall never know what your sweet nectar tastes like. Grrrr."

More laughter.

I look around the room. Caught off guard by a few of the grimaces. It hasn't occurred to me that not everyone has made it to the place of self-deprecating humor.

A friend who has not been able to beat her demons once told me she hated meetings because all the talk about drinking made her want to drink.

"I have to laugh or I'm going to cry." Back pedal. Back pedal quick.

"When moments like today come, I force myself to remember my drunk video. I can't entertain the fun part of a buzz without remembering I do not possess the necessary skill to stop. Period."

September 18, 2017

Super stoked to meet the fam tonight.

Phaaryl, Daaryl and their mom, Velvet, will all be at the Take Stock in Children Family Dinner. It's an opportunity for mentors and mentees to visit college vendors and hear a motivational speaker talk about post-secondary education.

In the past, I've worked the event. With the expectation that kids say the darndest thing, I recorded senior interviews. Questions like 'What's your most embarrassing moment?' and 'Do you have a date for the prom?' never disappointed.

I walk into the venue tonight wondering what they will do without me this year? I offered to freelance for the event but never received a response.

At the table Elizabeth and I got together, we are delighted to discover our mentees' families know each other. Bonus. Tonight is perfect. Or so I think.

On the way to the buffet, I spot a camera set up for interviews. I notice it is the college student Leah enlisted to do the interview with me last year. Before I can say hello, a familiar voice calls out.

"Tracy?" It's a woman my former boss has known for several years. A brilliant techie type with a flair for PR.

I glance down at the nonprofit badge around her neck. The same one I wore for four years. I am completely caught off guard. I can feel my face turning red. The humiliation. The embarrassment. The evil voice in my head telling me I'm not good enough. Again.

"Hi. What are you doing here?"

"I'm working." She points to her badge.

I know, Captain Obvious. I saw your stupid badge.

"As ... what?"

"Marketing Manager."

"Oh. Good for you." I have no idea what is left to say. I stick my tail between my legs and walk away. Good versus evil battling it out in my head.

See. I told you they didn't want you. Probably didn't even let anyone else go. Staged that whole meeting just to dump your sorry behind.

I bite my lip and search to find my group at the buffet.

Don't cry. Don't cry. It's for the best. God has you onto your next great adventure. You would not be doing it if you stayed at that job.

My sweaty hands shake as I pile spaghetti and salad onto my plate.

For the best? Are you kidding? They didn't even wait a month before they replaced you. You think that wasn't planned? And there you were all, 'Oh, what can I do to help you through this transition.' Doormat.

I force myself into the Serenity Prayer and take the outside aisle back to my seat where no one is the wiser of the war raging in my head. I smile and nod at the conversation though I have no clue what anyone is saying.

While the twin gerbils argue on the spinning wheel, the twin art students humor me with their sisterhood. Surrounded by a table of people, they carry on like long lost relatives scrambling to catch up. It's fascinating how much they have to talk about.

"Hey." I lean forward and interrupt them.

"Yes, ma'am." They respond in unison.

"Have you gotten a mentor yet?"

"No, ma'am," Daaryl says.

"How would you like me to mentor you, too?"

"Yes, ma'am."

It's so matter of fact, I'm not sure she means it.

"Are you sure?" Nose scrunch.

She reads the cue and adjusts her body language with a big smile and a quick succession of head nods.

"Oh." She laughs. "I mean, yes ma'am." This time there's gusto in her voice.

Their mother, Velvet, gives a nose giggle and shakes her head. She obviously knows her girls so well.

"That would be great," she says. "Thank you so much."

I get the warm fuzzies. The gerbils have nothing to say. Discontent cannot penetrate when your heart is filled with love. By taking the focus off myself, I successfully shrugged off any ill feelings trying to attack.

I am right where God needs me to be.

CHAPTER 11

IF YOU THROW UP ON SOMEONE,
YOU'LL FEEL BETTER

September 19, 2017

It's one thing to have your friends, also known as your 'yes' people, read the most vile, intimate, glorious, bougie escapades of your life. They'll love it. It's a given. They have to. They're afraid you'll release one of their skeletons on page 223 if they don't.

Tonight, I'm dumping a whole bag of my own bones on strangers. They don't have to like it. In fact, Lynn encourages them not to. What could you possibly learn from a good butt kissing by Shantyboat Writers? Nothing. You need the down and dirty. The disappointing break down of where you fell short.

Sadly, I never had the opportunity to see the boat in person. Hurricane Irma swept her away last week. An event so momentous, because of the talent educated on the floating office over the years, Lynn and husband Jim's heartbreak was broadcast on the 5 o'clock news that week. Tonight the sessions start, one week late, in her home.

A woman named April and two guys named Rick, all three seasoned authors, and Lori, a newbie like me, crowd around Lynn's workshop table, staring at my submission.

I bring the piece that I've already shown Lynn. I change the grammatical errors and keep some of the stuff she said I should change. Convinced it will be met with rave reviews the way it is written.

They take turns reading until the three pages are done.

Lori throws me a bone and points out the good stuff. As I with her moments ago.

I throw her a wink and make a quick tongue and teeth clicking noise. *Yeah, sister. We newbies got to stick together.*

April gives valuable feedback. The first Rick cracks a joke, his signature modus operandi, then also gives good feedback. Then it is second Rick's turn.

Out of the corner of my eye, I catch Lynn at the head of the table lean forward like a cat ready to pounce. A matching Cheshire grin reveals her tongue shifting back and forth between her front teeth.

What is happening here?

I look over at the second Rick. My papers upright in his hands. He winces. Looks at the ceiling. Selects his words carefully. And I will be danged. He says the same things Lynn said three days earlier.

Lynn slams her hand down on the table. A true and defiant nonverbal Yes! A show, don't tell Yes! She shifts in her seat with excitement for her turn to talk.

"I can explain," I say.

"Shush." Lynn snaps a finger to her lips. "No talking during feedback. If you have to explain what the book should have explained, you're not writing it right."

I can't help but smile. *Lesson learned.*

September 22, 2017

I'm starting to feel the pressure again of sharing my truth at the birthday party. It's not a fear of the reveal. It's fear of the interpretation.

I imagine some will believe I have put myself in an ivory tower, preaching the sermon of abstinence.

Look at all you sinners, celebrating my birthday with your devil's juice. How dare you.

It's important to me that they understand the intention of my project is not turn the whole world into a society of teetotalers. That I loved alcohol. That I miss it. The romance of wine, the celebration of shots, the good old American past time of cold beer.

Nearly every one of my friends drink. And they're good at it. They are weekend warriors and weekday unwinders. They love a good cabernet to complement a meal. Mimosas are a staple for brunches. Champagne for opening night galas. Crack a 10 a.m. beer at a tailgate party? No judgement here. It's game day for Pete's sake.

I loved it. I'm jealous of it. I wish I could do it. But I can't.

Once I start, I cannot stop.

The delivery of the message has been weighing heavy on my mind. It's time to quiet the beast through action. I put my fingers to the keyboard and start typing out a prequel to the book. An abbreviated version to share with them at the party. Once I start, I am all in. The words flow easily.

It's my 22-page love letter to the people I adore. And an abbreviated helping hand to anyone who needs it now.

I share the highlights—or, lowlights, rather—including the crapping all over the floor incident, which my neighbor may or may not have seen. I never asked her. I was too ashamed.

I pour my heart out with the story of my father saying 'I love you' and the subsequent shame 10 days later when I unknowingly abandoned my mother on the day of his death for a 4-hour trip to drunkard island.

And tears flow as I relive the look in my sister's eyes, so broken and pleading, as she begs me to stop killing myself, swearing if I do, she will die, too. And I know she means it. I'm too afraid to ask how.

I wrap up the booklet with an invitation to follow my journey along the way in an online blog at TheCrushedVelvetProject.org.

My last task of the day is to check in with Mike and Tammy Heath to make sure we are still on for filming tomorrow.

In true broadcast fashion, I'm going to produce a video with their help. A 6-minute glimpse into my life, and it is not going to be pretty. But I've committed to myself, it will be funny.

After all, I am still me. Just not as sloppy.

September 26, 2017

Another round of manuscripts fills Lynn's inbox. We go around the room. Reading and commenting. Learning from other's rights and wrongs.

.I breathe in deep. The lingering scent of Marlboro Lights from Lynn's back office mixes with the sweet and salty snacks on the plate in front of me. I clench my teeth.

"I want you to sit back, close your eyes, and listen." Lynn's voice is stern.

I bet she's going to tell me not to keep my mouth shut.

"And keep your mouth shut."

Her scolding spurns a nose laugh.

Since our first meeting in July, I fought her like a drunk refusing the surrender portion of a 12-step program. She responded with military discipline. My constant excuse interruptions were met with, "Shut up and listen." She wasn't asking for opinions on her editing. She was telling how it was going to be. I thought it was Lynn's way or the highway. I learned in this class, it was Lynn's way really is the right way.

My submission is a three-page portion of the book. Including a description of the opening scene to Sandra Bullock's *28 Days* movie about an alcoholic. Lynn has already edited this chapter outside of class and told me to take it out. She said it didn't fit. Sidetracks the story.

I believe I shall get a second opinion.

Seated on the edge of my seat. Smiling. Patiently listening while the group takes turns reading the paragraphs out loud.

Let me have it. Give me the feedback I know is coming. It didn't work out last week, but this is a chance to show Lynn the chapter works. As is. No changes.

"This is a good piece," the serious Rick says.

Yeah. That's right, Rick. Drink it in. Every last word.

"But, what is the deal with this movie scene?"

My smile fades, transfers to Lynn's lips. Silence follows. Knowing nods. Glowing in affirmation.

"You've got a good flow, and then suddenly we have to stop to and switch gears and picture this movie in our head, and then get back to your story." Rick's brow furrows. "I don't get it."

Maybe I'm not good enough to pull this off. If people don't get it, what's the point. I won't be able to help anyone. Can I write sober? What if all of my creativity is tied up in the euphoria of a drink.

The negative self-talk hangs on through the night and lulls me to sleep.

September 27, 2017

"Do you think God would give you a vision to allow you to fail?" The pastor's words hang in the silent breeze of the air conditioning. "Think about it. If He gives you an idea. A business. A calling of service. The adoption of a child. If He has called you to make a change in life. Perhaps it is a moral conflict raging inside. An addiction to drugs or alcohol. A struggle with a family member that is tearing you up."

He's speaking to everyone. In this moment, I feel like he is only talking to me. Addressing my fears.

"Do you honestly think your Heavenly Father, the one who loves you more than anyone in the world, would press upon you the desires and hopes and ideas to build your life." He pauses to look around the room. Making eye contact. Connecting with the congregation. "Do you think that is the same supreme being who would set you up for failure?"

Lynn has been on me about not writing every day. It's hard to be creative when you lose faith in yourself. Today's message is exactly what I needed.

September 29, 2017

Confidence begets confidence. I am on a roll with nothing to lose.

I pick up the phone and dial Sharon Siegel Cohen's cell phone. The longtime executive producer of the number one morning show is very well respected in the industry. And one of the nicest in the biz.

Eight years ago, at the recommendation of WJXT The Local Station's zany, fun-loving morning meteorologist, Richard Nunn, she brought me on board to do an entertainment segment every Thursday.

The first episode, I was so nervous, giant moon-shaped pit stains poured through green chiffon. One little stumble and I was off to the races. Loving every minute of it and making better color and fabric choices. I loved it right into a full-time position at another station. Though always staying close to my Channel 4 family. So, reaching out to Sharon isn't at all awkward. It's phoning a friend.

"I'm on my own now," I say. "I lost my job."

"Oh no. I'm sorry."

"I'm not." I quip back, still stinging from last week's encounter. "I was wondering if you would consider renewing my segment, Are You Ready for the Weekend?"

She says she will think about it and asks to call me back.

Ten minutes later, Nikki shoots a text. It's a screen shot of an exchange with Sharon.

Sharon: Tracy Collins is interested in coming on previewing weekend happenings. I like her. Wondering what you thought?

Nikki: Love her. She has amazing energy. And she's a great friend. Would love it.

Yaaay! Sharon likes me. Barely time to gather my thoughts, the phone rings.

"Let's do it," Sharon says. "You'll start Thursday."

I am over the moon and landing smack dab in the fluffy gooey center of Cloud 9. I've missed being on television so much. I feel like a sailor back from deployment. Falling in to the loving arms of home.

October 9, 2017

Unbeknownst to them, I continue trying paragraphs on my fellow Shantyboat Writers Lynn and I are at odds over. They reject them. I pout. We move on.

So far, the score is Skapyak on top 3-0. I am out of fight. Tonight, I'm ready to do it her way. I close my eyes. Lori, April and the two Ricks take turns reading 10 pages from the beginning of this book. Uniform voices in a monotone speech.

What are they thinking? Do they like it? I can't tell.

I squint one eye open to study their faces. Blank canvases. First Rick starts the feedback.

"When you were questioning if you are an alcoholic and reference the questionnaire," he says, "I thought it was a little too cutesy."

Too cutesy? It's funny. And you're the funny Rick. How can you, out of everyone at this table, not think it's funny?

"It was meant to be flippant," I say.

"Nope." Lynn shuts me down. "Not your turn. Does anyone have anything positive to say to this writer?"

"Yes, definitely." To my surprise, the serious Rick responds before anyone else can. He's an accomplished writer. An incredible writer. His ability to paint a colorful landscape with minimal words using lavish adjectives and visual verbs accentuates the importance of every sentence. Although I learned a lot from him, my sense is that new writers must bore him.

"I'm not partial to this type of writing," he says. "Memoirs. Autobiographies. Biographies."

Oh, no. I knew it. He hates my kind of writing. Or just my writing. Period. Is it because I'm new? Or because I'm not good?

"But when I read these entries each week." He shakes the pages with his left hand. "This character is interesting enough that I want to know what happens next."

My right hand goes to my chest. "Really?"

"Yeah."

"Does the writer have any questions?" Lynn asks.

I turn back to the first Rick. A dog with a bone she won't let go.

"It was meant to be flippant," I say. "You know, because the questions seem so silly." I reference the paper. "Like this one, 'Have you ever missed work?'" I look back at Rick. Give him a look that says, *Really?* I read the response.

I'm sure once he hears it with sarcasm, he'll get it.

"There's a reason the day after the Super Bowl is the most missed work day of the year." Eyebrows raise. "And it ain't the chicken wings." I tilt my head and nod it. "Know what I'm sayin'?"

"Yeah, I know what you're *trying* to say," he says. "But it doesn't work here."

I squish my face at the foul odor of criticism. His response is not computing. His weekly aid when a fellow writer is getting pelted with negative feedback is to counteract with a joke. If anyone sitting in these mismatched chairs was going to get it, I thought it would be him.

"This is a serious topic." The second Rick, the most stoic of our group, pipes up to explain.

"I know, but my go-to is humor," I say to Rick one, then turn to Rick two. "That's why I thought you would get it. If you don't get it, then I'm pretty convinced no one else will either."

"You can use your personality," first Rick says. "You've done it well in several areas we've read prior. This isn't the place for it."

"So, the question is," Lynn asks, "do you want more?"

"Yes." Rick nods. "I want more."

The brakes squeal on the rollercoaster of insecurities I have been on for the past several months. The ups of feeling empowered by sharing my story with a stranger who says they really needed to hear that today. The lows of realizing I am just days from telling all of my friends the truth, not knowing what the reaction will be. The ups of finding the sweet spot of a scene that I know in my heart will motivate change in another human being. The lows of feeling like I'm burning up the computer keyboard, then realizing I have so far to go before the book is finished.

Rick is not a lip service critic. He says it like he sees it. Or in this case, reads it. This assessment puts more fuel in my fire.

The workshop is exactly the way Lynn described it. Unbiased, straight forward expectation of how readers will react before sending off the final project.

I'm ready to keep pushing to the next goal: The birthday party chap book, a compilation of a work in progress. Hopefully, my friends will see things Rick's way.

October 14, 2017

"I'm fifty." I bark it out in a feigned Irish accent. Push my hands down on the vanity chair. Lift my barely-covered bum and kick my thigh-high leather boots in quick succession. "And I luhv it, I luhv it, I luhv it."

Kimberly giggles at my Sally O'Malley impersonation (one of Molly Shannon's famous Saturday Night Live characters).

"Okay, you're done," she says. "Who's next?"

Kimberly is my stylist and one of my best friends. We met through a mutual friend, a local radio personality named Amadeus, who says he always knew we would be perfect together. Thanks to him by, the time I met her in person at a Toby Keith concert, I felt like I already knew her. She felt the same way.

Kimberly is exactly how Amadeus describes her: The most beautiful girl in the world. She was Nashville-glam ready for the show the night we crossed paths.

Honey blonde hair dripped meticulously down her shoulders. A neon red daisy clipped over one ear and neon teal daisies dangled from both lobes screaming, "Look at me. I'm different. Polished. Nothin' but top shelf here, baby."

Her bold blue eye shadow choice exemplified country-sexy. Her black tank top thread count was tested by full tan breasts. Tight jeans ending in blinged-out cowgirl boots completed the package.

This is a girl I want to know.

And that face. Giant brown doe eyes, perfectly shaped eyebrows, big full lips. Every feature is big and bold and flawless from forehead to nose to chin. When she walks by, heads turn in sequence. Like the wave at a football game.

Tonight, Kimberly welcomes my mom, my sister and me over to her mansion. She's making all of us beautiful for the big event at the stylist vanity in her giant bedroom. Her gift to the 80s party is my giant curly wig, reminiscent of Whitney Houston's "I Wanna Dance With Somebody." Teased to the Himalayas. Just the way I did it in high school. I look at my reflection in admiration.

There is something so transforming about wearing an extra inch of makeup and seven more inches of hair. I'm rockin' a mini skirt at Kimberly's insistence because "your legs are your best feature." A crossover leather jacket with faux rivets hides any love handles five decades parceled out. Bonus. A smile wider than Steven Tyler's and toothier than Dee Snider is plastered on my face.

I'm feeling bulletproof. That is. Until I look out the 10-foot arched window just as a crack of thunder cues the clouds to dump its contents out with my confidence.

"What's wrong?" Nancy asks. She takes her turn in the vanity chair.

"I don't know." I stare past the pool. Past the oak tree. Past the third tee. Onto the green that's getting darker and darker. "I'm getting nervous."

The rain is abnormally torrential. I can no longer see the golf course.

"Why?"

"People in this town do not like rain." I search the sky for any sliver of a break.

"It's true," Kimberly says. She grabs another fist full of hair and keeps teasing.

"Well, I'm sure they'll still come," Nancy says. I can feel her watching me in the vanity's reflection. "Won't they?"

"Yeah." I breathe the word past my lips with a sigh.

Fail. The word keeps spinning through my head. Nancy, my mom and Kimberly are whirling words past me. But I'm stuck in my funnel. Sucked down into insecurities I don't know how to shake.

This is more than a birthday party. It's a coming out party. A love me or leave me party. Right now, I am terrified. I might not be surrounded by enough of a support system to cushion the blow of my ego. It is about to jump off a skyscraper.

People are expecting a big announcement. Check that. A BIG ANNOUNCEMENT. I was sure to put it in all caps every time I promoted it. And boy howdy, did I promote it. Social media. Electronic invite. Email. Snail mail. That's right. I mailed out 100 postcards with my giant '80s Glamour Shots head plastered on 8x5 cards. They read: We're Gonna Party Like It's 1989!

I put so much pressure on filling the venue, I think I lost sight of the fact this was supposed to be fun. Now this rain is drowning my dreams.

I turn around to survey the here and now. My mom, my beautiful mom, who wasn't even planning on making the trip east until the day she got that silly postcard. She sits on a chair in the middle of a giant area rug, laughing at something Kimberly said. I instinctively join in with a chuckle. I don't know what was said. I only know it makes my heart happy to see her smile.

My sister. The girl I worshipped through childhood and barely knew until this past year in adulthood. She was the first to say she wouldn't miss it for the world. Her eyes glimmer with amusement.

Kimberly. The most beautiful girl in the world. She is so much more on the inside than any amount of makeup or hair dye can make her on the outside. The most beautiful part about her is her heart. It's the part about her I love the most. It's our mutual core principles of honesty, fairness, positivity and creativity. We root for the underdog, defend the bullied, raise up the righteous, believe in Jesus. Understanding that looking better, dressing better, smelling better and getting paid better earns you the right and responsibility to go out and help those less fortunate. We are champions and cheerleaders forever in each other's corner.

Now. Right here. Right now. As I trade glances back and forth with my sister and my mother, I realize it doesn't matter if no one else shows up. The important people are here.

"You can't be early to your own party." Kimberly fakes disgust when she hears my plans to man the welcome table. "You've got to make a grand entrance." Dramatic hand goes up in the air. "A theme song." Another hand follows. "An announcement." Repeats hand one. "A fog machine." She stops short of repeating hand two and giggles midstride. Both hands drop. "Okay. Maybe that's taking it too far."

I do what she says and arrive 30 minutes late.

Mike and Tammy set up a kickass photo booth at the entrance with props: Aqua Net hairspray, neon sunglasses, '80s themed thought bubble signs, and my favorite, I giant handmade Rubik's cube.

Kerry plays sentry at a table flanked in VHS cassettes of *Cocktail* and *Miami Vice*. She greets guests by making them sign in with their addresses for thank you cards.

Inside Tammy also built the centerpieces. Square candle holders made out of old cassette tapes lit up by green LED lights. They fit on top of thrift store LPs.

I peer in expecting to see about half of the 125 or so who RSVP'd. My heart sinks. I look back at Kerry in panic. *Where is everyone?* My nightmare comes true. No one has shown up. I can see a few people milling around. My friends Richard and Samantha are standing at a cocktail table. Three bartenders shuffle back and forth completely bored.

Oh, God. I mentally slap my forehead. *I told the manager we were expecting way more people and she put another bartender on staff. I'm such an idiot. Nobody's coming to this party. What was I thinking? Nobody cares about my stupid party. I'm old and I'm an alcoholic. What did I expect?*

Mike stands next to the DJ booth and quietly yells to me, "Are you ready?" I nod. He signals the DJ. Nothing happens. I move to the entrance. Nothing. He motions to me again. "Ready?" I nod harder, angrier. He points to the DJ. Nothing. *What is that fricking DJ doing?* My frustration is starting to show. I am in full-blown freak-out mode in my head. I want to cry.

All at once, in what felt like a full, smooth transition of time, my eyes meet Richard's. He sprints the empty floor to comfort me. *Pour Some Sugar on Me* starts playing. I walk into his arms and grip him tight. Then his wife. Then another guest. And another. Then five more show up. Two couples walk in. Some singles. And so on. And so on. Until the place fills up.

After an hour of greetings, sandwiched in between the costume contest and the dance contest, it is time for "Tracy's big announcement."

The social time forces the butterflies to fly in formation, but a mutiny starts again in the pit of my stomach. It doesn't help that when I try to get the crowd's attention, no one listens. No one. Except the con artists in my head. They are on high alert.

These people don't care about you.

"Can I have your attention, please?" They keep their conversations in stride.

You probably won't get invited to parties once they find out.

"Hey." I tap on the microphone and ask the DJ to turn it up. "Can I have your attention."

I drop the mic to my side, let out a heavy sigh, and watch in horror as people ramble on. Nobody's even noticed there isn't any music playing. I'm invisible. Maybe nobody does care.

Kerry walks over with her cell phone held up in position. "You ready to go live?"

We had decided I would do the announcement on Facebook live for people who couldn't make it. In my video composition brain, the broadcast looked happy, joyous and free. The crowd would cheer at the revelation. Fans would weep with delight in front of their home computers. Children's choirs would break into song. Or. Maybe not.

"Hey," she says. "You ready?"

"No. Nah. Let's forget it." Dejected and drained, I start to wonder if I even want to tell the ones who showed up for it. *I can't remember why I believed doing this project was a good idea. Who was I to think I could actually make a difference in anyone's life. I can't even get my own friends to pay attention to my message.*

"What's wrong?"

My eyes scan the crowd. She follows them. Snatches the mic out of my hand. "Hey! Shut up," she yells. A few silences pass through. "Hey." She pulls the mic from her mouth and uses her height to yell above the crowd one more time "Shuuuuuut uuuuup."

It's enough to get us where we're going.

"Ladies and gentleman." This time her voice is comically low in the mic. "Tracy Dot Com Collins."

Everyone cheers. But I'm still shaken and unsure.

"Okay," I say. "Well, you've all been hearing me say for a month now that I have a big announcement. I know some of you have some fun ideas of what that might be. And some of you already know what it is. But I'm ready. So, if you're ready, here we go."

I point to Bill Bortzfield and he pushes the play button on the computer. Tammy and I pop up on the screen. With. No. Sound.

Like a swift undertow, I am abruptly pulled back into panic mode. I take a deep breath and stop. Anxiety needles are moving their way up my arms and reaching my head. *I can't believe this is happening. It's a nightmare.*

But Bill's a professional. There's a reason I asked him to be in charge of tech. It is his jam. He smacks the stop button and walks behind the DJ sound booth. *Ugh. That dang DJ.* If there is one thing this party has taught me, it's never scrimp on a DJ. In video, I learned a long time ago, people will forgive what they see, but they don't forget what they've heard. It holds true at parties, too. Especially if the one thing they've heard is … nothing. I can't blame her. It's her first gig. I got her because she was cheap. I'm her audition gig and I'm paying the price.

A few flips of some switches and he's back at the computer to start it over. The movie and my sanity.

Everyone is on their feet, crowded around the elevated screen.

Tammy enters the scene, carrying two shots. "It's your birthday, it's your birthday, we're gonna party like it's your birthday," she sings. Sits down on the couch next to me and attempts to hand over one of the glasses.

"No. Thanks." On screen, I put up a hand. In real life, I turn to watch the audience. I know what is about to happen.

"More for me." She cheers, asks what my big announcement is. She pours the liquid into her mouth.

"I'm pregnant."

The crowd goes crazy, screaming simultaneous 'whats' and 'ooohs.' I watch in delight as my college BFFs Brad Lahey and Amanda Warford, who I call my Lil' Sissy's, eyes slam open and meet his. Her mouth forms a giant O and he's full-barrel laughing. It's full-scale chaos for awhile and I start to worry that they're going to miss the real announcement.

Kerry quiets the crowd. "Liar," she yells.

"I went to treatment." I confess my fears and nobody says anything. Amanda's face is relaxed. Brad's is, too. I can't find anyone who looks surprised. I'm not sure how to take that.

But as the story moves forward, things change.

On screen, I sit on a couch. Alone. Explaining to the camera the fear and isolation I was living in. I tell the truth about the woman they thought they knew. I relive the story about stopping at the liquor store and grocery store every Friday.

"And then I would go home." I rub my fingers back and forth on my temple. "And close my curtains. I wouldn't open them again until Monday morning." I purse my lips and raise my eyebrows. "And that's it. That's the secret I've been keeping."

The room is completely silent. Totally engaged.

"So, what do you want to do now?" Off camera, Mike asks.

"What do I want to do now?" I repeat him. "Have you ever heard the story of the starfish?"

The picture fades to a beach scene. A close-up of a little girl holding a starfish. As a man walks up to her, she tosses it into the ocean. He asks what she's doing.

"Saving the starfish," she says.

"Why?" He shrugs. "There's thousands of them. You can't possibly save them all. What does it matter."

She looks at the ocean. Looks at the starfish. Contemplates its fate. "It matters to this one," she says unapologetically. With a heavy throw she returns the starfish back to its home.

I scan the party to see if anyone gets the metaphor. Mouths are open. Tears are wiped. My fears are quiet. Relief washes over me and I can finally enjoy my 50th birthday party.

"Who wants cake?"

CHAPTER 12

NEVER SAY NEVER

October 23, 2017

The aggressive post catches me off guard.

"PLEASE SHARE HOW THIS IS GOOD TO DEFLATE YOUR EGO? NOT!"

It had barely been 20 hours since I posted my first, of hopefully many, Facebook Live videos intended to keep the conversation going after my reveal video topped 5,000 views.

So far, nearly 1,900 people watched, 129 gave it the coveted blue thumbs up, and 53 took the time to post words of encouragement. But for some reason, all I could focus on was this man—who by social media standards is my 'friend'—and his three separate expressions of hate mail, one minute apart in the comments section.

"HOW ABOUT DO MEETINGS AND STAY OFFLINE UNTIL YOU HAVE 10 YEARS OF SOBRIETY!" was followed by "GO BACK AND READ AND STUDY THE TRADITIONS................."

I knew this was coming. I mentally prepared myself knowing not everyone will be riding the pink cloud with me. Still, it hits square in the gut.

Suddenly, without warning, I am broken. Every movement towards peeking from behind the curtain was with trepidation. Fear of rejection, surprisingly met with love and acceptance. Until now. Guard briefly relaxed and ... POW.

Why would anyone find pleasure in poking a hole in the life preserver of a stranger whose only goal is to reach someone else lost at sea?

I immediately call Nikki.

"I don't know why this makes me so mad?" I say.

"Jackass."

Nikki gets it. She comes under scrutiny on a regular basis. Being one of the most recognized TV anchors in Jacksonville has its challenges. She has 80,000 social media followers and not all of them are blowing sunshine up her butt. Many of them are darn right cruel. Taunting her about her weight, her parenting skills, her choice in cell phone coverage.

"I've got all these people cheering me on. I've had phone calls, private messages, emails, you name it. But this one guy," I tell her, "this guy—who, p.s. and by the way, sent me a happy birthday message in all caps with a thousand exclamation points nine days ago—this guy is all I can focus on."

"Do you *know* him?" Open disgust oozes from her words.

"No," I respond. "He must be a viewer."

"Oh. Well, obviously he's dumb enough to not realize he's Super Glued the caps lock on his computer," she says. "Forget him. You know what? You knew this was coming."

"Yeah." It doesn't make me feel better.

"I know it's easier said than done, but you need to focus on all the positive. You need to realize that when you are doing God's work—and you believe this is what God wants you to do?"

"Yes."

"That's when the enemy comes. When you're disrupting his evil plot." She sighs at my silence. "Look. I don't know why someone who is obviously in some kind of program—he knows the lingo, so I assume he is—would be against you wanting to help other people? But there is one thing I've learned. If you're right in your heart, you don't feel the need to strike out at others. You just don't."

"I think he assumes I'm talking about A.A.?" I say. "But I'm not. I'm only talking about *my* experiences in binging. I'm only talking about *my* experiences in putting my mind and my body and my spirit back together."

"Whatever. Even if you did accidentally say something inappropriate, if his intentions were sincere, he would have contacted you through private message to explain, not publicly shame you. He's just a jackass. Period. Ignore him. Focus on the positive."

We hang up. My mind cycles through a Rolodex of self-help notecards.

Positive? Um … Positive. Let me think.

Okay. Well. I did make a mental note about Miss America's TEDx Talk. At least I know I'm not the only one believing it's a powerful tool to pull back the curtain. If one is able. That's number one.

Number two. It's true. I won't have the same belief system in 10 years. I'll be stronger. Wiser. Seasoned. I am not going to be right about everything in my book in the ways of sober living. But that's not what my book is about.

It's about the ah-ha moments I'm going through. The missteps I'm making. It's about my journey in the first year. The good. The bad. The grotesquely green. It's about helping people who want to change know what to expect. To take away their fear.

If no one talks about it, how will anything ever change?

I go to bed thinking about his '10 years of sobriety' comment. Those four words bother me the most.

The person I am trying to reach doesn't have the luxury of giving me 10 years to catch the tips of her fingers as they slide off the ledge. She needs me to use my voice now. Her life is depending on it.

October 24, 2017

Tap. Tap. Tap. I spend the day aggressively banging out the passage you just read. This one is going to the experts. Can I capture the moment with the savage intensity I felt last night?

It's our last Shantyboat evening together. Blood rushes to my prefrontal cortex anticipating the feedback on this latest piece.

"Well." Rick shakes the papers in his hand. "I've been watching this character develop, and I can't say I didn't see this coming. It was really a matter of when. I'm glad I got the opportunity to read about it before the class ended."

"Do you want to read more?" Lynn asks. As soon as Rick replies the affirmative, she smacks a righteous hand down on the table. Grinning ear to ear.

After we finish, Rick and several others buy a chap book. Now, I'm the one grinning ear to ear.

I walked in furious. Hurt. Defeated. Thanks to my literary tribe, I'm walking out strong. Happy. Justified.

October 25, 2017

Giddy bubbles in my belly. I don't walk into the WJCT studios. I float.

Melissa Ross. Jacksonville's sweetheart. Host of the cray cray popular First Coast Connect. She made it to the party. Missed the big announcement. Gasped when she got a private proclamation over the phone two days later. Then agreed I should be on her show.

Her NPR junkies are my people. Intelligent. Accomplished. Possibly hiding a secret? In need of a fellow flawed professional to rescue him or her before the world realizes they're a fraud?

"First this hour. She is the lovable personality known to one and all as Tracy Dot Com." Melissa reads from a script with the gift of sounding like an impromptu conversation. "Tracy Collins has appeared on local TV for years. Always with a smile and a bubbly personality."

My lips press against a spit guard mounted on a fluffy studio mic. Anticipating a question from the host. Padded earphone cans muffle everything except her soothing voice.

"You've seen her covering every event you can imagine all around town for different media outlets over the years. Take a listen."

An enthusiastic voice fills the headset.

"I am Tracy Dot Com, your official funologist." Producer Kevin Meerschaert plays a live shot I did the day before for my Facebook page The TDC Experience. Child-like excitement over the impending holiday. "I'm at The Party Shop. They're moving, so you can get your

Halloween costume cheap, cheap, cheap."

I smile and hold back a giggle.

I really should look into fulfilling that lifelong dream of car sales spokesperson.

Melissa describes to the listeners my secret life. The story setup is on point. Smooth. Direct. Using phrases "behind the smiles and packed social calendar" and "she hid the problem until it was impossible to hide anymore."

Kevin pushes a button on audio from the video Melissa missed at the birthday party. I'm describing how I only have two speeds. Zero drinks or blackout to pass out. There is no in between.

"It wasn't going to continue." I hear myself take a pause in the video. Self-aware of impending demise. "At least I wasn't going to be alive at the end of it."

"It was that realization, Tracy knew she was going to die." Melissa turns her attention to me. "People all over town, including me, did not know what you were dealing with."

"People would come up to me and say, 'You're so happy all the time.' I would give them a closed-mouth smile and say, 'Mmm-hmm.'"

I watch in awe as Melissa navigates the info coming in on her computer, listens to the producer in her ear, and still manages an engaged, active-listening conversation with me. Head nods and verbal affirmations in all the right places.

"I was not faking it when I was in public," I say. "I am a social person. That is what makes me happy. But once the door closed, that was it. I don't have a significant other. I don't have children. My family is far, far away. When it came to my friends, I organized a very manipulative calendar according to my drinking schedule. That is what alcohol does. It isolates people."

She asks about rock bottom. I offer the conversation with Nancy. The agreement I made to stay alive to save my sister. She asks about my renewed purpose in life. I tell her about the car accident at 13 that, to this day, still drives me to be a champion of the community.

"I've loved God since I was a kid. I learned in church, take your God-given talents and use them for your purpose." I hold up a finger to count down mine. "I know how to write. I have a microphone for the city." Point to the mic. "I am going to let people know the face of alcoholism is not the guy under the bridge." Same finger runs in circles. Forehead to chin. Chin to forehead. "This is the face of alcoholism."

"This bubbly, beautiful face that we all know and love." Melissa points to me.

Oh, gosh. How do I respond to that? Don't say yes. Don't say yes.

In my head my eyes are big as saucers. Caught off guard by the compliment. It feels like a lifetime of dead air. In reality, it's a necessary pregnant pause. I opt for a quiet thank you.

Calls start pouring in.

Here we go. We're doing it. We are making a difference.

We talk to people in recovery. People who have a loved one they are trying to save. People tweet appreciation for the topic. However, no one has called to ask for help.

Maybe they're not up this early? Or fearful their voice will be recognized?

Melissa announces we will take one last call. It's June, a woman in a car accident who got addicted to opioids.

It's a subject Melissa is intensely familiar with. She recently had a guest on to talk about the overrun Jacksonville morgue. Bodies all over the floor. Heroin overdoses. Too many to process.

June is in recovery. Her experience has not been as joyous and free. Family members shame her for addiction. Her dad died this year. The list keeps going.

"I lost my house in a hurricane. I'm getting a divorce. And. Um." June's voice starts to shake. "I don't have anyth…"

June starts sobbing. Melissa tries to calm her.

"Oh, June. I'm so sorry." Her tone is wrought with angelic empathy. "You feel so alone. I can tell. You're not alone though, June. You're not alone."

I wonder why she called in to a radio show? She must not have a support system. She's sober, but does she need help finding a narcotics anonymous group? I don't understand drug addiction. I don't have the answer for her problem, but I do have the drive.

"Send me your phone number," I say. No game plan in mind. Just determination to help. "I'll call you off the air."

Is this a starfish?

June leaves her number with Kevin. I call her. Leave a message. She doesn't call back.

Leaving the studio, I'm overwhelmed with how much happened in less than an hour since we went live. Live calls. Texts. Tweets. Private messages. Melissa's influence on the community is validated in action. Social activism. Financial support.

Before I can turn the key in my car to head home, my phone dings. A familiar ringtone associated with the GoFundMe app. Ding. And then another. Ding. And another. Ding.

The first two are book backers. Fifty dollars. Women who donate enough to receive a free chap book and a promise of a free completed book. Their donor level is affectionately called Book Backer. For obvious reasons. They each leave kind messages about why they donated.

"This is for my beautiful daughter-in-law who is in severe denial."

"Sending love and light."

The third requires no message. I hear it loud and clear. The amount says it all. Five. Hundred. Dollars. The most received to date from a single donor. Lifesaver level.

I speed home. Hands shaking on the steering wheel. I can't bust through my front door fast enough to mail chap book gifts.

Keys thrown on counter. Pen snatched from a drawer. Gushing appreciation inked on the inside. Three envelopes with return address stickers and $1.91 postage stuffed. I pull up the donor info to draw addresses from when I realize who the Lifesaver is. Phyllis Staines.

Holy cow. Phyllis Staines believes in my project.

Phyllis is a local agent, who not only runs a successful business like a boss, she also writes a weekly real estate column in The Florida Times-Union. While at the T-U, one of my duties, outside of the self-imposed task of fawning all over the Homes section, was to post Phyllis' column on Jacksonville.com.

The rest of the day more alerts come in. Not the playful music kind from GoFundMe. More like "My Heart Will Go On" from *Titanic*. A message tone denoting questions from listeners who heard the show. First in the morning. Another round after the playback show in the evening.

A resounding theme in all. How do I help my loved one?

October 29, 2017

Thank you for the excerpt from your book.

I have seen what alcohol can do to one's health. My father was an alcoholic and died at 72. And his father before him.

I think what you're doing is brave, but even braver still is taking responsibility now while you are healthy.

I wish you the best of success and look forward to the completed project.

Regards,

Phyllis Staines

My fingers can't type fast enough to write her back. She's been a hero of mine for years. When I think real estate, I think Phyllis Staines. I love homes. The exterior. The interior. Customized backyards with pavers and pools.

I looked forward to her words of brick and mortar wisdom in the newspaper every Sunday. To have someone of her caliber believe in me is huge.

I tap out my glowing affection in a return email and hit send just as the phone rings.

It's a number I don't recognize. I answer anyway. My cell number is listed on the website.

"I heard you on the radio." The voice on the line is hesitant. "I know you can help me. If you would call my daughter. Or, maybe ..."

She breathes into the receiver like a marathon runner. The sound of a mother desperate to save her adult child.

"You could go to her house? Pay her a visit and tell her your story? I know she would listen to you." After a moment of silence, her quieted voice begs. "Please."

My heart breaks for her. I clench my teeth to fight back tears. I bite my lower lip, searching for the right answer.

This is not what I signed up for.

I'm in completely unfamiliar territory. The closest I've been was right after my mom read the preview book of *Stumbling Into Sobriety.* Riding down the road in my back seat the next day, she used her quiet voice, too.

"I just don't understand," my mom said.

I shot a confused look to my sister in the passenger seat, then glanced up to the rearview mirror. Mom looked so small in the back seat. So small and so sad. She stared out the side window. Tears welled in her eyes. Right fist propped up under the chin. Her head slowly shook back and forth.

"I just don't understand how I didn't see it."

How could I ever make her understand that my only job, my one job in life, was to keep it a secret? I didn't know what to say to my own mother to reassure her my alcoholism wasn't her fault then. I don't know what to say to this mother now. But I try.

"Well. Uh, it doesn't really work that way," I say. "If she wants to quit, and she wants to call me, I will do everything I can to help her find resources to make that possible."

She hesitates.

"Oh." I hear her disappointment.

"But let me talk to my doctor." I make an effort to offer hope. "The least I can do is find out what *you* can do."

I hang up the phone and head to the alumni group meeting at Greenfield Center.

Until now, it hadn't occurred to me that there was a whole other community of sick people out there. The ones innocently sucked into our wake. Drowning in our pit of depression and our anxiety and our hopelessness.

This call was just one of a dozen since the broadcast. I am clearly in over my head. But I am determined to get answers for the next caller. And I know the man who can give them to me. Brian Jackson. Specialist in addictive disorders.

One phone call. He's on board. We start a game plan to get the info to families in need.

October 30, 2017

I made the decision early on to come clean with the WJXT viewers as soon as possible. I need to for transparency.

I feel pressure to explain I won't be leaving off events in my segment because liquor is involved. Party on, non-alcoholics. On the flip for my sober friends, I also explain I won't be declining invitations to attend balls-to-the-walls soirees. No cause for worry though. Water my beverage of choice. Sober Irish goodbyes to follow.

Sharon is on board for the reveal. Nik is the only one I agree to go live with.

I arrive incredibly nervous. No idea how hard the truth is on her.

We go through the same information on Melissa's show. At one point, she fights back tears. I jump in to fill dead air while she regains composure.

"Hashtag don't know why I'm still single." I joke at the ridiculous bloated face on screen from my drunk video.

She isn't laughing. Her right hand reaches out and grabs my left wrist. Lips pressed firmly together. She swallows hard.

It's the first time I see proof and comprehend self-centeredness. My bad decisions really do affect other people.

Off air, we talk about the Facebook fiasco and how his words still bother me.

"Don't let trolls take you off course, Tracy," Nikki says.

Later on, I talk to Brian about the post. Ask him why another recovered alcoholic would stir my pot. What good could come of this?

"Well," Brian says, "his sponsor probably taught him not to discuss his sobriety. Some sponsors won't let their sponsees talk in meetings for a full year."

"What?" I shout into the phone. "I wouldn't last a week."

"Well then." He deadpans. "I guess you better make sure you don't ask him to sponsor you."

We hang up and I go in search of spiritual guidance.

I find it in an excerpt from a pastor.

"All things work for the good of God," he says. "What things? *All* things. When He gives you an assignment, you don't ask, 'How?' You ask, 'How fast?' Be still. Listen for instruction. Be strong. Stand up to indifference. When someone questions your motives, you make sure your motives are true. Only then will you have the authority to say, 'Stay in your own lane. This is not your calling. This is my calling. Not anyone with bad intentions nor good intentions will keep me from accomplishing what God has set me to do.'"

It gives me peace. Conviction to fight another day.

November 1, 2017

Acupuncture should be covered by insurance. And neuromuscular massage. And Pilates.

Western medicine will have us taking pills for the rest of our lives. Band-Aids on severed arteries. Numbing agents masking infected cysts of the soul. Requiring ongoing treatment. And on. And on.

Alternative methods, in many cases, are so much better. They are truer aligned with the harmony of our mind, spirit and body.

Acupuncture helps with anxiety. Peace. Well-being. I've also heard it is great for PTSD. Yet insurance does not recognize this Chinese treatment as restorative. Deductibles didn't blink a financial eyelash adding Xanax and Ambien to my deadly remedy. But a $100 non-chemical, non-pharmacon human pin cushion solution? Not no. Hell no.

After hitting an all-time low in tolerance of the widespread pain radiating through my body, I finally walk through the door of Tehila's Pilates & Massage.

My friend Keith Marks has been pushing me to see him after I spent hundreds in co-pay fees for doctors to say they don't know why I've had progressive muscle and joint aches since getting sober.

Sugar infighting the chemical balance of my flesh undoubtedly responsible for much of the chaos. Brain receptors firing on all cylinders won't let go of the cravings. Since our visit to 904 Thin, Kerry lost 25 pounds. I, on the other hand, found them.

It's more than inflammation though. Each morning requires a pep talk to roll to the left, swing legs over the side, clench the teeth and gingerly push up to sitting position. A second pep talk and I'm upright. Shuffling like Tim Conway into the bathroom.

Watching my own grimace reflecting back, I stretch cramped fingers, contorted toes and a kinked back. It only takes a few minutes to feel better, but any measure of stagnancy, such as driving, evolves into cramping.

Neuromuscular massage pops up when I Google relief from these symptoms. A box-store massage friend confirms the benefits. And the cost is the same as her franchise pricing.

For 60 minutes, Keith moves his hands around the problem areas. Feeling each muscle. Listening to what the body is screaming. Adjusting and alternating pressure based on what he hears. No two massages are the same. Even on the same person.

When he finishes, I feel brand new. I can't explain it. I don't know how it works.

"Welcome to my world," Keith says. "The ongoing battle of trying to explain our industry in a self-medicating country."

He waves goodbye and I tell him I'll help spread the word.

November 2, 2017

Add another notch to the self-employed section of my resume belt, please. Public relations assistant.

My friend Michelle Gilliam, owner of Point Taken PR, hires me to sandwich my participation in Mutts & The Media with set up and clean up.

The gig makes me feel wanted. Accomplished. Valued. The pay rate is generous. A wink at my talent.

"Great job," Michelle says. "Send me an invoice and I'll get a check right out." She drops the trunk on her SUV. "By the way. I'll probably have some more work for you. If you're interested."

I'm not only interested, I'm counting on it. After two months of grinding away at various jobs (ride share, video production, bartending), the writing is on the wall. I'm self-employed. God will provide.

November 17, 2017

"I will *never* get a tattoo."

Sitting on the Jacksonville International Airport floor, cuddled up to an electric outlet charging the iPhone, the memory of my words stirs a chuckle as I draw a cross in the webbing of my right hand for the 148th day in a row.

It's not that I've ever been opposed to tattoos. I like them. On someone else's skin. Telling someone else's story. One application of someone else's ink at a time. That is, until someone else's permanent markings got me thinking about my own story. My own ink.

One hundred forty-nine days earlier I watched *The Passion of the Christ.*

Roman guards struggle to position the mangled, bloody mess of

Jesus' body on top of the grounded cross for crucifixion. His weak mass flops back and forth across the main post until his left outstretched arm is bound with rope to the intersecting beam.

I winced knowing what was coming next. A slow-motion montage. A thick, archaic nail positioned in his palm. The rise then lowering of a hammer.

BAM. Vibrating echoes with each pound drives the metal deeper into the flesh.

BAM. Jesus grits his blood-soaked teeth.

BAM. Red liquid spurt from his palm.

The next day I pondered the ramifications of watching this gruesome act of love. I couldn't unsee it. So. What was I willing to do? If He was willing to do that, what was I willing to do?

I was on fire to help snatch other alcoholics from the devil's jaws. But am I strong enough to pull the curtain back and expose my silent humiliation in order to scream, "You're not alone. I'm down here with you."

Yes. But I wanted a physical reminder for the days I knew it would be tough to stand in belief.

I prepped the tip of a Pilot medium tip pen on a piece of scratch paper and circled the fresh flow of blue ink over and over in the center of my right palm, showing homage to my Savior's scars. Before the day was over, I barely remembered the doodle session and condensation from icy water bottles erased any proof of it.

I reached for another sip. Looking at my grip, it hit me. A cross on the webbing of my drinking hand.

A well-known symbol in an odd location. A conversation starter to share a testimony. And, if I ever reached for a libation, an emblazoned reminder that God didn't save me for failure.

That day, and every day after, I manually draw a cross in the same spot.

Maybe one day I'll put my story down in permanent ink. Until then, I always pack an ink pen and enjoy the daily ritual of my temporary scar.

November 23, 2017

There is plenty to be thankful for as I look around the dinner table. My first sober Thanksgiving draws the expected questions. Are you okay around alcohol? Does it bother you that we're having wine with dinner? Etc.

My eyes bounce on and off the sweet red nectar. Taking careful precautions not to get caught.

Trying to explain alcoholism to someone unaffected requires analogies. A relatable scenario. Alcohol is like falling in love. The romance phase. When you think about her all day. Can't wait to see her. Taste her. You love the way she makes you feel when you're with her. Powerful. Creative. Handsome. And miss her when you wake up. She's gone. Until the coast is clear again.

I watch in fascination as Aunt Laurie sips in between bites. Tiny tastings. No sense of urgency. Occasionally when the conversation is good and distracting, only a swirl of the glass then back down. Wine notes singing in the air between her and the turkey.

This is so fascinating. How does anyone sip wine? That glass would have been gone before the salad.

Her husband is Mom's youngest brother. Uncle Rodney was the cool uncle. When Heidi and I were growing up, he wasn't married and didn't have kids. We thought of him as one of us. Fun. Carefree. He could play on the floor with us or toss our little bodies over his shoulder like a sack of potatoes.

By the time we put on our fancy wedding party gowns Grandma made us for his wedding, I already had one severe drunk under my belt.

A 5th grade slumber party. An absentee parent. An unaccompanied bottle under the sink. A lethal combination that led to an evening over the toilet. Dispensing red wine. Similar to the burgundy ex-lover setting across from me now.

I don't have the luxury of moving backwards and try to focus on something else.

I like the way I feel too much to take a drink. It doesn't matter how beautiful the crystal stemware presentation tonight. Or what delicious fruit infusion they add to Samuel Adams beer tomorrow. There is no taste bud temptation worth trading this high I'm on.

"Is it hard?" Uncle Rod breaks my concentration.

Mesmerizing, hypnotizing wine legs squiggling down the glass lose their grip. I turn my attention to his voice at the head of the table.

"Huh? Oh. Drinking? Or, I guess, not drinking?" I ask.

All mouths stop conversing and, for the most part, chewing. Curious eyeballs and ears turn my way.

"Not really." Nose scrunched, the words come out in the form of a question. The truth is more complex than yes or no. "It's not that I don't want to do it. I just know I can't."

More analogies are in order. I ask if they all love chocolate. Some heads nod. Others cock in confusion.

"So, I love chocolate." I pull my hands to my chest and fold them into a prayer grasp. Look skyward. Belt out emphatically. "Love chocolate."

Heidi blows a nose laugh out at the dramatics. I look over at her and giggle at her giggling at me. I love her so much, we have our own language.

"But if God said, 'You can eat or drink anything you want for the rest of your life. However, if you eat any chocolate, you will die.' You could put a triple-decker German chocolate cake with cream cheese fudge frosting in front of me and I'd say, 'No, thank you.'"

I shrug my shoulders. Let it sink in. Throw out a little humor.

"Honestly, if I had to choose between alcohol or chocolate, I'm not sure what I'd do?"

Laughter comes from those who would also not want to make the impossible choice.

"I'm serious. I've thought about it," I say. "Fortunately, I don't have to. God made it for me."

No matter what hardship we are given, the sooner we accept,

surrender and adjust our lives to accommodate, the easier it becomes.

Stop fighting the universe. Peace will follow.

November 27, 2017

My heart aches for parents who have children with addictions. It bleeds for children of addicts. What an insult to injury. Taking on all the weight for a problem you didn't create.

This is not my calling. I do, however, feel responsible to find answers for anyone who reaches out. Link them to resources. Utilize my spiritual gift as a people connector. Be a voice of encouragement.

Today I'm doing all three. Resource: Melissa's show. People connection: Dr. Brian Jackson. Encouraging voice: That's where I come in.

Before we go live on First Coast Connect, we go live on Facebook. Tell them what we're going to tell them before we tell them.

"The disease of addiction is a family disease." The doctor says often times the family members are as sick if not sicker than the addict. "They're anxious. They're worried. They're fragmented. It's difficult for them to get the loved one off their mind and get them some help."

He recommends Al-Anon. A group made up of anyone affected by someone else's alcoholism.

"Loved ones miss work. They sometimes suffer financial consequences as a result of the addict. The emotional toll can lead to the need for medications," he says. "Learning how addiction works, that it is an illness and it doesn't define who they are, can really help in overcoming the frustration."

Education in the do's and don'ts are important. Those who care about us the most can inadvertently enable us. Leading to more frustration.

During Facebook Live, a viewer comments he did not believe in treatment centers. Overpriced. Waste of time.

A.A. all the way, he writes.

I bolt to defend Greenfield Center and Brian's honor. He does not need it.

"Treatment is not for everybody. A.A. is for everybody who is suffering from the disease of addiction of alcohol. And a continuum of care with Alcoholics Anonymous is key to continued sobriety." He then loops back to my point. "Some people need treatment to get up and running. We highly recommend a 12-step program like Alcoholics Anonymous. Getting sober is one thing. Staying sober is another."

During Melissa's show, the calls to the show are encouraging. Fewer this time from family members. More about medical facts.

"We have a tremendous amount of overdoses from alcohol where your auto respiratory system shuts down," Brian says. "People like to think, alcohol. It's legal. It's social. It won't kill me. They did an anonymous survey of doctors where alcohol was a contributing factor, but they put stroke. Heart attack. Things of that nature."

We talk about that slippery slope of alcohol. Legal for some. Lethal for others.

"I still promote events that have alcohol," I say. "I recognize other people can drink responsibly. I, unfortunately, was not one of them. Once I start, I cannot stop."

How do you tell when someone is just having a good time? How do you tell the difference between a drinker acting out on a weekend binge from a problem drinker from a full-blown alcoholic? Where are the nuances?

"I had enough redeeming qualities, if I did have too much to drink and went overboard, I didn't even have to make excuses," I say. "People were making excuses for me."

You worked hard this week. You deserve to let loose. Everybody was getting crazy last night. It's a celebration. It's a vacation. It's the holidays. The forgivable catalysts were plentiful.

Melissa asks Brian about difficulty in recovery during this time of year. When a new party seemingly pops up every weekend.

He recommends arriving late. Eating plenty of food. Keeping a non-alcoholic drink in hand. Having an escape plan to leave if necessary.

"How are you doing here at the holidays?" Melissa asks.

"I'm doing great," I say. I haven't been to any parties yet. Educating myself on proper procedure is key for success. I change the mood to keep things light.

"My recommendation (if you want to quit) is to make a selfie video of you trashed like I did."

Our friendship is obvious. We both burst into laughter at the visual. I can barely make it through the follow up statement.

"You'll *never* want to go back to *that*."

I pull together composure and give a recap for any listener who doesn't know the drunk video story.

"It's 2 o'clock in the afternoon and I'm talking about how I better get some sleep so I can get to work the next day. My M.O. at that time was waking up about 10. Figure out how many drinks, based on one drink per hour, how many shots I can take to get a buzz. Then fall back asleep and wake up the next day to go to work."

Melissa shakes her head. Still in disbelief six weeks after learning the truth about someone she thought she knew so well.

"So, yeah. This was my life," I say. "Fortunate to be a woman because with enough hairspray and makeup I can pull anything off."

A woman calls in to ask about help for family members. Brian repeats his suggestions from the Facebook Live. Therapy and Al-Anon.

"The alcoholic is powerless to stop," he says. "The family members are powerless over, 'Why won't he just stop?'"

He discusses how people believe they are terminally unique. Shame and life responsibilities keep them from getting help.

"The good news is," he says, "in treatment, we realize we are not alone."

He responds to a conversation we had in the green room. Curiosity about the gap between whimsy and reality. Elation in early sobriety. Subsequent dips in mood.

"There was this ebb of maybe I'm not as much fun when I'm

drinking," I say. "And this flow of thinking, I'm back." Excitement discovering my authentic self. Learning about this new person I never knew. Giving my brain a break and forgiveness and time to heal.

"I think if they invented alcohol today it would not be legal," Brian says. "It affects the mind. The body. To the negative unbelievably."

I don't know if we solved problems. I do believe each of us played a part in being a stepping stone on another's journey. Perhaps many we will never meet or speak to. One listener. Or two. Or a hundred.

Still. I haven't found a starfish. That one person I can mark as saved. Changed. Transformed. Thrown back to the ocean. Living her best life God intended.

I don't need it for ego. I know we are helping people. Right here. Right now. I need it for validation I am doing it right. Proof to refer to when insecurities creep in. When naysayer voices are louder than the prophetic ones.

November 30, 2017

A conversation the day of our radio appearance has me thinking all week about various ways people get sober. Why does one program work for some people and not for others?

December 5, 2017

More buzz about the cause. This time in BUZZ Magazine, an entertainment publication. I open it to review my column and see my face. Twice. On the same page. Very exciting. Once as a thumbnail for my monthly column. Another smiling face shot right next door in Melissa's. She named me in her feature as The Most Interesting Person I've Interviewed This Month. Sweet!

December 7, 2017

Somebody's dad died today. While reading through the beautiful condolences, I realize I don't remember any of the messages left for me. None I can recall in the moment. I was too drunk. A cloudy medial temporal lobe. Mental note. Go back and look with a newly sharp brain.

December 8, 2017

It's only 5 p.m., but the day-long downpour and quickly sinking sun has me longing for my p.j.'s. Apparently my next Uber rider got the casual Friday memo.

A slight frame outline of what appears to be a tween boy or girl in pajama bottoms and slippers emerges from the darkened door onto the front porch of her tiny block home. Arms quickly cross as the cool air hits her. A grey hoodie hides her face. In a faux attempt to dodge the rain, she sprints to the rear passenger door. I can't confirm her assumed gender from the name on the waybill until she opens the door and peers sheepishly from under the grey hood. Even still, I'm not sure of her age, but she is definitely an adult.

"Did you make it a great day?" I ask as she shuts the door.

I turn back to face the front and put the car in gear. She lets out a heavy, doubt-filled grunt. Exhale releases the stench of alcohol into the cabin. I can't tell if it's old, slept-on afternoon morning breath, or a fresh batch of a new buzz. Her exhausted face tells me it's the prior.

"Oh. That good, huh?"

I click the start button on the Uber app and notice we've got two stops. I'm fairly certain I know what that means: round trip liquor store run. The place where everybody knows your name and nobody cares that you came to the party in your bath robe.

"I've got to work tonight," she says with another groan.

While the majority of the working class is getting off and heading home with a resounding "Thank God it's Friday," I imagine she wants to get a quick buzz followed by a short nap.

I don't want my presumption to be true, but it's fueled by the glowing neon sign at the end of our first stop.

She jumps out, promises she won't be long and closes the door. Leaving me to silently contemplate my options.

Do I say anything to her? Is it any of my business?

I catch glimpses of her through the glass openings in between beer promo posters. Pacing. Waiting for her turn in line to place an order to the man behind the bulletproof glass. She's dwarfed by all the normal-sized neighbors she greets as they enter and fall in line behind.

Do you or don't you have conviction for what you have been working towards? If you truly believe God's new calling in your life, then you have to say something. If not you, who?

The divine intervention command is unmistakable. Worry of what to say, how to approach it, vanishes. Faith in its place. Darkness and light cannot co-exist. I'm flying blind. But I'm ready.

I visualize her never darkening the door of this local business again. She's unknowingly saying goodbye to the familiar face behind the polycarbonate wall for the last time.

The other regulars will run into her at the grocery store with a *"where you been?"* Curious about her clear eyes and inner peace with a *"you look different ... did you color your hair?"*

I see it. My daydream is as clear as a real memory.

Windshield wipers repeat their perfect tempo as I watch her emerge. She scurries through the rain with a familiar smile. That elation. A surge of bliss. Bittersweet knowledge that it's only six short minutes home and she can feed the beast gnawing at her psyche.

She jumps in the back, tosses her clutch next to her, and pulls back her hoodie.

"You good?" I smile back at her. She sighs. The smile fades. Her face drops into her little hands.

"You okay? What's wrong?" I turn to put the car in drive and start the journey back to the block home.

She looks up and shakes her head.

"My boss wants me to come in an hour early."

"What? When?"

"Just now," she says.

"Just now? Like he called just now when you were in the store?"

She nods, leans her elbow on the door, chews on her thumbnail and stares at the passing trees.

"Oh, man. I remember those days," I tell her. "You want to have a little cocktail before the night shift. Maybe take a little nap."

Her rearview mirror reflection nods in agreement.

"The difference though is I was a full-blown binge drinking alcoholic."

The face in the mirror snaps to attention with wide eyes.

"No!" she hollers.

"Yes, ma'am. But I was bad off. I couldn't stop." I glance in the rearview.

Was that a glimpse of recognition I see?

She stares at me in shock.

"No. Not you?"

"Oh, yeah. I'm feelin' you. What time do you have to be at work?"

Her disbelief fades back to reality. She sinks in her seat and quietly says, "An hour."

"An hour?" It's my turn for the crazed look and wide eyes in the rearview. "Like an hour from now?"

She nods. I glance at the clock.

"Hold on. So, you have to be in around 6 o'clock?"

"Yes."

"But you were supposed to be in at 7 o'clock?"

"Yes."

I take an extra second at the stop sign and shake my head. There's nobody coming. I turn to look her in the eye.

"Okay. Because you do know you already smell like alcohol, right?" Her look says she doesn't.

"Really? You can smell it?"

"Oh, yeah. I smelled it as soon as you got in the car." Silence.

"I'm not judging you." I reassure her.

"No, I thank you for telling me that." She stares out the window until the next stop sign. Searching the empty streets for the answer of what to do now.

"So, you used to be like me? For real?"

"Oh, yeah."

Her barely audible voice creeps across the backseat, quietly screaming for help, "How did you quit?"

I pull into the drive and put it in park.

"There's my book right there." I point to the chapbook in the pocket in front of her. "You can keep it. Read all about it. I would make those corner store runs every day."

"No." Her jaw drops. She looks like I just read an excerpt from *her* chapbook, and she wants more.

"Yep. In fact, I can tell you exactly what happened back there." I point towards the direction we just traveled. "You were thinking you had a couple of hours." I motion to the clock. "So, you only bought a couple of mini bottles. No more than you drink right now and get away with it." I point to her handbag. "And you shoved them in your purse."

"How do you know that?" Her hand covers her mouth.

"Because I was you," I answer. "Just enough to get a little buzz, but you can handle it. You got this because you've got some time. Maybe a power nap before you have to go."

"How do you know that?" She slaps her knees twice with both hands. The rain starts to pound louder with every revelation.

"Because I did the same thing." I tap my hand on the center console with each word and smile thinking about my own insanity.

"And now your boss calls. And you're scrambling."

"Yes, Lord. Yes." She throws her head back, recognizing her own insanity.

"You're scrambling mentally, trying to figure out what to do now. Should you eat something? Brush your teeth? Chew gum? You're wondering, 'How did I get here today? How did I not see this coming?'"

"Yes, Lord." She closes her eyes and nods her head.

"Aren't you tired?" She continues nodding and I continue talking. "Mentally exhausted from that gerbil on the wheel. Spinning and spinning and spinning inside of your head. Trying constantly to stay one step ahead of how and when you're going to get your next drink?"

She opens her eyes, the eyes that tell of the wear on her brain. Barely audible over the drops beating the roof.

"I am."

Our eyes lock briefly. I wince at the pain I can feel filling the space between us. Suddenly, something catches my eye.

Fingers of electricity reach down from the sky on either side of her head. Moving swiftly towards the center. In the yard across the street, they culminate in a giant white fireball over her left shoulder.

I look like I've seen a ghost. Before she can register my abrupt emotional shift, a cannon-sized clap of thunder smacks the back windshield, followed by mountain-sized yelps from both of us.

We laugh at the sound of our own voices.

"That was God sending you a message." I giggle, but I'm serious. She knows it because she believes it, too.

"What can I do?"

I reach for her hand. "I'll help you."

"You will?" Her eyes aren't so sure. But I grasp her hand harder and shake it twice.

"Yes. Take my book. Here's my number." I scratch the digits on the back page. "Call me tomorrow and I will help you. I promise."

She takes a second to stare out into the rain one more time.

"Okay." She opens the door and dodges the rain back to the same porch I found her on 20 minutes earlier, stopping to wave as she climbs the steps.

She no longer looks like a child. But she does look like a broken woman. Even so, I see her how she can be. Brave. Beautiful. Healed.

I wave back and say a prayer.

"Please, God. Please. Please let me have save this starfish."

Until now, no one has followed through. All of the emails, phone calls, appointments for coffee. None of them have followed through. I'm not deterred by the inaction. I recognize that my role may only be to plant a seed.

This one is different. This is the first time I can visualize the results from start to finish. I would selfishly like to see it come to fruition. I have strong faith, but a little reinforcement I am making a difference can go a long way.

The next day, she calls.

My heart lumps into a ballistic motion. Ready to launch Stella Starfish back into the ocean.

CHAPTER 13

CO-DEPENDENCY, JUDGEMENT & OTHER FUN DEFECTS

December 9, 2017

Co-dependency is my middle name. Correction. *Was* my middle name.

"I'm better as a team." I always said when questioned about my need to be in a relationship. Boyfriend checklist: Hot. Likes to drink. End of checklist. "I don't wake up with ugly."

The shallowness of the criteria. Nauseating. The results. Predictable. One to two years, tops. Love spending time with me. Not in love with me. Really cool guys most of the time. Emotionally, and often times geographically, undesirable guys all of the time.

I had been that way for so long, I assumed it was a character defect. In sobriety, in discovering my authentic self, the lifted fog revealed a calculated subconscious plan to unite with surface partners. A perpetual state of the romance phase with men who would never get too deep. The thought still scares me. The difference? I'm no longer willing to compromise.

Gwen once told me after hearing my romance history, "You weren't dating men. You were dating alcohol the whole time." Now I recognize it in others. Shake my head in pity.

"Are you Daniel?" The clock strikes 2 a.m. as I roll down the passenger window to question the first person who looks to be intently following a little white vehicle icon on his smart phone and glances up simultaneously with my arrival.

The community center gravel lot is filled with young men in T-shirts and jeans and young women in tank tops, denim miniskirts and cowboy boots. Crushed cans and Solo cups litter their feet.

Who cleans this crap up?

I imagine what the janitorial staff reaction must be after a night of *Animal House* style partying at the cheap rented venue.

"Yeah." Daniel finally responds.

He seems in no hurry to get in the car. Holding on to an open beer in his left hand, his body sways unsteady as he leans back to pull an animated drag off the cigarette in his right hand. He twists at the waist to take in the commotion swirling around him as co-eds decide who is riding with whom. Their incoherent conversations make me anxious to get far away before any keys turn on engines.

What is he doing? Is he waiting on friends? Come on, rudeness. Time is money. Let's go.

After two more puffs, I hear his hand on the rear door. Then nothing. I lose sight of him in the blind spot. He finally opens the door. Sans beer and cigarette. I assume his DNA now litters the ground on his discarded butt and can amidst all the other trash.

As I pull out and turn left towards the university, I look at the kid in the rearview mirror and wonder if he's even old enough to be drinking at the frat party.

"Fun night?"

"Yeah." He leans his head back and sighs. The kind of sigh that screams, *I want to talk about it*. He slumps in the backseat. Rebel-without-a-clue attitude. He so desperately wants to convey he's got it together. But inadvertently shared his insecurities. The short trip to the dorm room will include a long story.

"She says she doesn't want to be with me." He starts in the middle like we're old friends picking up a dropped conversation from earlier at the party. "It's freakin' B.S." He grunts and grins out the window. Each passing street lamp reflects a strobe of light off his pale face and high and tight haircut. "I'll show her." He turns to lift his head up and meets my eyes in the mirror. "I'll screw somebody else and then she'll be back, banging on my door."

"Oh." *I'm not really sure what to say to that.* I look back at the road. "Okay. Well ..."

"Hey." I look back, but he's not talking to me. His voice is an octave higher. A classic tell-tale that a boy is talking to a girl. "Wass goin' on?"

Was he slurring that much a minute ago? Maybe he hopes to blow this off as a drunk dial if she rejects him.

"Are you coming over?" An inaudible female voice responds. "Why not?" More excuses. Something about hanging out with her friends. "Just come over." Her responses are quick and perky compared to his sloth cadence. He continues to grovel until she excuses herself from the call.

"Damnit." He smacks the leather seat beside him. "See, she does this." I can feel him looking at me again, but I keep my eyes on the road. "But you just watch. I'm going to find somebody else to hook up with." He rubs his lips in between the forefinger and thumb. "And then she'll be back."

His aloof confidence is all an act. I don't let on that I've had a starring role in that play. Many times.

"I ain't mad atcha, guy." I shake my head. "But I have to ask. Why do you want to be with someone who only wants you if somebody else does?"

He tries to backtrack and minimize the direness of this dysfunctional relationship he's revealed. But the damage is already done. I can't unsee his future. The countless hours he'll spend trying to fit his round peg into her square hole. The countless days he'll pine for what he mistakenly believes is the love of his life. That is, until the next girl comes along who fits the criteria: Beautiful. Likes to drink.

While Daniel drones on about how they are meant to be together and "she knows it but she's scared"—blah, blah, blah—I say a little prayer of gratefulness for the recent example God used to reveal to me how far I've come with self-worth in recovery.

It was the topic of discussion last week during another ah-ha moment.

Hanging out by the pool with David and Kerry at our friend Denise's annual Christmas party, we argued over a recent come on I turned down while driving. I gave him a Lyft. He tried to give me a lift. To his apartment.

The alleged suitor had a lot of checks in the right column: Handsome, nice condo, a boat. And, even though I picked him up at a bar, he didn't seem intoxicated. Didn't even register a scent on my ultra-sensitive smeller.

"I just don't get why you don't call him?" Kerry asked.

"Two strikes," I said. "I picked him up at a strip club."

She pointed her finger aggressively at me to counterpoint. "You said he was at a friend's birthday party."

David opened his mouth and leaned in. Before he could say anything, Kerry fired at him. "She did. She said, he said, he was at a friend's birthday party."

David laughed in disbelief, shook his head and regrouped his thought. He raised both hands in air quotes. "'A friend.' Right."

"And, he asked me to come up to his place and hang out." I shot them both a sarcastic grin.

Kerry's height gives her the advantage of feeling like she's the big sister who earned the right to speak before everyone. Plus, she can be loud in contrast to David's mild manner. He started to speak, but she jumped on top of him.

"But they just met." She looked at him like he's the judge and jury who will make the final ruling. "It wasn't like they had hung out all night and he was like, 'Hey baby, you want to come up to my place?'"

He couldn't help but laugh through his response. "It was 2 o'clock in the morning."

"But. They. Just. Met."

"It wasn't like he asked me to dinner, Kerry." I jumped in. "He asked me up to his place." Air quotes. "To 'hang out.' It wouldn't have mattered if it was two in the afternoon."

She dropped her shoulders in defeat. "Oh." She gave David a side glance. "I guess you're right."

At some point, Daniel stops talking. His weary head leans against backseat. Slits for eyes stare out the window.

Man, I remember those days. I chuckle audibly, but Daniel doesn't notice. *Those days when I craved any attention at all. If a good-looking man I picked up at a strip club would have asked me up to his apartment to 'hang out,' I would have jumped at the chance for fear this was the last handsome man in the world who would ever be attracted to me again for the rest of my life.*

I pull through the university gates and roll down the hill to the men's dorm rooms. I want to tell Daniel the story. He won't get it. Heck, he probably won't even remember it. For now, I just pray he, too, finds his way.

Maybe the stranger last week was a good guy with poor dating skills. Or maybe he was looking for a hookup. Either way, it's not my problem. It will never again be something I have to second guess the morning after. It is a sweet, deep breath of refreshing freedom.

Sometimes I pick people up and share my story, leaving them knowing God put them in my path to teach them something. Other times, I recognize He brings about people like Daniel, who end up teaching me something about myself.

December 15, 2017

If your best friend tells you you're not alcoholic. Don't believe her. The first friend I told said she would support me in my decision, but she didn't think I was an alcoholic.

On the flip. If an alcoholic tells you you *are* an alcoholic. Well, then. You probably are.

Take Michael and Carol for example. They were the unlikeliest of sweethearts. She a socialite. He a felon. But the heart knows what it wants. And when Michael got out of prison, Carol knew she wanted to marry him.

I'm caught up in their critics-be-damned love story on NPR's *This American Life* with Ira Glass when I hear one thing that stops my attention span.

"Michael drank too much at parties," Ira says. "Probably to ease his comfort level around her friends."

I can't tell if that is a personal observation the host came up with based on what he knows, or doesn't know, about alcohol use vs. abuse. Or if that is what Michael and Carol told him. Either way, it sticks with me through the end of the story. And believe you, me. I am fully invested in this story.

As the broadcast comes to a close, Ira's distinct voice comes back on with an update.

"This story was originally broadcast four years ago," Ira says. "Since then Carol has been diagnosed with cancer and Michael has gone to rehab."

Ah-ha! I knew it.

More and more, I find myself assimilating information. It's nothing I can put my finger on. Similar to detecting nuanced dialect and knowing where someone is from. Not in a way you can verbalize or understand yourself.

Like this UpLYFTing Anecdote from a recent rideshare.

Me: They're getting a lot of food trucks at the beach.

Passenger: Yeah. I almost got arrested for peeing on the tire of one last weekend.

Me: Hmm. You look too classy to pee on the tire of a truck.

Passenger: (After a long pause) Wow. That's the nicest thing anyone's ever said to me.

Me: (After an even longer pause): Well, that's just sad.

You may think this is the conversation of an alcoholic. I don't. I think he's making bad 20-something decisions after a night of drinking. That's a given. However, our prior conversations lead me to believe he's already growing weary of chasing his tail. Trying to keep up with the boys, and some girls, in his social circle.

I'm not a doctor. I don't pretend to know the difference between someone going through a phase to past the point of no return. When the conversation fits. If the person in my rearview seems open emotionally. I launch a dialogue about my journey. Allowing them to switch the focus internally if necessary. Never with judgement.

It's rare a real starfish will come clean during a 25-minute psychobabble backseat workshop. More typical they admit to needing a self-check.

"Have fun," I say. "But if you think you have a problem, don't hesitate to reach out."

Sometime they do. Then I never hear from them again. It used to bug me. My need to know the end of the story. I realize now, it's on a need to know basis. God's need for me to know. Or not. I'm just here to plant a seed. Provide options. Availability to a living, breathing person with a face. Answer questions. Bounce ideas. It's all some people need to take the next step.

Over the past several months, I have responded tirelessly to people I've known for a decade and people I've never met before. Anyone who reaches out for help gets an answer. Many of them share an apprehensive spirit. Fear of being badgered like a used car salesman looking to sign on the dotted line of Sobriety for Life, LLC.

They're drawn to a willingness to help but not hound. I'm willing to offer what I can. Only if they really want it. I keep it real. Especially those with a similar daily regimen to mine.

I've looked friends and strangers alike in the eye and said, "You're going to die. I'm not trying to be mean. I'm letting you know. If you keep up this pace, you will die. Your heart. Your brain. Your liver. We're not built to cycle this level of poison through our system."

I've also learned through the wisdom of my sponsor, Brian and Lynn, I'm too green to take the world on my shoulders. I use my people connecting skills to pull them out of the storm and get them plugged in to a shore they feel safe on.

No one is ever rebuked for not taking advice. All responsibility for action falls on the shoulders of the one seeking the help.

"I can only share with you my journey and the things I've learned," I say. "If you need more, I will work like crazy to find you the right connection. Other than that, it's up to you."

December 31, 2017

Last year, I passed out before the beginning of the New Year. This year, I'll be watching people pass out. What a difference a year makes.

I started bartending in October. Big events only. Including the World's Largest Outdoor Cocktail Party. Also known as Florida-Georgia weekend. When the Florida Gators take on the Georgia Bulldogs. Good rivalry. Great tips.

Six months sober and ready to add another job to my growing list, I jumped at the opportunity given to me by friends Janice and Mario at the Jacksonville Landing.

Any apprehension about being in close proximity to cohorts in crime Jack and Jim (Daniels and Beam, respectively) evaporated with the poisonous stench coming out of those bottles. Like its addictive predecessor I gave up years before, cigarettes, I no longer inhaled the fumes and thought, I gotta get me some of that.

Science now separates the abuser from its victim. Smells of damage. Toxicity. Deadly arsenic. My senses are no longer aroused. They are assaulted. It's time to gain back some of the money libations stole from me.

The party I'm working is private. A stunning second-story, floor-to-ceiling window view overlooking the St. Johns River. Boats lit up with Christmas decorations float past multiple barges. Floating fireworks platforms primed. Ready to explode.

While thousands crowd into the Landing's civic area below for free music, long liquor lines and standing room only fireworks, our upstairs guys and uptown girls roam freely from bar to bar. Enjoying balcony water views and comfy seating areas in their fancy gowns and silky ties.

No amount of glitz and glam can dull my drunk-dar. The ability to detect true problem drinking from the seasonal three sheets to the wind full sail into the New Year.

The man who bellies up like clockwork three times as fast as his co-workers for double Maker's Mark on the rocks. The woman who requests a celebratory shot on the side of her mixed drink for the sixth time with 60 minutes left before the celebration actually begins. The couple who drinks unevenly. He arrives at the bar each time to support her. Then stands alone at the window watching fireworks. Her limp body slumped over on the loveseat near him.

While the crowd swirls around, complimentary champagne flutes in hand, looking for a better spot to watch the colorful explosions, I empathetically watch her sleep. No one appears to notice her. I do.

I want to sit on the coffee table in front of her. Softly take one listless hand in mine. Gently stir her drooping body. Activate her mind from its temporary coma. Explain there's a better life waiting for her. A beautiful world expecting her. Missing her.

I don't think she will be appreciative if I do. I settle in to be appreciative of her instead. A serene reminder of a place I never want to visit again.

Mental note. Add all three to prayer list tonight. Thanks to a friendly self-introduction earlier, I will be able to do it by name.

Two hours later, grotesque fluorescent lighting kills the ambiance. Maker's Mark man summons a rideshare. The couch surfer rises from her slumber. Unsteady. Unashamed. At the end of the bar, another woman rambles in, trying to get a drink before last call.

"Sorry. It's after two," I tell her.

She doesn't have a wristband. I appreciate her moxie. A party crasher trying to get a final fix.

I would have done it.

She hangs out while we clean up. Making friendly conversation with the bar back.

Hoping to flirt her way to a final beer, I bet.

It works. He gives her one while my back is turned. I steal glances in between pulling pour spouts off and putting bottle caps on. She's very beautiful. Long, highlighted locks twisted into flowing curls sag from the humidity. Microblade eyebrows. Professionally attached eyelashes. Perfect pout lip fillers.

Too pretty to be alone. Yet. There she is. Sipping on a beer. Nowhere to go. Lonely. Drunk. Alone. Sad. We come in very different packages. Internally, we were once exactly the same.

January 9, 2018

Being a student at a specialized school is stressful. Fun. But stressful. In addition to core classes, the self-imposed expectation of standing out creatively while pursuing a dream in the arts can make it hard to be a kid. Once behind, it's difficult to catch up.

Phaaryl feels the stress. I watch, every Tuesday during our lunchtime, her fear building. Hiding behind a forced grin. A grin I am intimately familiar.

Today, her body language says different. Bouncing into the conference room wearing a Micky Mouse T-shirt and a smile, she piques my interest. Last week, her anxiety so strong, I felt it. Now? Night and day.

"What's going on?" I push through an incredulous laugh.

"Oh, nothing." She drops her book bag on the table. Takes a seat. Flashes intermittent eye contact. Sideways grins.

"Don't blow me off," I say. "Something is going on."

She shares she is feeling much better about the semester. She has a game plan to stay caught up. A committed schedule will take her out of her comfort zone as well as the procrastination circle.

"And I'm going to focus on the things I'm thankful for," she says.

"Oh, cool." I nod my approval for giving God the glory. "Like what?"

"Well," she says, "like you."

"Me?"

"Yeah." She gives it a *duh!* sounding flare.

I'm intrigued. Crossed arms. Pointer finger knuckle partially emerged in my mouth. Eyes scan the book bag. I don't know what question to throw at her to get the next clue. I stick to the basics.

"Like what? How?"

"Like, when you come here and we spend time together," she says. "It's great. It helps."

I swear this child is destined to be a high-stakes poker player.

Phaaryl crowned six minutes after her sister. Or as her mom likes to say, "Six loooong minutes." They shared a birth sac and they both wear glasses. That's where the similarities end.

I always know when Daaryl is excited, scared, happy, uncomfortable, empowered. I also know I can encourage her to stretch her boundaries and she will take heed. Phaaryl is tougher nut to crack.

"Me?" I ask. Until now, I am clueless to the difference I'm making. I only know the positivity she brings to my life. Then again, she probably doesn't know it either.

January 12, 2018

A big grin rolls across my face when I see the name pop up on my phone: Stella Starfish. She is a bright, sunshiny mark on this severe weather day.

"Hi, Stella." My voice exudes excitement.

I tried unsuccessfully for several weeks to reach her after our last get together. She answered once, but said she was sick. Probably detox, I told her. The doctor later confirmed. Subsequent calls and texts went unanswered. I was starting to wonder if she changed her mind. Went back to the path of least resistance.

"Miss Tracy." Her voice is barely audible. Melancholy. "What do you do when you really want to drink?"

Alarm bells go off in my head. BEEP. BEEP. BEEP. Crisis. Crisis. I've only heard about situations like this. Never lived through one.

A few months after treatment, Gwen relapsed. She called in the middle of the night. I looked at the phone. At the time stamp. 2:17 a.m. *This can't be good*, I remember thinking, and made the decision not to answer. I didn't feel equipped in that moment to say the right thing. And if Gwen was drunk, as I suspected, she wouldn't hear me anyway.

Today, I am in warrior mode.

"What's going on?" The rain is pounding the windshield, and the Bluetooth is turned off in the car. I'm listening to her on speaker phone through the rhythm of the wipers. I want to make sure I hear every word and pull over to the side.

"I don't know how I can do it," she says.

I flip the phone from speaker to handheld and pull it to my face. It feels more personal. Protective. Sincere.

"Have you drank?"

"No. But I really want to."

"Okay." My mind races.

Performing triage at a car accident would be easier. At least I know breathing trumps bleeding.

"Have you had a drink today?" Assessing the damage is the logical choice.

"No."

"Why do you want to drink today? Did something happen?"

"Yeah," she says. "My daughter got into a fight at school."

Oh, shoot. I got this!

"Stella. Okay. We got this." I snap my fingers. "Yes, I know you are upset. But Stella, this is just a blip on the map of your life. A year from now ... check that, a month from now, you won't even remember this."

"You think so?" She sounds hopeful.

"I know so. I have been exactly where you are at. Everything feels so gigantic when you're in the moment. You're overwhelmed right now."

She confirms I'm right.

"Tomorrow you are going to feel completely different. Completely."

"You think so?"

"I know so. We can talk about it again tomorrow, but let's not worry about tomorrow. Let's only focus on today. You have *not* had a drink today, correct?"

"No. But I want to. That's why I called," she says.

"You did exactly the right thing. Exactly the right thing. Do you hear me? Can you promise me you won't drink? Just for today."

"Yeah, I can do that. But I'm scared. I don't know that I can keep doing this. What if I can't keep doing this?"

Think. Think. Think. What if she can't? How do I convince her right here, right now, she can? And then I remember. I don't have to.

"We're not going to worry about tomorrow." I throw my right hand up like I just solved the million dollar question. "Or next week. Or next month. Okay? We are only going to worry about today. You told me you can stay sober today. Did you mean it?"

"Yeah. I can do that."

Her confident voice gives me pause to take a deep breath and exhale audibly. The rain band passed, and I finally notice the windshield wipers are still on high and shut them off.

"I'm scared though," she says.

Staring at the warm exhaust coming from the parked car in front of mine blowing clouds of smoke into the cold air, I try to think of where to go next with this intervention.

"I read the whole book …"

"You read the whole book?" I cut her off in shock.

Dang. I haven't even read the whole book. And I'm the one who recommended it.

In treatment, I learned about the *Alcoholics Anonymous Big Book*. It's considered a must-read for anyone wanting to get and stay sober. Along with *Twelve Steps and Twelve Traditions*. That one is something I've come to consider an educational guide to ongoing self-growth.

But the Big Book? I have struggled with that one. First, it's not just a quirky name. The book is freaking huge. Second, I don't lie awake at night pining for that style of a read.

However, just like the original big book in my life, I know I need to read the Bible daily and I know I should read the A.A. book, too.

I decide to keep this information a secret.

"I read it the first week we met," she says. Her conviction quickly turns to self-loathing. "But I feel like I haven't made any progress."

"What are you talking about? You picked up the phone." I'm practically yelling. "Stella. You picked up the phone instead of a drink."

"Yeah?"

"Yes. That's huge," I say. "Huge. You barely know me."

"I don't really know you at all." She chuckles.

"Exactly. You don't really know me at all." I pause. I can't figure out if I'm offended by the comment. She's been on my mind every day, I feel like I know her. I don't think she was reciprocating. "Instead of picking up a drink, you picked up the phone. That's incredibly brave."

"Yeah?" She thinks about it. "I guess you're right."

"Absolutely, I'm right. You are brave." I sound like a high school basketball coach. "You are too precious to allow this disease to take you, Stella. And it's going to keep trying. Every day."

"Every day?" Fear in her voice returns. "For the rest of my life? I have to deal with this for the rest of my life?"

"Yep."

I hate being so real. But I realize I can't blow sunshine and rainbows up her butt.

"I don't want to think about it anymore." She's barely audible again.

"We need you thinking about recovery. Not addiction," I say. "Right now, you're obsessing. And you're going to continue until we get you embedded into a program. So, here's what we're going to do."

I give her a chronological list of proposed events over the next few days. A phone call tomorrow and a meeting on Monday. She agrees.

Before hanging up, I give her one more rah-rah tidbit. It's starting to sound corny.

"When we get together," I cradle the phone with my shoulder and grab the car wheel with both hands. "We are going to lay out a game plan that includes getting you a sponsor and going through the 12 steps, okay? You are not alone."

She agrees and we hang up. I put the car in drive and pull out into traffic with no real direction in mind. I can't remember where I was headed before the phone rang, and quite frankly, right now, I don't even care. Right now, I just want to share the excitement with my favorite sober friend. I pick up the phone and call Lynn. Surprisingly, she does not share in my glee.

"Well." She let's out a frustrated grunt. "You didn't even ask her about her struggle."

"I talked to her about the solution."

"Who cares," she says. "Who cares what you're doing tomorrow. What happened today? Did her daughter get in trouble? Did she get expelled?"

"I don't know."

"Exactly." She practically interrupts me. "You don't know. Don't you think she wanted to talk about it? Wanted to know you were there to listen? When you were getting sober, didn't you want somebody to listen to you?"

"Yeah."

"Of course you did. You didn't want someone sing-songing, smiling on the phone, telling you everything's going to be great."

I drive in silence. Listening to her rant through the car stereo. My hyperactive bubble deflating.

Lynn's right. I didn't even take a second to ask about the situation. I need to slow my role. Understand if I'm going to be out there, how best to guide those who trust me with their truth to those with more experience. Put the oxygen mask on myself before attempting to put one on Stella.

"She's calling Monday," I say. "I'll do what you said. I'll take the time to listen. Find a way to get her to my sponsor. Work on my own steps in the meantime."

"Good." Lynn always snaps her reply when she knows I get the lesson. "Slow down and remember, these people are hurting. You're doing a great job. I love ya."

We hang up and I wait. Wait for Stella to call. Wait through Monday. Tuesday. Wednesday Thursday. Wait through voicemails. Text messages. Prayer chains for her to call. She never does.

January 19, 2018

I jump on the early morning flight to New England with visions of an AFC Championship and the sweet sounds of "DUUUUVAAAAL" dancing in my head.

Though disappointed by the lack of Jaguars hats bobbing atop rows and rows of Southwest passengers, I'm holding out faith the Davis brothers—we met at check-in—and I will be joined by more fans headed to our Boston Teal Party on the connecting flight.

I find a window seat vacant in row 22 and snuggle in for the all-too-familiar 75-minute flight to Nashville. My heart hurts knowing my feet will stand in the same town as Robb for a brief layover. Actually, it's more of a dull throbbing. I've grown fond of it since my last drink. I'll probably feel different when I see the Tootsie's sign and tiger lily logo in the airport bar that once owned part of my paycheck waiting on departing flights every couple of weeks. This too shall pass. In about 15 minutes. Like any good craving.

"Would you like something to drink?" The flight attendant passes honey roasted peanuts over the empty middle seat and I order orange juice. Normally, it's water or coffee, but I'm feeling especially festive.

A few minutes later, she passes by to retrace her steps with deliveries. Non-descript colored liquids line her serving tray. But it's the two champagne split bottles that catch my attention.

Whoa. I glance at the time on my phone. 6:58 a.m. *That is just ... wow.*

I crane my nosy neck. *Who is drinking this early?* Realization sets in. With a shake of the head, I settle back in my seat. *I ain't mad atcha. That used to be me.*

Heck, by now, my belly would be lined with three shots for breakfast before leaving the house. The airport bar doesn't serve until 8 a.m. I know this because I have sat on a stool, impatiently checking the time for 10 minutes straight, calling out my order three minutes early, asking "can you go ahead and make it and give it to me right at 8?" So, this morning I would have stuck a couple of minis in with my liquids hoping to get through TSA Precheck since I'm not required to pull them out. One would go down en route. The second in the airport bathroom. The third in my seat under the cover of a blanket because "that stewardess is taking an awful long time with those drinks. Did she go to Finland to distill the vodka?"

By the time she makes it to our row, I've lost track of which lucky ducks get to exert their right to public displays of early morning bottle poppin'. But I do notice the lady in the aisle seat is one of them.

I barely have time to imagine how good her cranberry mixture would salivate the taste buds before flight attendant lady reaches for a vodka mini, scans her courier notes, and begins another arm extension in our direction.

Oh, wow. Aisle lady looks so innocent. But here she is. Obviously about to chug one straight from the bottle. Or sip on it. Or dump it in her poinsettia. Yeah. That's what I liked to do. Order the innocence of champagne with a juice and then dirty it up with the clear stuff.

I shoot quick glances all around the circle of movement. Aisle lady. Her drink. Flight attendant lady. Her extended arm. *Why is that arm is not stopping at aisle lady?* She pushes the no-name vodka past the empty middle seat. *Is she passing that to me?*

I stare at it. Eye level. Furrowed brow in comical disbelief. *Does she think this is for me?*

It's what happens when you're looking at your neighbor with those judgey, self-righteous eyes. God throws up a mirror.

"Vodka orange juice, right?" She shakes the bottle in my direction to take it from her.

"No. Just orange juice."

She keeps her arm out and looks back at the list. Her shoulders drop and she retreats the bottle to her tray.

"Oh. For some reason, I had vodka and orange juice." She passes the cup of orange liquid across the same path.

"I probably look like a screwdriver kinda gal." I laugh and then I lean in to make sure she hears me correctly this time.

"In full disclosure, I need to tell you I am an alcoholic. So, I have to make sure, there's no liquor in here?" I point inside the cup.

"No. No." Her long blonde locks sway back and forth with her shaking head. "I wouldn't do that to you."

I giggle at her exuberance since she kind of, almost, did. "Don't make me go and blow my 9-months of sobriety now." Everyone in earshot laughs with us as she walks away with the lone mini soldier standing proudly unopened on her tray.

"Wow. You're so brave." My row 22 neighbor is a beautiful 40-something with shiny reddish hair. If I didn't know she had to be at the airport by at least 6 a.m., I would have sworn she went for a professional blowout prior to boarding.

"Oh, I don't know if I would call it brave." Without eye contact, I grab the signature SWA heart on the end of the red stirrer and swirl it out of habit. "More like self-preservation." I lick the lonely OJ off the end and set it down on a napkin. A look over. A shrug the shoulders. And I decry. "Sometimes. You gotta fight. For your right. To *not* paaaaawtay."

I give her a sideways glance and grin. Her chuckle says she gets the twisted Beastie Boys reference and relieves my potential for social awkwardness. I'm able to take a sip and verify the juice is, in fact, not spiked.

"I think I'll just stick to water and coffee from now on." I laugh and take another gulp. "It's safer."

January 28, 2018

Seven days since the Jags lost. Eleven days since my last anti-depressant. Ten months and 22 hours since my last drink. And they are all colliding today.

On the plane to Boston, I realized I forgot to take a daily dose of happy pill. Worse, they weren't packed for the trip. By Monday, the error forgotten. In spite of a fourth quarter debacle that dashed our hopes of a first-time appearance in the Super Bowl, I left Beantown in a relatively good mood. Unlike my fellow black-and-teal-bleeders.

The airport crawled with dejected faces dressed in unwashed Bortles, Ramsey and Fournette jerseys. They lined the airport barstools like birds on a wire, hunched over Bloody Marys to match their blood shot eyes.

I do not miss those days. We came. We lost. We move on. Without alcohol in my system, my perspective lost its ability to look in the rearview mirror for too long. So, I kept typing. Tap. Tap. Tap. All the way home.

Skapyak is on my tail. If I don't get this chapter in, she'll wake me up with the Emperor's March ringtone and demand I drop and give her 20.

The rest of the week I worked around the clock to get goals accomplished, conveniently forgetting meds along the way. A discussion with Lynn about my latest submission. Fail. Meetings with my high school mentees, my sponsor, my producer. Success. A phone discussion with a surefire fit of a financial sponsor for the book. Fail. Nothing was getting me down. Or too high up. I felt just right. *Maybe I don't need medication anymore?* Wrong.

Friday started the struggle.

I'd been collecting video for news stations for money the past few weeks. An alert came in: Can you get video of an accident on I-95? I looked at the time stamp. Seventeen minutes had passed. *It's probably cleared.* Then another: Girl Scouts are arriving to pick up truckloads of cookies. *I've got all day to get this. Maybe later.* Then another: Jacksonville Boat Show. *I would have to pay to park and possibly again to get in. Not worth it.* Each time I rolled over and closed my eyes.

By the time Saturday Night Live signed off, I wondered if my lack of enthusiasm for a paycheck this weekend was justified by a need for rest. Or the depleting serotonin in my brain. I did a great job gathering news footage on Saturday. It didn't all get purchased, but that's the game. However, one thing was noticeably missing. My passion to keep the gravy train rolling with an 8-hour Uber run.

Goals. I told myself last night. *Tomorrow I will go to early church service to get my day started in the right direction. That's all I need.* I've committed my future to squelching the stigma that alcohol is a moral choice. But I'm embarrassed that I'm not strong enough to combat depression on my own. How messed up is that?

Awake at 8:15 a.m. Plenty of time to get up and make it. But the start time is a moving target. I negotiate with myself for the second service and fall back asleep.

Surrounded by pretty people, excited and moving swiftly on light feet, I'm swept up in the celebration I can't comprehend. They're not from here. They need a guide to tour them to fun. "Oh, how fortunate," I say. "I. Am. Your Official Funologist." They laugh. They like me. I want them to like me. I need them to like me. "I can get you to the beach for brunch," I say. "We can go to Zeta for mimosas and then the Lemon Bar for Sunday Funday." Time collapses. The sound of drunken laughter assaults the silence. A shot of Jager in my hand. A jubilant clink. Syrupy bitterness on my tongue. Cheers from the crowd. A stranger's voice. "Another?" I grab the second round that came out of nowhere, throw it back and bolt awake.

I'm not supposed to be doing this. What am I doing? My heart pounds. Guilt rushes in. *Why did I throw all of that sobriety away? Why? Why?* I feel like sobbing. But the tears won't come. My mind tries to wrap around the story. *It's real. I know it's real. But I don't recognize those people. But I know them. Right?* I cannot comprehend. My mind wavers. Grasping in equal time at reality and the realness of this memory.

I look at the clock on the dresser. 10:32 a.m. *Oh, thank God.* Relief flows over the guilt like a blanket pulled from head to heart to stomach to toe. I should get up. I've learned from newcomers and old-timer alkies alike, this is the time I need to reach out for help. The choir will start singing in less than an hour. However. The procrastinator service is still three hours away. There's still time. I roll to the other side of the bed, readjust my pillow, and pull another in between my legs.

"What seat did you get?" The guy next to me is cute. I hope mine is next to his. "A17," I say. By Southwest standards this would mean I am in complete control of where I sit. But I've never flown this no name airline before. I'm not sure what A17 means. "It's a cool flight," he says and coolly props his arm on the chair rest. "There's a kitchen. And a full bar. And a swimming pool." *A swimming pool? What is this EverBank Field? How big is this plane?* We're in a windowless waiting room. I can't see what's waiting for us outside.

The time collapse finds me in a darkened gangway. Claustrophobically tight. My new friend mysteriously absent. A tingling of anxiety runs down my spine. Space opens up as I board the front of the plane. Like, way up. The starboard side on my left is lined with first class seats. To the right, patrons surrounding a four-barstool cocktail area raise their glasses to me in a toast. I smile in return and keep moving past kids jumping straight down into a perfectly squared 5-foot pool of water.

How cool is this?

"Watch your step," a flight attendant says.

I stare down a steep staircase inside a metal hatch and take a gulp of saliva before steadying my weight through the restricted space. There is a considerable difference in the haves and have nots on this plane. I glance around the fuselage at the seats arranged in a semicircle on either side of the aisle. It's slightly cramped, but the guests look happy to have their legs stretched out as far as they want.

"What seats are these? I think I want to book this area next time." A stranger yells, "B," as I approach the next hatch marked A. The stairs are not as steep. When my right foot hits the floor after only four steps, I find out why. Head and shoulders hunch over to avoid the overhead. The walls are closing in. This is the end of the plane. The chairs are noticeably closer. I sit down in a seat that cramps my 5'4" frame and has me nearly knee-to-knee with the faceless person across the aisle. I strap in my seatbelt and sit back. Breath quickens in and out through an open mouth. Two people immediately flank me, their overlapping shoulders have me pinned down. Hyperventilation kicks in. I wrestle my shoulders back and forth. Pull frantically at the seatbelt. Scream out to the flight attendant. "No! Noooo! Let me out of here!" Ignoring my pleas, she continues closing the hatch and stealing all light of day from our windowless compartment. I can feel the tin coffin filling with evil.

I bolt awake for a second time. But this time, I jump out of bed. Cold sweat drips from the back of my hairline. The dream wasn't real. The hyperventilating and rapid heartbeat is.

It's not real. It's not real. It's not real. My mind tries to convince my vitals as I blow in and out. Action. Immediate action is my only sense of recourse.

Brush the teeth. Swallow 10 mg. Escitalopram. Jump in the shower. *It's not too late to make today a do-over.* There's plenty of time to make it to the 1:30 service, but first, I have to do what I learned in treatment and call someone.

"Well. Congrad-u-effing-lations," Lynn says. Her raspy sarcasm spurns a nose giggle from me. "I've been sober 30 years, and I still have dreams that terrify me." She pauses to release a cough. "Not you, my abnormal alcoholic queen." She laughs. She either just made up a new term of endearment or accidentally revealed a secret one. "It's about dang time." Sweet words of backhanded encouragement. I live for them.

I finish getting dressed just as RALLY FOR CHANGE at 2 P.M. pops up on my video app. A surge of creative excitement gets my happy dance rolling.

I'm on it. There's always the 5:30 service.

CHAPTER 14

THIS MORAL DEFICIENCY LOOKS AN AWFUL LOT LIKE A DISEASE

No eye has seen, no ear has heard,
and no mind has imagined
the things God has prepared
for those who love Him.
1 Corinthians 2:9

January 29, 2017

Anna Faris is going to read my book. She said so. I heard it on the *Mom* star's new audiobook *Unqualified*. Disc one. Chapter four. Three-minute mark.

"Dear Listener," she says. "You and I will be best friends after all this is over. I would like it if you would send me your autobiography, too."

So, on a personal note. Hello to you, Ms. Faris.

If I had to make a wish list of people I would want to read my book, people who positively affected my decision unbeknownst to them, it would be, in no particular order:

- Anna Faris – Not only is her television program great at using humor to show what recovery looks like, she also did a CBS Cares public service announcement with Allison Janney and the U.S. Surgeon General in 2016. "Addiction is not a moral failing. It is a chronic illness." Anna's words made a huge impact on my self-worth.
- Allison Janney – I love her Bonnie character on *Mom*. I think Bonnie and Allison would get my flippant humor and appreciate the need to use it as a shield of protection from getting too close to myself.

- Elvis Duran – Former co-host Bethany Watson did Dry January once. No alcohol for 31 days to kick off the New Year. The conversations through the four weeks were spirited and wistfully honest from the rest of the morning show crew who would not, some admitted could not, participate. His syndicated radio show reaches millions. He would be a fantastic advocate to get the word out.

- Terry Gross – I'm obsessed with NPR's *Fresh Air*. Terry is one of the finest interviewers in all the land. She brings about learning through exceptional, though-provoking questions. Breaking down complex subjects into bite-size knowledge. I have no doubt she would take a common story like mine and turn it into audio cotton candy.

- Ellen DeGeneres – I don't know if there has been a person who has gone through so much public crap to live her truth. She always handles it with grace. I've learned a lot about forgiving myself and others through her actions. Good always prevails.

- Oprah – Quite honestly? Just because she's Oprah. She would have my next move mapped out in a seven-step game plan and a slew of people lined up behind her to make it happen. She would shout to the audience, "You get sobriety! And you get sobriety!" And it would happen.

For those not confident in the way prayer works, in speaking your truth into existence, this probably just seems like a fun exercise to name drop and fantasize. It's more than that. It is about creating possibilities.

Before I got sober, I fantasized about what sobriety looked like. I pictured a sober, loving, Christian husband. I visualized speaking to thousands, sharing my story of hope. I imagined a ripple effect. Being brave to come out of the shadows to empower others to do the same.

Rich Ray, my mentor from my Florida Times-Union days, taught me Prayerize, Visualize, Actualize. Pray about it. Picture yourself doing it. Do it.

Doubters wonder why staying sober comes easy to me. It's because by the time I made the decision to go to treatment, I was chomping at the bit to get in there. I had seen myself doing it so many times in my head, I was on fire. In essence, I did (prayerfully) all of my relapsing for 39 years until I grew brave enough to actualize the solution.

Similarly, if you're in a blissful union, you don't wake up and wonder, "Let's see. Do I want to stay married today?" You just do it. That's how I approach sobriety.

However, like a marriage, I tend that spiritual garden. I tend it good. With prayer. Big book study. 12-step assignments. Church attendance with other Christians. Meeting attendance with other sober people.

I am very aware my mission has made me a target. The devil is a patient, diligent stalker.

January 30, 2018

What. The. Hell.

Resentment wells inside of me. It has been less than a year Laura and I overcame our feud. I swallowed pen-knife razorblade pride to repair it. Now this.

Watched your FB cast.

Hmmmm…Someone in the

Midwest states called you out

years before your dad did.

Honesty first, journalist.

Credibility makes for a better

memoir.

Makes me question the

authenticity of the book to

come, since you're consistently

pegging on that mistruth.

Heard you mention that about

your Dad on a few public

forums.

Regardless, stay smart and

strong. Keep up on the good

cause Your hair looks glorious!

Love you.

The text sent from Nebraska chaffed my hiney all weekend. I fully expect strangers to give me crap. Heck, after my video troll incident, I expect self-righteous sober people to demand I live with my disease in quiet shame for—what did he say—10 years. But my friend? And so soon after we repaired our relationship that broke four years ago?

It happened December 31, 2013. You often hear moaning around the middle of January from the sad few. Those who just weeks earlier hung on to the ridiculous concept that watching adults in diapers waiting 12 hours to sing Auld Lang Syne in Times Square would somehow magically transform their fortune. My moaning started less than two hours after the stroke of midnight.

I landed on a snow-dust covered Omaha tarmac in the late afternoon on New Year's Eve. A $30 tab at the airport and one to match on the plane had me feeling pretty good when I jumped in Laura's car. By the time dinner was served, I had already downed a quadruple tall (I remember Laura gasping, "Oh. Okay," when I poured it.) and shamelessly fallen asleep on the couch while guests arrived. Eventually I got up, we had a great meal, and a fun game night. (I also remember I was having too much fun. I laughed uncontrollably at everything everybody said. Inexplicable crying laughing. Asking myself, "Why am I laughing at that. It wasn't even that funny?")

The guests cleared the house. Go Big Red college football party for tomorrow was set. All I needed was one more nighty-night shot from the kitchen bar before retiring to the guest bedroom downstairs.

"I'm not doing this." Laura's voice was soft. Her lanky figure leaned over the breakfast nook. One hand on the counter. The other gripped a nearly empty bottle of cheap vodka. Her back to me. Shoulders hunched over. Head hung low. Her husband stood on the other side of the nook directly in front of her. Sad eyes shifted back and forth from her to me and back when she spoke words I couldn't comprehend.

"I can't do this. I'm not going to."

They must have had a fight. I'll lighten the mood. I snagged a used shot glass next to the stove. Not sure who drank out of it last. Don't care.

"Who wants a nightcap?" I sang the words, rocking the empty vessel playfully between my middle finger and thumb. I started to step forward but got knocked back by her surprise attack. She spun around hard and shoved the sloshing liquid at me.

"Here." She screamed. I rarely heard her raise her voice. It startled me. "Here. Drink it. Drink it all." She leaned her face into mine. Red with fury. I looked down at the bottle and reached to cradle it from her as she stormed away, screaming all the way to her bedroom. "And when you're done with that, I'll just run over to the liquor store and get you some more so you can kill yourself."

"What did I do?" I whimpered the question to her open-mouth husband frozen behind the nook. Walking forward, I set the bottle in front of him. Stared at it. My mind trying to make logic out of her illogical reaction.

Did I hit on her husband? Definitely not. But dang, it had to be something huge for that outburst. Did I say something inappropriate to her visiting sister-in-law? Maybe that's it. She did retire to her guest room without saying goodnight. Crap. What did I do?

The shrill orders started again. From the bedroom to the kitchen. "Pack your crap. Get out of my house." She pointed to the door. "I mean it. Get the eff out." She stormed back to the bedroom and slammed the door.

"What am I supposed to do? I don't have a way home." I searched her husband's eyes for the answer. He looked broken. A trojan left alone in the lion's den to pick up the bloody pieces from a battle he saw coming, but had no idea how it would play out.

"You do realize you have a problem," he said. He leaned closer to search my down trodden eyes for an answer. "Right?"

I looked back to search his eyes for my answer. "How am I supposed to get home?"

"Tracy. You do realize you have a problem, right? She's worried about you."

"Yeah, I know." I brushed him off with a wave. "That's what we were supposed to talk about on the way home. That was the game plan. Now." I shook my head in desperation. "How am I getting home? I don't have a plane ticket home."

I arrived in Omaha only eight hours earlier. Now I was, in a sense, abandoned halfway across the country. I felt like a sucker. I had let her talk me into flying in for New Year's and taking two precious days of vacation to help her drive back to Florida to visit family.

"She promised she'd pay half my ticket here." My inner calculator tried to figure out how much this good deed was going to cost me.

Eighteen hundred in case you're curious: $400 for the plane ride West, $1,200 for the last-minute return East, $200 for a rental car because the closest I could get to Jacksonville was Orlando.

She never did give me the money promised. And I had to take a cab to the airport because how I got there, she said, was "not my problem."

I spent the week making excuses to friends why I returned early. The story varied but always ended the same. "That girl is cray cray. I'm done with her."

I quit drinking. I quit drinking for 30 days because "I am going to show her. I'm going to show her I am not an alcoholic." Wag the finger. Stomp the right foot for effect. "Could an alcoholic do that?"

It took four years to repair the friendship. During the four years, I *proved* I wasn't an alcoholic by not drinking for 30 days three more times. It's no coincidence it was every year directly after the doctor told me my liver enzymes were elevated. The last time I was sent for a sonogram and subsequently had an MRI scheduled after the results didn't look good. But I gave up the fight before it was necessary to go that far. I still don't know what it would have shown.

Sulking in the days after Laura's text, I moved from anger to acceptance.

How dare she try and make this all about her! turned in to *How is she understanding my story different than what it is?*

The question in interviews is direct: What did it take to finally admit you have a problem? The answer is a conversation with my Dad catalyzed a traceable series of events that plopped my butt in The Greenfield Center.

But thin threads of God weave us to where we are supposed to be and includes the seeds that are planted along the way. Laura's was the size of a palm tree seed with the strength of a mustard seed.

I still don't agree with the way she did it. But I have to respect that she was watching a friend die in front of her and she had to make a decision. She had to ask herself, 'Do I care enough about Tracy to tell her the truth so she won't die? Even at the cost of our friendship?'

So, yes. She is a stone I stumbled over on the way to sobriety.

Three weeks later, I'm at the WQIK studios, getting interviewed by longtime friend and radio personality John Scott. In addition to hosting the station's popular morning show, John headlines a weekly public affairs show.

We stand across the desk from each other, speaking into large mesh microphones. I like standing during interviews. I can use my body language better and really get into story telling.

John asks me the usual questions. We establish the story about my dad et al. And then he says something that catches me off guard.

"Did anyone ever tap you on the shoulder?" He reaches back and taps himself on the shoulder. "You know, earlier in life when you were younger, and say, 'Hey, I think we've got a problem here.'"

"Uh." I look at the ceiling. In a split second, I see a barrage of flashbacks. An ex yelling on a dirt road. *No one is ever going to want to be in a relationship with you until you get help.* Hank pleading. *I'm begging you. You are going to die.* From the smashing glass and twisting metal of a '70s sedan to an $1,800 New Year's Day ride home.

He interrupts my thoughts. "You said you started drinking really young. What is the first time you remember somebody tapping you on the shoulder?"

"Well." I draw the word out and then chuckle in disbelief at what I'm about to say. "It's not the first one, but can I tell you about the worst one?"

Laura gets her 15 minutes of credit. Condensed to five for the sake of time.

I had hundreds of seeds planted along the way. I may have acted like they were poured on stony ground. But they were planted. Planted deep inside. Each growing strength from the next. Dorothy needed every slab on the yellow brick road, not just the final ones, in order to find her destination. I needed every single seed. Every single brick.

None hit as hard as Laura's. She says she wasn't getting through. Went for broke. Pulled out the shock factor. I was too proud to admit it worked. She was willing to lose me as a friend over watching me die. The least I can do in return is forgive her for ruffling a few feathers over semantics.

February 4, 2018

In *Pretty Woman*, Julia Robert's character Vivian tells Andrew Gere's character Edward how an intelligent, beautiful 20-something can find herself at an all-time personal low. Hollywood hooker.

"You could be so much more," he says. Soft piano music fills the pauses.

"People put you down long enough, you start to believe it," she says.

"I think you are a very bright, very special woman." He gazes into her eyes.

"The bad stuff is easier to believe."

It's true. Sadly, it's often our own voice hurling the insults. Murmuring doubt. Scenarios of failure. On the cusp of potential success, Gwen is currently being her own worst enemy.

"I probably won't get a call back." Like Vivian, she's taking the path of least resistance.

Sheesh, girl. It's not even the end of the first quarter and you're throwing up the white flag?

"I'm sure there is probably some other candidate with more experience," she says.

Over the past couple months, Gwen has been allowing herself to dream. Plan for the future. A life beyond her mistakes. She's been working in the hospitality industry. Her eyes on a new department. Goals to move up quickly in the company.

"It's an entry-level job, Gwen. How much more can one candidate have over another. You've got a college degree."

"Not in hospitality." Her dejected face is a polar opposite to the excitement she exuded after applying a short 48 hours ago. She's given her head time to spin. A chess game of possible outcomes. She's on the losing end. Not even realizing, she is the puppet master.

"Exactly." I plead with her to see it my way. "Anyone coming in with a degree in hospitality already had an internship. They're looking past entry level."

"You think?" Her face softens with hope.

Perfect. All I need is a sliver. A tiny opening to slide in my spiritual shucking tool.

"No." I deadpan.

Her eyes pop open. "What?" She draws the question out in a laugh and I join her. Busting out a giggle before getting serious.

"I don't understand why your head is going to the dark side. Why is that the first place you go?" I ask. "Isn't my scenario as likely as yours?"

"Yeah."

"Okay. Then what?"

Then what? is a technique I learned from my cousin Heidi. A Proverbs 31 woman. A pastor's wife. Heidi is more of a sister than a cousin. Only a few months my senior, she is a thousand years ahead of me in her faith walk. She gets up early every morning to give her first and her best to God. It's those around her reaping the benefits.

She taught me this simple phrase that steals power from complex problems. Then what? As in, "Hey, Heidi. I think I'm about to lose my job."

"Okay. Let's say you do lose your job. Then what?"

"Um. Uh. I. I guess I get another one?"

"Great. Problem solved."

It is a solution-based question designed to pull you out of the gutter of the unknown.

Gwen looks as confused as I did the first time I heard it.

"You get a call back. You don't get a call back. You choose. Then what?"

"I get all the way through the process. They do a background check. I don't get the job."

Whoa. Sharp dark turn stage right.

"What kind of background check do they do for entry level?"

"I don't know."

"You don't know?" I'm shocked. She's strictly going off assumptions. "You don't know and you've convinced yourself you're not getting the job."

"Well, when you put it that way." She laughs at how silly it sounds. Words of reason make more sense when they come out of someone else's mouth. I'm happy to help. Ribbing her a little along the way.

"Gwen, you are sober. You have faithfully taken care of your judicial commitments. You go to church every Sunday. You've been working diligently to rebuild your life."

She nods. Stares quietly into the space in front of her.

"Why wouldn't you believe God is ready to reward you?" My pointer finger snaps in her direction then, for effect, taps in rhythm with my words on the table. "If He decides this is your job, the rest will fall in place. How do you know the person who approves your hire isn't in recovery? Or has a child who died from addiction? Wants to make a difference in the life of someone who deserves a second chance. You just don't know."

"Yeah. I guess you're right."

"What if you don't get the job? Then what?"

She looks over. Eyes meet mine.

She's probably thinking, aw crap. Not this question again. That's what I would be thinking.

"Then what?" I push. "You don't get the job. Is this the only entry level job in this particular department in all of the hospitality industry in all of the world?"

Gwen releases a quiet chortle.

"You're thinking small," I say. "God has big things planned for you. Way bigger than an entry level job. Be patient. Do the work. Applications. Interviews. Let Him do the rest. Then hang on, sister."

We choose to be our worst enemy or our best friend. The choice is reinforced by the world vomiting negativity at every turn. Do we buy into it or walk away? Try this. Give someone a compliment today. Watch with amusement the confused look and subsequent genuine appreciation.

I encourage you, anytime you think a positive thought about a friend, say it out loud. We are a species starving for love and acceptance.

February 21, 2018

The quickly approaching one-year anniversary sparks new jitters. Different organizations offer a variety of recognition tools. Chips. Key chains. Certificates. They vary in time. They vary in color. They don't vary in capping out at one year.

I've been reading articles about the pitfalls of blowing out the first candle on the recovery cake. Dips in mood. Feelings of invisibility. After regular incremental slaps on the back, congratulatory celebrations and conversations, followed by a note on the calendar for the next milestone, the fanfare abruptly stops at month 12. Leaving some looking around for incentive to stay on course.

My concern is warranted. Ego has been a major character flaw. Reliance on attention and admiration from others to feel alive. It's why I called myself a tragic binge drinker in the beginning. I thought I was special. I'm not. I thought nobody drank like I drank. Turns out, I'm just like every other alcoholic. Ego is why I am diligent about second guessing my motives in everything I do with The Crushed Velvet Project. Keeping my prayers focused on others. Meditating on decisions before acting. Prayerfully pleading for divine guidance to keep the focus off me and brightly shining on God.

Today I'm visiting an inpatient treatment facility. They do not use a 12-step program. Facilitators empower patients and teach tools and techniques for self-reliance. The conversations are passionate and very green. I like it. Hearing the women describe ah-ha moments reminds me of items that should be added to my grateful list. The fears. The struggles. The challenges of everyone new to recovery are deranged reminders of a past I am living to kill.

In return, those of us on the outside encourage these women the fight is worth it. Today's topic is self-talk.

"What things are you telling yourself that you know is a lie." The class leader is a hipster black man teetering one way or the other on 30. He's in recovery, as is almost everyone at every facility I've visited.

I think it would be impossible for a person who doesn't know what is like to be out of control. To feel his skin crawl with anxiety. To vomit in front of strangers. I imagine that person would not be a great resource when treating addiction.

One-by-one, the women shout out their single-word insecurities and lasso full phrases roaming the wasteland of their semi-cloudy brains while the hipster writes on a fresh, white flip board.

Worthless. Not pretty enough. Overweight. Ugly. Synonym variations follow.

My hand comes out from under the roll of flesh resting on my lap. I put it to the sky. Reluctant. Fearful I may be overstepping boundaries. The hipster points to me and I introduce myself.

"I will be alcohol-free for a year next month."

The crowd smacks hands in unison. I hold out both of mine to slow them down.

"Thanks. Thank you." Embarrassed by the attention, I move quickly to the point. "I keep hearing you guys give up what's occupying your brain time. Repeatedly, it's something external." I point to the marked-up paper whiteboard. "All of those fears are real. I had them. I raised my hand to tell you, if you stick to your program, everything on that list is temporary."

Trying to make eye contact with all 24 people in the room, it's neck-and-neck for blank stares and knowing nods.

"Ever since I quit, I am addicted to sugar. My body cannot get enough," I say. "I'm heavier than I have ever been." So far, the count is 30 pounds. "Before I got sober, my entire identity was tied up on the outside." I circle my stomach with an open palm. "But as the days turned into weeks and into months, I started to like myself. The more I like myself ... I don't know." I shake my head, searching for inexplicable answers and start again. "The more I like the person I'm becoming. The outside doesn't matter anymore."

February 26, 2018

Disease or not a disease? That is the question.

Another successful radio interview followed by a passive aggressive critique has Gwen visibly upset and ready to pounce.

Earlier today a Facebook note dinged my phone. A stranger, with no profile photo or posts, thanking me for my candor in sharing the message of hope on John Scott's show yesterday. But the accolades quickly turn to casual uncertainty. The social media account is a fake. The comments are real.

When is the medical community going to recognize that alcoholism is not a disease but a moral choice? My wife has been sober for three years, and I'm grateful, but A.A. has her brainwashed to believe it's not her fault.

I read the entry to the Greenfield alumni gathering and plead with

Brian.

"I need to learn the medical description of disease. If I'm going to be an advocate, I have to know what I'm talking about when this question comes up." I hold the phone out. Point to the message on the screen. "What if this were someone raising a hand when I'm speaking at a church?"

Before he can answer, Gwen, sitting directly across from me at the round table, snaps her tongue on the roof of her mouth. Rolls her eyes. Releases a sigh of disgust.

"Gwen?" Brian turns from me on his right to her on his left. "Thoughts on this?"

"Well." She lets out another grunt. Takes a minute to gather her thoughts. References my breast cancer analogy. "Did I ask to have this disease? No. Did my mom ask to have breast cancer? No."

Weeks earlier, Gwen's mom, a beautiful dead ringer for Academy Award winning actress Holly Hunter, Texas twang and all, had a double mastectomy.

"Did my mom do anything that caused her to have breast cancer? Not that I'm aware of. Did I do anything to cause my disease?" She throws up a hand and drops it on the table. "Well, yeah." As in, well, duh. "I could have *not* picked up a drink in the first place."

Gwen had never negated my parallel metaphor of their mother-daughter health problems before. However, she's now willing to dissect it for the purposes of this argument.

"So yeah, maybe I do have some culpability in why I'm sitting here." She throws up a finger at my phone. "And maybe that guy's wife does, too." Her slumped body snaps to attention. Another revulsive outburst. "But what the hell does it matter? She's sober? Right? Isn't that what he said?"

"Yeah." I look back at the typed words to confirm. "Three years."

"Then what the hell does it matter?" She looks around the table at each of us. Nobody responds. Or breathes. "This guy's wife is sober. She's going to live. She's not going to die from cirrhosis." One finger goes up. "Or by cracking her head falling down the stairs." Two fingers. "Or a drunken car crash." Three fingers. Then reality sets in. She almost went out that way. Her hand drops loudly in front of her.

When Gwen first shared her story, months ago in IOP, about the fateful night she gave Austin, Texas, collision experts multiple new clients playing pinball with parked cars during her last DUI, I told her to her shocked face I was grateful she crashed. Grateful she had to lug around that annoying 'breathalyzer baby.' Grateful she caused thousands of dollars of damage.

"All of that can be fixed," I said. "It's just money. Without that accident, I have no doubt pills and booze would have killed you. You needed to cheat death to live."

Tonight, she's getting that same kind of protective emotion for our internet mystery man's bride. She is no longer the shy, quiet, guarded little girl I met in the spring. I guess we are all coming into our own.

"Your wife's sober, dude." She glares at my phone as if he can see her. "Who cares if it's a disease or not a disease. She's sober. Get over it. Get on with your life."

The group takes a collective breath. I look at Brian and raise my eyebrows for confirmation it is okay to speak. He nods and I open my mouth in response. Gwen cuts me off.

"And what kind of jerk says, 'Tell my wife she has moral problems.'"

It's hard to explain to non-alcoholics the cause and effect happening in our body when we take a sip. It's an allergic reaction.

A peanut allergy in a colleague creates external reactions we see with our eyes. Hear with our ears. Hives. Swelling. Labored breathing. These symptoms alert our cerebrum to take in the sights and sounds. Search our memory banks for information. Deduct what is happening to our friend. Get them help. Immediately.

An alcoholics allergy is internal. Psychological. An abusive communication between the body and the brain you will never see or hear. But it is just as real as your peanut allergy friend twitching in the corner.

"Alcoholism is a type of substance addiction." Brian gives us his standard answer. A more palpable definition than I found with Google. "This means alcoholism, like other addictions, is a chronic disease affecting the reward, memory, and motivation systems of the brain. This, in turn, leads to dysfunction for individuals who are struggling with it. In addition, as with other chronic illnesses, there is no cure for alcoholism; however, there is treatment available that can help individuals manage the condition."

March 3, 2018

So. This. Just. Happened.

TEDx Jacksonville opened applications for the fall conference yesterday. First thing this morning, John Phillips, a TEDx alum for his talk about racial injustice (America's Greatest Enemy: The Unevolving Virus of Prejudice), listed his top picks. He included my name, along with Jordan Davis' parents and Erin Brockovich.

I am blown away. And I say so in this post: I am blown away by this endorsement from our pillar of the community, John M. Phillips! I'm all in!

TEDx is a dream of mine. Just like he did when he nominated me for *Folio*'s Best Righteous Crusader, John's belief in me takes Ted off the wish list and writes it in thick, black marker on the 2019 niche list.

March 6, 2018

While the married, shacked up, and 'it's complicated' try to learn a new dance with the partners they barely know amidst new mental clarity, I'm struggling to do the same with my tribe.

I didn't believe things would change. Naivety on my part, I guess. At my birthday party, I told the crowd my only wish is to be treated the same. In their eyes, I should be the same person, If, that is, I hid it as well as I thought.

"Some alcoholics in recovery cannot be around drinking," I say. "I bartend. I'm good. Please don't leave me out. Likewise, don't be offended if I choose to decline. I'm still figuring this out."

A sea of understanding heads bobbed that night. Yet sadly, birthday party invites got lost in the mail. Group outing pics that will never hit my Timehop get posted. Invites to dinners are extended in front of me, not to me. It hurts.

Kimberly and I talk about it while she stirs up a goopy concoction designed to strip the teal out of my hair. I tell her I'm relying on *The Four Agreements*. A book with a few simple rules. Life changing rules. Like don't make assumptions and don't take anything personally. Today the rules are a tough sell on my wounded spirit.

"I can't hold them hostage in a friendship with a stranger." I rationalize that although I may see myself as the same person, I'm likely not. Priorities have shifted. I'm living like I'm dying. Embracing each day at sunrise and riding it hard until sunset.

Crinkling aluminum salon sheets with paint brushed locks snap close in Kimberly's palms. Snap. Snap. Snap. Right side. Left side. Fold in half. One after the other, quickly around my scalp.

"I've been trying to figure out why the romance has died. Maybe I am boring now?"

"Well," she says, "I don't think it's that. Not everybody feels comfortable around people who don't drink."

"I would say that's true," I say.

"They're looking at you and thinking, 'She's got a problem? What does that say about me?'"

"Right. Right," I say. "Because they have no clue what was happening after the party. They only see me drinking the same amount as them."

"Exactly." She leads me over to the dryer.

"Okay, so back to the reason I read it to you." I sit in the seat. She pulls the plastic bowl over my noggin. "I feel like I've learned so much this year about how the world works."

"Oh my gosh, girl. Yes. You and me both."

Twelve hours earlier, she sent me the Corinthians verse at the beginning of this chapter. Out of the blue. For no reason. Boom. Just like that. It fit perfect for what I was writing. Strange. Or is it?

The more I am still in the Word, the more I recognize how all of us ebb and flow. In and out. Crisscrossing a loom. Thin threads of God. Weaving the canvas of a bigger picture.

"Like the verse," I say. "It's a crazy beautiful lesson that I learned this year. To let go and let God."

Her doe eyes explode at the revelation. She yanks the plastic bowl back. Making sure I can hear her.

"Me, too." Her soft yell cuts through the humming blower.

"I feel like I would hear that phrase and roll my eyes. I didn't get it until now."

"Me, too. Oh my gosh, girl. Yes. Yes." She wiggles her crooked pointer finger. "C'mon. Let's rinse you. We're going to have to take this teal out in phases. I don't want to damage your hair."

I lay back on a super comfy black recliner. Drop my neck into the welcoming cup of a porcelain sink of the same color.

"Can you believe how much our lives have changed in, I don't know, two years?" she asks.

"I'm overwhelmed. I've given up trying to make plans." Both hands flip in surrender at the wrists. "God's got this. I wake up every day wondering what great adventure I get to experience today."

"Dr. Wayne Dyer says ... do you know him?"

"Yes."

Fragrant botanicals fill the rinse bowl. Her nails scrub my foamy scalp.

"I love his audiobooks. He says, 'Row, row, row your boat.'"

"*Gently* down the stream." We both enunciate the same word and crack up.

"'Gently,' he says. Not 'roughly.' Not ..." I search for a visual descriptor. Dig into it with a raspy voice. "Not 'grind against the current as often as possible.'"

Her body shakes with laughter. She turns the rinsing faucet away from my head to avoid spraying me in the face. Her loss of control cracks me up. I love making her smile.

Kimberly taught me the phrase, "Hurting people hurt people." I think of it often when someone is not kind. And when they are not acting the way I want them to?

Don't take anything personally. Ego will trick me into believing it is all about me.

Don't make assumptions. I've learned whatever the story is in my head, whatever I can come up with, no matter how realistic or how outlandish, I am almost always wrong. Whatever I think. Place your whole paycheck on it. It's wrong.

She blows my hair out. I hit the door. Fresh and fabulous. A good laugh-cry cleansing release.

Down the road a few miles, I meet up with my new sponsor. An adorable, sassy 25-year old with three years sobriety. For me, she's the perfect template of what I need to be equally yoked.

I love my first sponsor. She's a comforting motherly woman with a spitfire personality. I'm forever grateful for her getting me started. Doing step work. Nurturing the habit of calling each day to be accountable. She came to the table with a lot of knowledge and frequent daily requests. Her requirements seem perfect for fostering a young alcoholic struggling on a daily basis. That wasn't me. I grew weary of the back and forth of what is best for me. Two type A personalities better off as friends. We parted with promises of celebrating my one year of sobriety at lunch next month.

At this first meeting, my new sponsor has us take turns reading out of the Big Book. She reads a page. I read a page. The sheets we leaf through come alive with her side notes written in the margins. Fascinating facts she learned from her two sponsors.

When we wrap, I go over with her what I am willing to do. Boy howdy. That statement will have someone riled up tonight. Similar to legalistic Christians, I have met people who do not veer from the Big Book as the Bible. I think that is great. If it works for them. It doesn't

231

work for me. It creates animosity. Resentment. A desire not to continue. I cannot be smothered with restrictions. I have to be me. Me with boundaries. But in the end, me. A square peg that does not fit in a round hole.

I don't know about tomorrow. I can only be accountable for today. Today is a calm spirit flanked by balance and appreciation. The sheer peaceful joy I've searched for my entire life.

March 20, 2018

Phaaryl's angelic face tenses when she's stressed. She makes erratic movements, too. Bookbag flipped on the table. Dropped to the floor. Back to the table. Back to the floor. Her internal conflict forces second guessing of every motion.

She has a project due. I can tell she's been procrastinating. The answers are short and never solid.

"When is your movie due?"

"I don't know. Before grades are due, I think."

"Does that include editing or do you have more time for that?"

"Uh ... I'm not sure."

"You're not sure? Or you don't want to tell me?"

"Yeah. That."

"That what?"

It's an endless circle. I opt to drop it and add something positive.

"Don't worry," I say. "I do the same thing. It always works out."

I hope I'm right. I hope creativity builds up at the dam she creates in her brain and comes flooding in before the deadline passes. I'm ready to push her boundaries.

"You wanna do the 48 Hour Film Project?" I nonchalantly gather some of my belongings from the conference table and stuff them into a big black carryall.

Her elbows squeeze against a tiny ribcage. Shoulders scrunch.

"Uh. You mean make a film in 48 hours? No."

"No." I blurt out surprise. She's never said no to me.

"Well, we do the 72-hour film project here, and." She stops. Chooses her words wisely. "It's hard." Without warning she does an about face before I can even think of a rebuttal. "Okay. Yeah. Let's do it."

Again. Here's me. Shaking my head. Clueless. No idea what just happened on that gerbil wheel of hers.

"Ok. Let's do it." I repeat.

CHAPTER 15

READY FOR MY NEXT GREAT ADVENTURE

March 27, 2018

Happy birthday to me! A sober anniversary is referred to as a birthday. A re-birth of the you God created. I'm used to having blowout birthdays. I don't need anyone to throw me a party. I am perfectly capable of telling you how we will be celebrating me. Not just one day either. Nope. Typically, a week. A minimum of four.

However, the 365th day alcohol free finds me taking care of Momma Dot Com days after a full knee replacement in Phoenix. Surprisingly, no fanfare for my accomplishment. More surprising, my ego doesn't need one.

I'm not sure what I'm expecting today. No. That's not true. I *was* expecting to get a tattoo. I made the decision early in the New Year. I wanted to make the temporary ink cross on my drinking hand permanent. Then I proceeded to change my mind every day for two months.

I've grown fond of the ritual. One more measure of accountability. A single line down. A single line across. A tattoo would steal the ceremonial act. Until I saw Kendall Jenner on *Ellen* days before I board Southwest Airlines for a Southwest state.

In addition to her cringeworthy inner lip tattoo, Kendall boasts a white tattoo. Practically invisible. Unnoticed until attention is drawn to the drawing. That night I had a dream, waking convinced this is my best option.

I'll have it permanent in white. Draw over it daily in blue ink. Seems like the perfect way to celebrate. Except the nurse is saying Mom is forbidden to go anywhere yet. Oddly, the news doesn't faze me. My former perfectionist self, guided by ideals rather than practical considerations—like your mom probably won't be road ready five days after a major surgery—evaporated in the dry Arizona dust. I schedule an appointment for a week from Thursday and get on with my day.

I plan a trip to two organizations to collect annual sobriety coins in their varying colors and mission statements. The first I bring back and gift it to Mom.

"You deserve this more than anyone," I say. "Putting up with my crap and loving me anyway."

She sets it next to a crystal triangle recognizing Dad's post-mortem eye tissue donation.

We celebrate with a giant waffle cone cup of Cold Stone Brewery's Birthday Cake ice cream with brownie pieces and colorful sprinkles in spite of the additional five pounds I've packed on since arriving. I now weigh more than I ever in my lifetime. I remain unphased. Happy to be healthy.

We wrap our day. Uneventful. Not really journal worthy. I would be lying if I said I'm not disappointed. The goal of this book is to share my missteps, ah-ha moments, struggles and triumphs during my first year of sobriety. A dialogue from my perspective of what to expect if your fear is the unknown in getting help.

It's been great, but dang. How do you finish a book if you have no ending? It's disconcerting.

I tuck my mother into bed. I can't get enough of her sweet, gorgeous face. It's a new obsession. Not long ago, I dreaded the ride from the airport to my childhood Montana home. We lived 10 minutes away. Plenty of time for her and my father to take turns pushing my buttons while I scowled in the back.

I paid to come home for this?

Now that I'm sober, she is completely delightful. Weird, huh?

I strap her new knee into a motion machine. It will provide bending therapy. Rocking back and forth as she dreams. She's supposed to have it bending up to 90 degrees in two weeks. She wants to be there by the end of the week.

I'm starting to recognize where my tenacity comes from.

"Mom?" I pull her covers over the contraption and hand her the television remote. *This is really uncomfortable. Take a deep breath. It has to be asked.* "Did I hear you say you're an alcoholic?"

She takes a beat before she answers. Stares at the wall like she's looking for writing.

Oh my gosh. Is she going to deny it?

It wasn't once. It was twice. I overheard a phone call when she came to Jax for Christmas. Then another since I've been here.

"No," she told the unknown person on the other end. "I won't be drinking anything at the get together. I'm an alcoholic. Once I start, I keep going."

Maybe that's what she's visualizing now. Wondering how I know. She finally nods.

"Yeah," she says.

"I didn't wake up craving it like you did," she says. "But, yes. If I started with a glass of wine or a beer, I wouldn't stop. I don't mess with it anymore."

She's braver than I. If I could drink, even if it meant binge, but it lasted that night and that night only. No repercussions. No obsessions until I made the choice to pick up again? It would be impossible to stop. I'm grateful for my disease exactly the way it was planned.

During my time at Greenfield Center, no easy detectors popped up. I graduated not feeling comfortable understanding why me.

"If you want to become a millionaire," Brian said, "you can buy a lottery ticket. Or, you can work really hard at it, until eventually you become a millionaire."

I didn't like the idea I had worked really hard at it all these years. Inferring if I had lived a better life, I had a choice. There is something comforting in knowing my mom is in the foxhole with me.

"I'm proud of you, Toots." Mom's head is nestled comfortably on her pillow.

I stare down at her with a serene smile. A quiet moment between mother and daughter. Seeing my mom look at me with respect is a feeling like no other. I can't buy it, drink it, pop it or snort it. There's nothing like it.

We spend the rest of my trip binging on ice cream, playing the HQ trivia app, and laughing at Judge Judy.

We bond over my tattoo, which she insists on paying for. I tell her she will be with me for life, her gift inked on my drinking hand. She loves that. Though not enough to get one herself when I offer.

We cry when it's time to leave. An intimate moment to never take for granted again. I may have wasted a lot of time. I can't change the past. But I can vow to be generous with my time for the rest of the time we have.

June 1, 2018

My sponsor suggests I write an essay: What is my idea of a sane life?

Before she can explain why, I tell her no further instructions are necessary. I spent a lot of time fantasizing what a levelheaded, logical, lucid life looked like while curled up in sweat and body oils three days old.

I had a clear vision of what I could do if alcohol wasn't always in the driver's seat. Determining and demanding the constricted parameters of what could realistically be accomplished.

I write the words in blue ink on the college-ruled lines. The same blue ink I use to draw the webbing cross.

To wake up each day with the intent to be sober and honest. To make decisions that are faith based. To fight every day for peace and happiness in my soul. To chase my passions. To follow the purpose God stretched out in front of my path. To be dependent on no one. Not in relations. Faith. Money. Emotions. To work like crazy to save one more woman. Hold her hand. Guide her to freedom. A new, fresh, beautiful life that God intended for her. For me. The hounds of Heaven hunted me down. I will hunt her down. Stand in her place. Until she is strong enough to stand on her own.

I sit back and read the paragraph. Something is missing. I reread it. Again. Leave it for a day. Reread. It hits me.

The twins. The twins were part of the visualization. I continue with my assignment.

I longed to make a difference in a child's life. God doubled down. I got two.

Daaryl and Phaaryl could not have been more handmade for me if I birthed them myself.

And bonus. I fell in love with their mom, too. Velvet is a strong, funny, talented black woman, who has taught her daughters the value of natural beauty and the power of "Yes, ma'am." They go to church every Sunday. They do not gossip. They build each other up in the single parent home. A trait I recognize from my past.

I love them like family. They are my definition of what a sane life looks like. Fulfilling a flow of humanity that is harmony with how humans come together for a common good.

While the ink dries, I head to the Jacksonville Landing to meet the Wilsons. The 48 Hour Film Project fuses our strengths in creativity.

By the time the final 12 hours rolls around on Sunday, we've already been done for three. It is the easiest film production I have done in the past decade. Phaaryl had the idea of magic socks. Daaryl suggested she, the lead actress, would get three wishes. The concept of magic socks molded from our magical minds into a complete screenplay in two hours flat. We filmed on Saturday for six hours at five locations. Phaaryl and I edited while Daaryl went to a birthday party and play practice. Filmed a couple more scenes and finished editing at 4 a.m. Done. That was it.

Easy peasy. Sweet and breezy. One of those moments you never see coming because you don't really know what's going on behind the scenes. That's what happened when I overheard a conversation last night.

We were getting close to completion when Phaaryl got on the phone. Her excitement caught me off guard.

"We're almost done," she said. I could hear the mumble of another teenager on the other end.

I wonder who she's talking to?

"Yes," she said. More mumbles from the receiver. "I know. It's crazy." Her head bounced up and down. "Yes." She can't contain her delight. "We went to the TV station and then one of Tracy's friend's house, and it was huge." Her right hand held the phone while her left pumped up and down in a frenzy.

Huh. Very out of character.

"And then a hair salon and then our lobby." Mumble from the other end. "No, we have a little more to shoot when Daaryl gets home. But we've already edited a couple of scenes."

And then I heard something that made my heart float.

"Tracy taught me to edit scenes separately. We are so going to kill at the next 72-hour film fest. It makes it so easy."

Oh my gosh, I think I'm going to cry. I didn't react. *Don't let her know your listening. Do. Not. Scare her off.*

I could barely believe it. This is exactly the result I wanted. Remove the ceiling on her belief system. She is talented. She can do it. It will be great. Time does not matter. I was having so much fun, I forgot why I offered it up in the first place.

My actions affected a child in a positive way? Thank you, Jesus. Thank you.

I truly live my life doing things for others, placing no expectations on them. My sponsor taught me any time you put an expectation on a reaction of another human being, you set yourself up for a resentment.

I really encourage you to reread that last paragraph. It can change your world. With no expectations, when it goes well, it is crazy good. I was on top of the world and barely slept last night. Now, back at the Wilson's, I can't wait to show them the final edits I made.

Velvet giggles. The girls cringe.

"Wait 'til you see yourself on the big screen." My words do not comfort. Velvet and I laugh in unison.

I pick up our team three hours later to submit their final product. Not only on time. Early. They present me with three things they each learned in the last 48 hours. Including the value of planning ahead and believing in themselves. I am overwhelmed.

"I always try to live in the present." I talk to both of them in the rearview mirror. "But I found myself thinking about how I only have you for two more years." They look at each other and giggle through open palms. "And then what? I'll never have mentees as good as you."

"You don't have to worry about that," Velvet says. "You're never getting rid of these girls."

My heart is full.

June 9, 2018

Add it to my resume. Dogsitter. Thanks to Nikki, I'm staying at her friend Julie's beautiful Ponte Vedra Beach home with a community pool for the next seven weeks. The dog is gorgeous. The home is gorgeous. I'll be in heaven while I finish writing about hell and the grace that followed.

I'm also going to put my home up on Airbnb while I'm gone.

I am in awe. Every month I am blessed with another opportunity to make sure I can pay the bills. It's been almost a year since I lost my job. I made the decision at that time to keep allowing the church to take out the tithe amount I made while working fulltime.

It's obviously more than 10 percent of what I've been making. I don't know for sure. I haven't done any calculations yet. I'm afraid if I figure out the numbers, it will all crumble. I stepped out on faith to keep the funds coming out of my bank account. I'm perfectly content living in ignorant, grateful bliss. Until tax season.

The freedom it has afforded me to help others without the bondage of time clock can't be a coincidence. I feel like somebody pulled back the curtain on life and I'm able to look at the world with a bird's eye view. My eyes are open to little winks from the universe on a daily basis.

It's impossible to rattle me. When unexpected bills crush my budget, I embrace the concept it's God's money, not mine. When plans don't pan out, I'm excited to see what's next instead. When challenges slam my confidence, I take a breath, jump back up and slay the barriers to capture the lesson.

I continue to consume knowledge as fast as I can. Honoring my commitment to help others through understanding all the resources available to alcoholics lost in the details. Drowning in fear of the unknown. Determined to snag them before they go under.

June 25, 2018

Jason Gaes died today. The child prodigy, who folded 10 pieces of typing paper in half to create in crayon a message of hope for kids with 'cansur' in 1987, took his final breath at age 40 surrounded by family.

His story is an example of following your heart and allowing God to take care of the rest.

Jason never guessed his book would be printed in five languages. That he would spend his time speaking at conventions, schools and summer camps for kids in treatment. That he would field thousands of calls and letters. That HBO would create an Academy Award winning documentary about him called *You Don't Have to Die*.

God may not have made him seven feet tall. But he lived to be a giant to families in the child cancer community.

He died being an example and inspiration to my mission.

CHAPTER 16

DON'T WAIT UNTIL YOU DIE TO
REST IN PEACE

July 22, 2018

It's been one year since I walked into Lynn's humble abode to start a journey. I hoped and she seconded, together we could create a ripple effect to save lives.

I've said it already. A story isn't complete without an end. I've been anxious about what would bring this journey full circle. I trusted God would show me in His time. However, I would be lying if I didn't say I smacked the back of my right hand into my left palm several times over these past weeks, looked to the sky, and said, "C'mon, dude. Deadline's comin'."

It's true. I talk to my Higher Power like a friend. Joking. Laughing. Crying. Thanking. In the end, always respecting.

It's been a quick year and a long haul for Lynn and me.

To show appreciation, I bring her an anniversary card. The cover reads, *For My Wife*. I cross out ~~Wife~~ and handwrite *Editor*. On the inside, *I Feel Lucky to Wake Up ~~Next to You~~* is changed to *I Feel Lucky to Wake Up to Your "Where's Your Next Chapter?" Phone Calls*. I leave alone the sentiments *You Warm My Heart, You Fill Me with Love*, but add on *And Occasionally Fear*.

It ends with *I Wouldn't Know What to do Without You*. I draw in *#truth*. Because it is. She became more than an editor. She's a friend. A guidance counselor. A sobriety coach. A mother figure.

There were times I wondered who was working for whom.

If she hadn't stayed on top of me when I was feeling uninspired with my story. And again, when I felt insecure about my writing. And again, when it seemed like there was all the time in the world. These words wouldn't exist.

So, no surprise. I tell her I'm having a difficulty with the end.

"Come sit down." She shuffles me past the dining room table. A lit cigarette burns in the ashtray. A cup of coffee steams next to it.

Turning into the kitchen, husband Jim gives a quick wave and escorts their black Standard Poodle, Beau, out to the patio.

"Coffee?" she asks.

"Yes. I want it in my mug."

"What mug?"

I reach for the same one used on our first meeting and read it out loud. "I know what my problem is. What's yours?"

We laugh and return to the table.

"You need to tell them where you're at," she says "What's changed in you over the past year?"

Now, why didn't I think of that? I'd ask, but she would just say that's what I'm paying her for. Again, #truth.

"Reading the beginning of this book is like a voyeuristic look at a stranger," I say. "A person I don't know. An eagle eye view of a woman I don't recognize." My eyes drop to the floor while my brain relives the shame. "Sinful. Broken. Scared and confused."

Lynn's recent editing of the first 100 pages elicits fervent head bobs.

"But determined to fight for her serenity in a way she would previously only do for another," I add.

"Think about who you are writing this for." She takes a drag off a Marlboro Light. Residual smoke billows out with her words. "What do you want them to know after they've read this book?"

"Hmm." I search the floor for answers. Memories flood. Reliving the yearlong process of quieting anxiety, sleeplessness, night sweats, depression.

"My therapist friend, Amy Decker, who's currently working on a book about the subject, says if you ask anyone in therapy—any kind, for any reason—what they hope to gain," I say. "She says, nine out of 10 will say peace."

When a storm is brewing in our mind, or body, or soul, the imbalance throws off the entire agreement of harmony.

"Think about it," I say. "When your mind stresses about a problem, the body craves nothing at all or everything in the fridge. When your body is under stress, your mind races to find a rescue path. It's equally consumed when actions are not in alignment with spiritual beliefs."

How can I get that across? Find a way, a different angle, to make people understand action creates reaction creates change.

"Um." A childlike shoulder shrug. A scrunched nose. "I want them to know I currently live in a tranquil form of mental, physical and spiritual homeostasis like I've never known and I want everyone to feel this way."

"Ah, bullcrap." Lynn shoos away the comment.

Laughter fills the dining room space between us.

"The audience you're going to reach, I believe, are people either thinking about sobriety or in their first year," she says. "This is a good example for what a first year of sobriety looks like."

A tiny tobacco stained hand extinguishes her white soldier.

"I can see treatment facilities issuing it, especially to women," she says. "They need to know what you're thinking now looking forward."

Hadn't really thought about that. Teeth gnaw on a thumbnail. *Too busy living in the moment.*

"Do you have any cravings?" she asks. "People are going to want to know."

"Hmm." Thumbnail slowly retreats to my lap. "I can't say I don't still look at drinking situations and wish I could partake. But after gaining 50 pounds, I'm back on my weight loss program, and I also look at chocolate cake the same way."

"Those sugar cravings never go away." Lynn takes a sip of coffee.

"The difference is I dated alcohol. I'm married to sobriety. People in a healthy marriage don't wake up and ask themselves, 'Let me think. Do I want to be married today?' They get up another day and tend that beautiful garden to reap the benefits. This is how I treat sobriety. I water it. Feed it nutrients. Avoid situations I know to be temptation."

Knuckles tap in quick succession against my chest.

"It's within my power to keep my eyes on the goal instead of the cocktail or the cake," I say. "My focus deters my disease. Positive and negative."

"What do you mean?" she asks.

"The negative is easy to identify." I point to the Florida room. In the direction of the television. "When a commercial comes on showcasing sexy people living a large and happy life because of the cocktail in their hand, I visualize my drunk video. The way the story really ends for me."

A couple of clicks on the iPhone and an electronic list appears.

"I also make mental notes of grateful moments," I say. "You know. Experiences available only to a person blowing a 0.00. When the Jags game is over, I can go to the late church service. A call for a freelance gig can be fulfilled any time of the day or night. Being of sound mind and a spiritual heart to come to the aid of a friend. Knowing that as much as I hate getting up early, once I do, my healthy body loves to be in motion. Lotsa stuff like that."

Phone screen times out. Goes black.

"My mind can still recall the suffocating feeling of knowing my day was handcuffed by taking that first drink. The entire day. Completely hijacked." I draw my wrists together. Bound with invisible rope. "The sensation is like treading water with no land in sight. Fully aware, any moment, I'll tire out and go under."

Hands drop in my lap. Eyes focus on hers.

"A drink? It's not worth it."

"Well, that's great for today, but you've only completed your first year." She pulls another smoke from the pack, resting it between two fingers. "You've likely got 30 or 40 more. What about that? What about fears? What are you afraid of moving forward?"

Fears? I don't harbor any fear. Gerbils sleep. An eerie calm. I visualize a glassy Tennessee lake. The quiet moment when enough darkness has passed to see but right before the light wakes the birds.

Memories of fear are still fresh. Lingering paranoia. Feelings of unexplained doom. Out of body experiences. Standing on my bed. Tugging on my own limp arm. The sound of my own voice screaming in the distance. "Tracy. Tracy." It creeps closer. Until "Wake up!" jolts me upward to the sounds of hyperventilating coming from my heaving chest.

It's been more than a year though.

"I guess I don't have any fears," I say. "And that kinda scares me."

"It should." She parts her lips. Inserts the waiting stick in her hand. Flame from the lighter glows off her elfin face. Her warning looms. Weaving its threats through dirty white clouds.

"You're on this high." Her vocal chords tighten around the first puff. "You're bouncing from here to there. But you're riding a horse that might buck you off at any minute."

Her eyebrows raise and hold. Waiting for confirmation.

"Yeah. You're right." I surrender to her way of thinking. "It's why I'm in no hurry to find a relationship. I'm scared to death."

Another brow raises. This time, giving confirmation.

"It's a trigger. Breakups, that is. I'm scared to death to try."

"You're lonely." Sounds like a statement. Not a question.

"No," I say.

"Not alone, but you are lonely."

Is she trying to convince me?

"No. I'm really not," I protest. "I haven't stopped long enough to be lonely. I've been consumed with this project. Helping people find resources. Maintaining my sobriety. Writing this book."

"Do you think the book has helped you?" she asks.

"Definitely. It's cathartic," I say. "I can't stress it enough when I meet new people. Journaling is where it's at. I look for one takeaway from each sermon and record it in a journal. And then I add in peaks and pits throughout the week. It serves as a personal pick me up when I need it."

"You do it every day?"

"Not every single day."

"You should." Lynn walks into the kitchen. "It's parallel. Writing and sobriety. It's parallel." She pours another cup of coffee and returns. "Think of all the disciplines you learned in the writing class. Crafting technique. Reading the articles I sent you. Required parameters for your submissions. Getting feedback from the group."

"Emotional setbacks were the worst for me," I say. "Not being disciplined and getting behind wasted so much mental energy. But once I powered through and got back on track? I couldn't figure out why I didn't just do the right thing in the first place."

"Yep." Her entire body rocks when a student has an ah-ha literary moment. "It all ties together."

I take a sip of coffee and admire her happiness.

"What about friends?" she asks.

"What friends?"

"Your friends. People are going to want to know about your friends. And family. They'll want to know that, too." Her voice drops like she's telling a secret. "What they really want to know is what's going to happen with their friends and family."

"Oh. Well. That's a complicated one." There's definitely a shift in dynamic. Each is different.

"My family is easy. I can't get enough of them. I would have us all under one roof if I could. At least in the same town. I cringed at the thought of hanging out. Talking on the phone. Now I call or text my mom almost daily." Forefinger and thumb pinch nervously at my lower lip. "But my friends? Hmm. It varies."

They all still drink. Except Lisa "The Boatanista." She never did drink. And she's probably thrilled I'm no longer lying face down in a pile of cabin cruiser pillows while she's left on top navigating sunset buoys alone. Others I don't see as often.

You really do find out how much you authentically have in common with someone when you're clean. Plus, I enjoy my alone time. Now that I'm spending it with someone I like.

"Hanging out with friends who drink is not a problem for me. But, like, Gwen? She can't do it. Some people can't. So, we do other things together. Like movies. Hanging with sober friends at least four times a week is a must for my sanity. It's more than companionship. It's a way for us to share our stories of success and bounce struggles off."

A sour stomach full of resentment feels so good after vomiting the problem all over people I can trust.

"With your serenity, it's how you deal with crises that matters. I mean, look at you." Lynn waves a small white nub of smoldering tobacco in my direction. "You lost your Dad. Your good friend Tom committed suicide. Your aunt died. You've been through a lot in one year." She smashes the filter. It disappears beneath her fingers. She pulls them out of the ashtray and points to me. "But you didn't drink over it." A broad smile widens in unison with her posture.

She rises from her chair. Reaches for a hug. I mimic the motion.

"I'm proud of you, baby."

We walk towards the door.

Who would have ever known I could have learned so much from the person I thought I was hiring to put commas in all the right places.

"What are you going to do now?" She opens the door. "Now you'll have all this free time."

I stop short of the exit to contemplate the question.

"I've got some ideas." A bag filled with paper remnants of our blood, sweat and tears hangs from one shoulder. "A TEDx submission. Or another book." Stepping outside the door, I turn back to her. "Maybe a comedy routine." A giggle follows.

"Just remember, I love ya." Her hand rests on the doorknob. "Life is going to go on. Stay ready for it."

"I know I'll always be a drunk." Hands raise in surrender and slap against my legs. "There's nothing sexy about it. I've been blindsided before. Only time will tell."

One last hug and I head to the car.

"You know what they say." I holler over my shoulder. "One day at a time."

***

When I started this book, the goal was simple. Find someone like me. Suffering in silence. Hiding in plain sight. Invisible under the radar.

If you're wondering if I found a starfish, I did.

She turned out to be a friend I've known for years. Both personally and professionally. A blind study of our resumes and our drunk logs would make you see double. I didn't know anything simmered under her surface. She didn't know about mine. But when I shared my story of recovery, she knew alcoholics are not only found on the street benches and homeless shelters. They are found in the mirror. The relatability gave her freedom to take a stand against the bottle.

Walking through decades of heartache and shame is worth every penny and brain cell wasted when I see her smiling, peaceful face.

We are currently stumbling through the sobriety steps together.

AFTERWORD

If you are someone who loves an alcoholic—a child, a parent, a sibling, a lover, a spouse, or a best friend—and you stuck around for their start of "Stumbling into Sobriety," then you know it wasn't the beginning of *our* journey. Our journey started long ago, watching someone we love, who didn't love themselves anywhere near as much as we love them. Slowly, methodically ruining their lives and attempt to commit deliberate suicide. For those of us loving an alcoholic, every sip chipped away at our hearts.

When Jake called on March 4th to say she wouldn't answer the door, I thought—I mean truly believed—when we got in her house, she was going to be dead.

I knew this was *THE TIME*. I was sobbing, already mourning the loss of her, something I'd been doing inside for years. When it turned out she was alive, I was relieved. And angry. Really angry. When I spoke (I'll admit, I yelled a little, too) with her on her way to the airport for her father's funeral, I was still crying. Begging her to get help.

I believe she finally understood my fear of her imminent death was real, and not unrealistic. She promised she would discuss it with her mom, and get help. We talked about her possibly staying in Arizona, and a myriad of other options. What we didn't talk about, but I think she understood, this was it for me. Either I would have her Baker Acted (for her own protection) when she returned or I was walking away. I simply could not handle watching her kill herself any longer. Thank God, she chose sobriety.

Tracy's decision to get sober, as with any alcoholics, is recovery for all who love her, too. We're in this together, as we always have been. When she boldly announced to the world she was an alcoholic at her coming out party, I couldn't have been prouder. Her unabashed, forthright conversations have helped to take away the stigma of reaching out for help from addiction.

Our community has rallied behind her in an amazing fashion, but she knows that's not a luxury that every person has. She is using her status as a local celebrity to reach out to those who don't have the kind of support she has. This book is a way to let others, who are struggling with addiction, know they are not alone. For those who have and love their own Tracy, this book is insight into the struggle of addiction—and might help you understand your loved one a little better.

Today, I still cry for Tracy. I cry in thanks that the grace of God saved her life. I cry in happiness that I have my best friend back. I cry with pride that she has taken an addiction, turned it around, and found a way to help others. I cry with love in my heart that this wondrous gift from God has freed herself from the chains of addiction. Now she is the soaring, beautiful butterfly she was meant to be.

Henrietta (Hank) Watson